I0423034

Me Three
Return to
Darkness

David Driggs

Copyright © 2014 David Driggs.

All rights reserved. No part of this book may be reproduced, stored, or transmitted by any means—whether auditory, graphic, mechanical, or electronic—without written permission of both publisher and author, except in the case of brief excerpts used in critical articles and reviews. Unauthorized reproduction of any part of this work is illegal and is punishable by law.

Because of the dynamic nature of the Internet, any web addresses or links contained in this book may have changed since publication and may no longer be valid. The views expressed in this work are solely those of the author and do not necessarily reflect the views of the publisher, and the publisher hereby disclaims any responsibility for them.

Any people depicted in stock imagery provided by Thinkstock are models, and such images are being used for illustrative purposes only.
Certain stock imagery © Thinkstock.

Lulu Publishing Services rev. date: 05/16/2014

Chapter 1

He knew it was a bright sunny morning even without looking out 8 am and it was too hot for sleeping in the small aft cabin of his 29' Searay Sundancer. Even on Lake Michigan in June the sun heated up the cabin quickly. Sure the boat was air-conditioned, but he rarely spent his days on board since he had started building his dream house the timber frame home he had wanted all his life, now almost a reality. The contractors could have finished it two months ago but that's not how the dream had gone. It took Doug Hines twenty years to become a master craftsman and cabinetmaker. Ten years of building other peoples dream homes and ten years of building high-end wooden store fixtures. Doug didn't mind the work he had come from a long line of hard workers and was proud to carry on the tradition. Doug wasn't the one the bosses pushed to get the job done, Doug was the one they relied on to get the job done right. Now at 42 he had the time and money to make some of his own dreams come true. The world had never made sense to Doug, 22 years to make $16.35 an hour with a few thousand in the bank. Then Doug decided to follow another dream and wrote a novel. A book deal, a movie deal and a few book signings later and he had $7.8 million in the bank. Twenty two years to earn less than 17 bucks an hour and five and a half months to become a millionaire.

Doug lay in his bed for a few minutes trying to decide whether to work on his house today or scrape the algae from the bottom of the boat. He had spent the last two weeks "mudding-in" the walls of the house so he decided it was time to take a break from it. Besides, he thought, it would feel good to take a swim. After fifteen minutes he climbed out of the aft cabin and went into the galley. He got a small sauce pan from the cupboard and filled it with a few inches of water before putting it on the stove. He then got two eggs and the package of English muffins out of the refrigerator. He put the eggs in the sauce pan, turned the stove on high, and put two halves of a muffin in the toaster. Then he went to the fore cabin to see if he had any scuba tanks filled with air. Two full and two empty, enough for the day's labor, or at least he hoped they would be. Doug went back to the galley and put the toasted English muffins on a plate and scooped the somewhat-near-three minute eggs onto them. After covering his eggs with a generous supply of pepper he got a glass of milk and went topside to eat.

Doug was greeted on deck with the temporarily blinding sunshine. The temperature in Grand Haven Michigan this morning was only 61 degrees, typical for early June, but with the clear skies it would be 70 to 75 degrees by noon. The dew on the boats deck showed what little remained of the night's fog.

Doug sat at the pilot's seat to eat his breakfast. After the heat of the cabin the cool air and slight breeze felt refreshing. He sat listening to the sounds of the marina. Even the protected marina couldn't keep the power of Lake Michigan at bay. The sound of small waves kissing the boat could be heard, the gentle rocking of the boats causing the bumper guards to squeak and the lines of the sailboats to slap against their masts. The wooden pier creaked with the gentle waves and the sound of gulls foraging for their breakfast could be heard from every direction. Doug knew it was going to be a good day; the gulls hadn't found him yet, or more to the point they hadn't found his breakfast.

The morning had always been Doug's favorite time of day, a peaceful time of reflection. Since gaining his financial freedom he now had time to watch the well-orchestrated morning rituals.

Funny, he thought, it had always seemed hectic and rushed when he was a participant. Now he sat on his boat and looked past the other boats to the shore where the small shop owners of the coastal town prepared for another day. Signs were being carefully placed outside the shops telling of the wonderful treasures to be found inside. The sidewalks were being swept or hosed down and the windows cleaned. A few of the merchants were standing around sharing the morning news. Only the open-air cafe was busy with the breakfast crowd. Soon the coastal resort town would be bustling with tourists, bustling by Grand Haven standards anyway.

Grand Haven is a small town stretched along the Lake Michigan shoreline where possibly 10 thousand hardy souls brave the Michigan winter and the average 140 inches of lake-effect snow that comes with it. The town grows to about 15 to 20 thousand residents every summer with a few thousand tourists. They come for the white sandy beaches, the boating and sailing, and of course for the legendary fishing. The lake keeps the night temperatures cool enough for sleeping and the sun warms the temperatures to the mid to upper 70s during the day. Never too hot and rarely too cool for the active lifestyle the people enjoy along the coast. The town's one fault, if you can call it a fault is that it tends to get windy in the afternoons. The resilient folks of Grand Haven take advantage of the wind by coloring the sky with an amazing display of kites. Kites of all shapes, sizes and colors. Kites that can be purchased at several of the town's tourist shop.

Grand Haven is probably best known for its Coast Guard Days Festival in late July. Along with the hydroplane races and the normal array of small town activities the Coast Guard usually brings one of its larger boats for the people to explore. The festival is West Michigan's way of thanking the Guard for the many services they provide on and around the lake. The men and women of the Coast Guard are more than willing participants and seem to enjoy their time in the spotlight. Other than this one week of the year Grand Haven is about as laid back a tourist town as you can find.

Doug finished his breakfast and watched the sleepy little town wake up. As he sat he reflected on his strange life. Four year earlier his life had changed when a doctor diagnosed him as bi-polar and started him on a drug called Lithium. It was as if a veil had been lifted from his eyes. He remembered that the first change he had noticed was that salt and pepper had different shapes. Salt was a crystal and pepper was granular. He had probably noticed it before but this time it was incredibly clear. A few days later he noticed the wrinkles in people's hands and faces. He could tell if people worked with their hands or if they had lived hard lives. He saw lights and heard sounds in a way he had never experienced before. Before he would go to the mall and the lights, sounds and rush of people overwhelmed him, often forcing him to leave, sometimes causing a panic attack. Now he went to the mall just to gaze at the lights and watch the people. These observations came in the first week of taking Lithium. In the following weeks he found that his memories were coming back to him. It's not that the memories had been erased it was that his thoughts had been racing for so long that he had no time for memories. For the first time in his life he heard silence and he liked it. The constant dialog of thoughts was gone. He called it linear thinking, a thought came into the back of his head and traveled forward gaining shape and clarity as it traveled. There was no more interference, no sidetracking, no multiple thoughts, only a peaceful clarity. Unfortunately, his fantasy life vanished as well. It was like waking up from a dream and now having to face reality.

Doug's reality hadn't been that good when he first experienced a quieter mind. He had few friends, male or female, preferring the solitude and his hobbies. He went to work and preformed his job with almost robotic efficiency, never standing around or talking to the other workers, even taking breaks and lunch in his car so as to keep to himself except when the job dictated otherwise. Doug's home life had been even more secluded, a small apartment in Grand Rapids, Michigan and a garage he rented and turned into a woodworking shop. His mind never at peace, the constant fantasies that ran like songs that you can't get out of your head, only these songs were in story form like constantly running movies that could last for months. Even in conversation the movies never ended. For Doug this had been the normal state. It was only through tremendous force of will that he had been able to function at all, his obsessive or robotic work habits the result of that force of will and his stubborn resolve to keep going on.

Part of the problem was that Doug liked the fantasies. It wasn't like reading a book or watching a movie. He was living in the stories that he created in his mind and they allowed him to escape the loneliness of his reality. His fantasy world had become both the cause of his isolation and an escape from his lonely existence. The problem was made even worse because Doug enjoyed the fantasies. They were good, far better than the movies he had seen or the books he had read. It had always occurred to him that if he could just write one of them down he would be able to sell it. Unfortunately, the fantasies would not subside long enough for him to put his thoughts together or to write much of anything.

To some extent, evidence of future problems had always existed in Doug but they grew progressively worse with time. In high school Doug was considered a normal kid with a strong interest in sports, accomplished in art, good scholastically, all in all a bright and promising future. He started college in architecture, but drinking problems and an ever-growing social inferiority complex had forced him to drop out. He was able to stop drinking at age 25 and he put all his energy into work, where he found a great deal of success and personal pride. While Doug's successes at work grew, his home life became ever more isolated, the fantasy world that would soon consume his mind growing stronger with the passing years. At age 30 the old and the new caught up with Doug, the old, a relapse into alcoholism; the new, disabling panic attacks attributed to agoraphobia or "fear of the marketplace." The panic attacks prevented him from doing such simple tasks as grocery shopping or going for an eye exam. The fear and anxiety of being around other people would often prevent him from even leaving his apartment long enough to collect the mail. The next three years were spent battling both the booze and the panic attacks. Doug was successful in dealing with both of these issues but in the end it was the fantasy world that would control the next decade of his life.

Doug had found the treatment and counseling he received intoxicating, not only from a personal standpoint but also from watching the progress of others. Group counseling was especially enjoyable for him, not only for the help it provided him and others but because in his isolated world it was the one place he felt secure with other people. It was in private counseling that Doug learned the relaxation and meditation exercises that allowed him to defeat the panic attacks. Systematic Desensitization, the process of going into situations that he knew would induce an attack and allowing the attack to happen, all the while trying to recite his mantra for the day or find the peaceful spot he had practiced finding hundreds of times during relaxation exercises. Then when he could get the mail consistently without an attack he moved to the mall or the grocery and starting the process all over again. While Doug found recovery to be one of the hardest things he had ever done, he also found that the process enticed him. Years later when the final piece of his psychiatric adventure was added, that being the bi-polar diagnosis and medication, Doug found himself back in college studying psychology in the hope of becoming a counselor and sharing what he had learned to help others. After one year of school he left when he realized that what he had seen and experienced in the real world of clinical psychology and what he saw and heard in the ivory tower world of experimental psychology had very little in common.

As he sat in the sunshine at the captain's seat of his boat Doug realized that his thoughts were taking him down an old and worn path. It's too nice a day, he thought, to waste it on feeling depressed or to run the old shoulda-coulda-woulda-beens tapes. He would save that for another time. Unfortunately he knew that day would come. Doug gathered his dirty dishes and headed for the sink in the galley to wash them. Then he got his phone and headed back topside. He found the phone number of Stan's Rental on speed dial and called. After all the equipment he had rented working on his house, the voice on the other end of the line recognized his immediately.

"How goes the house?" asked Stan.

"Not bad, finished mudding in the walls yesterday, now she's completely dried in, except for the fireplaces." answered Doug. "Now I can take my time with the rest, get it right ya'know. Figured I'd do a little work on the boat today."

"Shoot, son, you don't know what a little work is," laughed Stan.

"Maybe true, but it's the only way I know that things get done. I also know it's easier to get the algae off the hull once a month than once a summer when that stuff turns to cement," Doug told him. "Wrong again, it's easier to get someone else to clean the hull for you," Stan joked. "Suppose you'll be needin' the hall buffer, then."

"Yeah, right, if I hired someone to do it you'd all be saying I let success spoil me," Doug joked "And yes to the buffer."

"True enough, but we'd be green with envy when we said it," Stan replied. "Come on down. I'll put everything you need to the side."

Doug thanked Stan and hung up the phone. Doug then called his publisher, Jim Spears. He had managed to write a few chapters of his next novel, more to keep Jim happy than anything else. Writing might pay better than woodworking, but in Doug's heart he was a craftsman. As usual Jim liked the work and asked when he would see more of it. Jim reminded Doug of every contractor he had ever worked for. You could finish a house in a day and they would still complain about how long you took for lunch. One thing he does like about Jim and about writing and cabinetry work is that quality really is job one. When it's wrong you can feel it in your soul.

Before leaving the boat, Doug grabbed the two empty air tanks. Might as well get them filled, he said to himself, I'll be right there anyway. He walked through the security gate of the marina and headed to the 1984 Ford pickup he had just bought at the auto auction for $1,200. Granted, the truck wasn't much to look at but the tires were fair and the engine ran pretty smooth. He had a newer truck and an expensive new convertible but most of the time he was hauling stuff for the house and he didn't want to trash them. Securing the tanks in the bed of the Ford he climbed in and started it up. The older engine sputtered and coughed a few times before catching. Three tries, he thought, she'll do better when she's warm.

Kim James and Ashley Johnston are looking for something; they're just not sure what it is. They have been in a loving relationship for a little over six years, living together for the last five, yet there is something missing. They have tried various men but most seem to want to either dominate them or split them apart.

Kim is a 36-year-old registered nurse who has spent most of her career in cardiac ICU. She is a beautiful woman of Irish decent with green eyes and shoulder length brunette hair. A bit of a tom boy, she comes from a large athletic family and loves to shoot hoops, golf, or rough house with her brothers as much as she loves to dress up and stun in an evening gown-and she has the looks to pull it off. Raised in a traditional Catholic home and married at 19 to a boy she met at church and had dated since middle school, Kim's world came crashing down at 22 when she found out she was sterile. The grief of knowing she would never have children and the betrayal she felt when her husband filed for divorce took her years to overcome. She had several different relationships after the divorce, but none lasted very long. Work became her refuge, her reason to go on. She was good at it and it gave her life meaning, but not fulfillment. Then she met Ashley. It was to be her first experience with another woman, one that would change her life.

Ashley is a high school English teacher in the ladies' home town of Overland Park, Kansas. An avid reader from an open-minded artistic family, she dreamed of being a writer someday. Her flowing writing style could support her dream, but her imagination, or possibly her limited experiences, had so far had fallen short. She was left to critique the works of her students, which more often than not made her cringe. Ashley had long, platinum-blond hair silhouetting a face that was between cute and pretty. Her body wasn't as curvaceous as Kim's, Ashley being a little bit skinnier, but she could still hold her own against most of the high school girls. No doubt Ashley had been the object of several of the boys' early sexual experiences, even if it was only in their dreams. At 33 Ashley had not given up on having children but with a sex drive that leaned more towards women the prospect did pose an interesting problem.

The ladies had just gotten out of another failed relationship with a man named Bob. Bob had seemed perfect at first, understanding, gentle, and kind with a good job and an outgoing personality. Overall he had great potential. But not long after the three moved in together Bob seemed to stop seeing Kim and Ashley as individuals and seemed to be there only for the sex. It was a story the ladies had repeated several times over the last five or six years. It was after the breakup that Ashley convinced Kim to take the summer off and do some traveling. They would set out on both an adventure to see America and a test of the strength of their relationship. If the two could survive three months in a car together they would start planning the wedding. So the ladies packed up Kim's Audi Q5 Crossover, mostly with cloths, and set off to find America. They planned to stay at bed-and-breakfasts as much as possible, hotels when needed, and campout when they could. Neither of them had much experience camping but they wanted to give it a try.

Their plan was to go north to Michigan and the Upper Peninsula, then West to Seattle, down the Pacific Coast Highway to Route 66 and then back east to the Outer Banks of North Carolina. The plans were tentative at best. The real plan was to go wherever the wind took them. The lack of planning was unusual for Kim and Ashley, but Ashley had made Kim read an amazing book about the free-spirited adventures and deep thoughts that took place on an unplanned bicycle trip across the country. Written by an author named Doug Hines, the book was a cross between "Zen and the Art of Motorcycle Maintenance" and "Travels with Charley"

"...even with rationing my water was running low. I am down to about 2oz for every five miles and with the dessert sun and the 95 degree temperatures it is not enough. There is hope, I just passed a sign advertising a gas station and bar 10 miles ahead. If true it will make 86 miles of hot dry dessert between water stops. The age and poor condition of the sign worries me. If the station is not there it will be another 10 miles into town.

Great news-the bar is open. Bad news-there is a line of about 20 Hogs with Hells Angels written all over them out front. Time for a plan: get in, get a gallon of water, get out alive. Granted it wasn't one of my best plans but it was the best I could come up with at the moment. When I walked into the bar the first thing that caught my eye was six glass doors revealing shelves of refrigerated beverages. Five and a half of those doors were filled with long-neck bottles of Rolling Rock Beer. I saw what I was after on the bottom two shelves of the door to the far right. Looking a little farther to the right and into the deep "L" that gave the building its shape I could see four or five pool tables, leather, beards, tattoos, and some of the meanest looking sons-of-a- bitches I had ever seen in my life and they were all looking at me.

With as much bravado as I could muster I ambled up to the bar. There in the corner of the refrigerator not filled with beer lay my desire a six pack of Squirt. I did my best to get the attention of the barkeeper, but he had no interest in serving me. It was then that I realized that I had gotten the attention of one of the big uglies, 5'8", dressed in leather, long hair, tattoos, full beard and boobs.

When it started hitting on me I knew that my life as I had known it had come to an end. Then I noticed another of the uglies approaching, 6'2" and dressed in leather, long hair, tattoos, full beard but this one didn't have boobs and didn't seem very happy about me talking with the one who did.

"Where ya from?" he asked in a menacing voice.

"Well I started riding in San Francisco, then down the coast to L.A. and now I'm heading to Phoenix," I said almost paralyzed with fear.

"What kinda bike you got?" The loathing in his voice was matched only by the angry look in his eyes.

"A Trek" I answered, noticing that all the people who had been playing pool where now gathering around to join in the fun.

"What's that, one of those Jap bikes?" he challenged angrily, thinking he had found an avenue of attack. At this point I decided my best bet was to lie and told him it was made in Wisconsin. He then asks me some questions that a motorcyclist might know but as a bicyclist I couldn't answer. I finally told him it was an 18-speed touring bicycle.

"A peddle bike!" he exclaimed in surprise. At this point a few of the others left the bar and quickly returned with my bicycle in tow. Smart, I thought, Get rid of the evidence. To my shock and relief they all started inspecting the bicycle and asking me questions about my journey. They even bought me a hamburger and fries and a six pack of Squirt before sending me on my way.

In the world of psychology it's called Peer Group Recognition. In every high schools all across America the jocks, the nerds, the egg-heads and the shop rats all have their own place in the social order of the school. These larger groups are then broken down into smaller groups based on popularity, socioeconomic factors, taste in music, or any number of other factors and eventually they break down into small groups of friends. While there is crossover among the groups, an individual student is most likely to find his or her group of friends through trial and error in navigating this system. That student then becomes part not only of their group of friends but also of the peer groups surrounding their group. It's a circle with another circle with another circle around it, then another circle around that one, and another circle around that and so on. The inner circle is their small circle of friends. The next circle might be labeled friends of individuals in the inner circle. The next circle might include their friends and all of the shop rats who like rap music. The next circle could include all shop rats. In a school the outer circle will be all of the kids who go to that school. If any of these circles are threatened by an outside force individuals within the circle will band together to defend it. If a member of the small group of friends is threatened the group will tighten around them. If the circle labeled shop rats who like rap music is threatened, then all of the individuals within that group will band together to defend it. If the school is threatened, perhaps by another school at a Friday night football game, then the whole school will form a peer group and defend its honor.

Peer group recognition is an inescapable part of being a social animal. You will face it at work, at home, at the kids' soccer games, and everywhere else you go. You will even find it in a motorcycle gang like the Hells Angles. On this hot day in a bar in the Mohave Dessert, this thirsty, overheated bicyclist was accepted as part of some outer peer group by a band of Hells Angles and for a half an hour was welcomed to get a bite to eat and something to drink before continuing on his journey. An acceptance that I have often thought about but have chosen to never pursue again.

The book had instilled in Ashley a desire to undertake an adventure of her own. She had gone on other people's adventure tour packages and she had enjoyable vacations and fond memories from them. This time she wanted the real thing, the freedom to make her own rules, follow her own path, let the wind be her guide-only without the exertion of bicycling and the need to break through the ice of frozen streams to bath in. She wanted to awaken the free spirit and possibly even the author she felt inside her but couldn't quite touch. Kim loved Ashley and was certain that Ashley was already in close enough communication with her wild side; it was part of why she loved her.

Kim agreed to take the summer off and travel the country for deeper reasons. The dreams that were planted in her by her family, her friends, her church and society had all seemed to crumble at her feet-but not for lack of effort on her part. Now approaching 40 she was considering marrying another woman, an idea that would have been unthinkable a decade earlier. Ashley was taking the trip to fulfill one of her dreams. Kim had already found her dreams. She had found them broken and she needed some new ones.

Kim and Ashley left Kansas on a Monday morning in early June, taking I-70 to St. Louis, Missouri then turning north on I-55 to Chicago. Even though they both liked the city life they were eager to get away from it all. They spent the first night near Gary, Indiana then took I-94 to the sandy beaches of the West Michigan shoreline. Stopping early on the second day to get in some sunbathing, the ladies were able to find a room with a view of Lake Michigan at their first bed-and-breakfast located half way between Holland and Grand Haven Michigan. With no plans or schedule to keep, they decided to spend their third day exploring the shops and marinas of the coastal town of Grand Haven. Around 10 a.m. the ladies stopped for coffee at an open air cafe overlooking a marina.

Doug picked up the hull buffer from Stan at the rental shop, then had the two scuba tanks filled and headed back to the marina. On the way he remembered that he had promised Karen, the owner of the small book boutique located on Grand Haven's waterfront and near his boat that he would stop in and sign a few copies of his book. Doug found it amazing that people who hadn't read a book in years would jump at the chance to buy one that was autographed. Karen looked at it differently; it might be Doug's first novel but it made it to number four on the New York Times best sellers list, and a lot of people saw an autographed copy an investment.

Ashley loves books. She loves to read them, she loves the way they look and most of all she loves how the old-leather bound books smell. She couldn't afford the more expensive first edition classics, or the autographed copies the collectors bid on, but every once in a while in the corner of some used book store she would find a copy of a favorite book from a beloved author. They were usually too far gone for the collectors to have any interest in them, so Ashley would purchase the book and give it a good home for another generation. When Ashley saw Karen's Book Boutique down the street from the cafe where she and Kim were having coffee, it was a must stop for the ladies. Kim loved the look and smell of the old books as well but mostly she loved how happy the books made Ashley.

As the ladies walked up to the book boutique, an old worn out truck with bald tires and an engine that was obviously in need of repair pulled up and parked in front of the store. They wondered what this man could possibly want in a bookstore. He was kind of cute, though. He had light brown hair and was wearing tan shorts and a yellow polo shirt, six feet tall and a little over 200 pounds. He obviously worked hard or worked out. He held the door for Kim and Ashley, giving each a smile and an approving glance as they passed. Inside they saw a woman they correctly assumed was Karen. Karen was with another customer, but gave the ladies a welcoming smile then waved to the man and motioned him to her desk. The man must be her husband, they thought, as they began looking through the racks of books. Kim tapped Ashley on the shoulder and pointed to a tabletop display of "Thought on a Long Lonely Highway" by Doug Hines. Unfortunately, the man started collecting the copies from the display. It made them sad to think the book wasn't selling anymore and was being replaced with a newer title. Then, to their amazement, the man stacked the books on the desk, sat down behind it and started writing on the inside cover of the books. It hit them both at the same time. They looked at each other, it couldn't be. They both jumped when Karen asked "Is there anything in particular you're looking for today?"

Kim pulled herself together first and asked, "Is that Doug Hines?"

Karen realized why they had jumped, and with a chuckle said, "Yes it is. Would you like to meet him?" Without waiting for a reply she called over to Doug, "I think your fan club is here to meet you, Doug." With that both ladies blushed.

"Can't be my fan club, there's one to many." Doug said, looking up from his work. "You're not going to tell me you actually read my book, are you?"

"Not only did we read it," Ashley chirped, "we're on a trip trying to revive a little of the magic for ourselves."

"Magic," Doug repeated with a hint of query, and then jokingly said, "I strongly recommend you read it again. I think you missed something. So what kind of trip are you on?"

15

"Sign a copy of your book for us and we'll tell you," Kim answered with a smile.

"One book or two," Doug probed, already guessing the answer.

"One will do nicely," Kim replied with a meaningful smile. "I'm Kim James and this is Ashley Johnston."

"So Kim and Ashley," Doug said while writing a note in one of the books, "how are you two reliving my journey?"

"Kim and I are taking the summer off and traveling around the country," Ashley said with just a bit too much enthusiasm. "Only we're doing it by car, not on a bicycle."

"Yeah, probably a better way to go," Doug said looking up from his work. "I haven't really figured it out myself. I've traveled the country by bus and by bicycle. I even drove a semi for a year. Travel by car, interesting concept. I congratulate you on your spirit."

With a polite laugh Kim said, "Ashley is a high school English teacher and uses your book in her class."

"I didn't know they learned to read by high school," Doug said, wishing he could stop being sarcastic. "You must be a good teacher," he added with sincerity looking at Ashley.

Ashley rolled her eyes and responded, "Sometimes I wonder, you should try reading some their stories."

While Doug continued autographing the stack of books for Karen the ladies told him their travel plans. He mentioned several places that he had found worth visiting that were on their route and might think about including in their plans, and several places that were just tourist traps that he recommended they avoid. After 20 minutes he ask Ashley and Kim if they would like to continue the conversation over a cup of coffee at an open-air cafe just down the street. With a playful smile from Karen, the three left the book boutique and started down the sidewalk towards the cafe. Along the way the ladies pointed out some of their favorite boats and Doug told them who owned them. Doug pointed to his own boat and asked if they would like to see it. After entering the marina through the security gate the ladies soon found themselves surrounded by hundred thousand dollar boats of every size and description. Doug could tell they were more attracted to the sailboats than the power boats, but when they came to his they put on a good show. Once onboard they were surprised at how much room was in the cabin and impressed by the controls.

"It's a calm day on the water. If you'd like we can take a short cruse," Doug offered.

"It's almost lunchtime we could make a picnic of it," Ashley suggested after glancing at Kim to make sure she wanted to go.

"Yeah, that sounds good," Doug agreed. "I have to get some gear out of my truck first." So it was decided that Doug would retrieve the scuba tanks and hull buffer from his truck while Kim and Ashley got three boxed lunches from the open-air cafe. It also gave the ladies a chance to get some things from their car.

"I can't believe we actually ran into him," Ashley said excitedly once they were alone. "And he seems like a nice guy. A lot of times you meet these people and they're kinda jerks."

Always the more conservative one, Kim replied, "Let's don't be too quick to judge, he might want more than just lunch out there."

"I'm not so sure that's a bad thing, he is kinda cute," Ashley said, putting her arm around Kim. "Besides, we came on this trip for adventure. What better way to start?"

Kim couldn't argue with that. She shrugged and said, "Let's go with the flow."

When they were all back on the boat, Doug started the engines and called to the ladies to release the mooring lines and quickly get on board just like he had shown them. Keeping the speed slow so as not to disturb the other boats, they soon cleared the harbor entrance and headed into open water. Once clear Doug throttled up the engines to make 23 knots and headed south-southwest to a small lagoon he often used for fishing and diving. Stepping away from the controls he convinced the ladies to take turns at the helm. He showed them how to work the Doppler radar and the sonar on the screen built into the dash. Mostly they just talked and admired the large houses that lined the coast. The ladies were surprised to hear the names of the many big celebrities who owned some them.

When Ashley asked him which one of the mansions was his, Doug did his best to change the subject. He wasn't entirely sure how they had all wound up on his boat. He wasn't ready to invite them to his house, not yet anyway. "Let's see how the afternoon goes," he told himself. Approaching the lagoon, Doug took over the control to navigate the rocks guarding the entrance. He was glad to see that nobody else was in the lagoon and that they would have it all to themselves.

"This is one of my favorite places on the lake," he told the ladies. Both ladies agreed it was beautiful.

"Can you swim in here?" asked Ashley.

"It still might be a little cold. The water is only about 15 feet deep but there are some deeper holes down there that are fun to explore. I've got a couple extra wet suits if you girls scuba dive," Doug said

"I'm licensed," Ashley told him, "but I haven't gone since my open-water certification. I'd love to do it again, though."

"This isn't a bad place to learn," Doug prompted Kim. "The water isn't too deep and it's as clear as anyplace on the lake. If you want to give it a try this is the perfect opportunity."

Kim was reluctant, but with Ashley's assurance that it wasn't hard she finally gave in. Doug collected all the scuba gear he would need for three divers from the cabin and began setting them up on deck while Kim and Ashley went below and changed into the swim suits they had gotten from their car. He was glad that he had pulled his wet suit half way up when the girls emerged from the cabin in their bikinis. "These two are hot," he thought to himself as he handed them each a wetsuit. As Kim and Ashley struggled to put on the heavy wetsuits, Doug reeled in the 12 foot Zodiac he used for a life raft. Loading the scuba tanks, buoyancy vests, and other gear into the Zodiac, he explained to the ladies that he had taught other people how to dive and had found it worked best if they started from the shore rather than the boat.

Once aboard the zodiac, Doug reached into a satchel he brought and pulled out six 8" long fishing bobbers, fishing line and a frozen store bought fish fillet. "The cafe makes good sandwiches but fresh fish is better," he said with a smile.

"Your bait is frozen," Kim pointed out.

Doug picked up the package of frozen fish and played with it 'til the ladies figured it out. Finally he said, "Where do you think frozen fish comes from? Sorry," he said sheepishly "It had to be said."

"No it didn't," laughed Kim.

Baiting the hooks with one-inch chunks of the frozen fish, he then threw the six lines toward the opening of the lagoon and headed towards the beach. Once on the shore Doug fit the ladies into the scuba gear. He began the instructions by showing them how to equalize the pressure in their ears by pinching their noses and turning their heads from side to side and blowing like they were blowing their noses. He then showed them how to use their buoyancy vests. He finished the instructions by showing them how to breathe through the respirator. With the restrictive movements caused by the wet suit and the weight of the scuba gear, the ladies put on quite a show getting into the water, but with effort they were soon all underwater. Even with the wet suits the water of Lake Michigan in early summer is frigid, but it was clear and the initial shock of the cold water was soon replaced by the awe of the new world they were exploring. Kim and Ashley were amazed to see the amount of life just below the surface. Due to the lagoon being heavily explored, the fish that made it their home were accustomed to people, and the three of them were soon surrounded by schools of fish. Doug produced two zip lock sandwich bags full of fish pellets that he had brought with him and handed them to the ladies. Soon Kim and Ashley were being besieged by Walleye, Trout, Bass, and Perch, and even a Coho Salmon stopped by for the treat. He could tell the ladies were having a great time and backed off and watched them jester and point, all the time bumping into each other excitedly. With the fish pellets gone and the Coho in no mood to be petted, Doug signaled the ladies to follow him. They explored the rock formations and the deep holes that made up the lagoon. The tanks they were using held enough air for a 30 minute dive, but for Kim and Ashley the time passed in an instant.

"That was incredible," Kim shouted excitedly when they reemerged near the zodiac.

"And you thought it was too dangerous," Ashley teased her. "It is too dangerous," Doug said "People get into trouble all the time, then they panic and forget the proper procedures for getting out of trouble."

"Do people die out here?" Kim asked as she and Ashley started removing the SCUBA gear and weight belts and putting them in the Zodiac, following Doug's lead.

"Occasionally," Doug answered. "Most of the time they eventually regain their bearings or they're with someone who can help them, but you hear a lot of crazy stories, especially when they try to explore ship wrecks before they're ready."

"That's what would be really cool. Are there any ship wrecks around here?" Ashley asked excitedly.

"All kinds, the Great Lakes are both a grave yard for ships and because the cold freshwater reduces decomposition, it's also a historical preservation site. Let's build a fire and I'll tell you about some," Doug suggested.

As the three of them gathered drift wood, Doug told them of some of the wrecks he had explored and the tales of some of the heroic rescues by lighthouse keepers in the old days. The ladies listened intently as he started the fire. With the ladies huddled around the fire to warm up after the chilly dive, Doug took the Zodiac out to check the fishing lines that he had set earlier. The lines produced five good-sized walleye, the perfect amount for a fish stew. He headed back to the Searay to get what he would need. When he arrived back on the shore the ladies had spread two beach blankets and were lying out in the afternoon sun. They watched as Doug filleted and cubed the Walleye, chopped an onion, diced three tomatoes, wedge-sliced two potatoes, opened a package of frozen shrimp, and stirred all but the potatoes together in a bowl with the contents of a can of chicken broth and some basil and pepper. Doug then used the mixture to fill most of a rectangular package he made out of aluminum foil. He then put the potatoes in one end of the rectangular package and sprinkled them with Rosemary and margarine, then tightly sealed the package. Their curiosity was piqued when he started digging a hole with his hands in the sand. "What are you doing?" Ashley asked.

"I forgot to bring a pig," Doug replied as he filled the bottom of the hole with coals from the fire. Placing the aluminum foil package on top of the coals, he then covered it with sand and joined the ladies on the beach towels. "Probably should have marked the spot," he said trying to look concerned. "You can't believe how many of those things I've lost."

"We still have the sandwiches," Kim said casually, and rolled over. Kim was acting nonchalant, trying to hide the fact that she was in heaven. Doug sat down next to Ashley and the three of them talked about adventures and jobs and romances and anywhere else the conversation took them for the next 40 minutes. As Doug dug up his fish stew, the ladies set out a bowls and utensils from the picnic basket that Doug had brought. Doug asked for the sandwiches and slaw they had bought from the café earlier to go with his stew, but as soon as the ladies got one whiff of the stew and potatoes they put their sandwiches back. "This is delicious," Kim admitted. "Where did you learn how to do this?" she asked.

Doug looked at Ashley but he didn't have to look long. "On a long lonely journey," Ashley answered with a smile. Doug returned the smile, but he couldn't help thinking that she was more right than she knew. When their lunch was finished and Doug had loaded everything back into the Zodiac, he looked back to see if the ladies were coming. When he saw they were still on the beach blankets and sharing a deep kiss, his heart almost skipped a beat. When they gave him an inviting look his heart almost stopped. Soon it would be Doug that would spend some time in heaven.

When they were back on board the boat and returning to Grand Haven, the three of them sat a little closer than on the way out. This time none of them had any interest in who owned the big houses that lined the shore. The ladies were engulfed in Doug's description of the timber frame house he was building when Ashley abruptly asked, "Have you ever had a relationship with two women?" Doug was momentarily stunned by the thought of entering a relationship with these two.

Quickly recovering, he answered "I've been with two women before but never in an actual relationship. It was more of a physical thing."

"Your choice or theirs?" Kim asked.

"Life's, it just wasn't there. I'm not even sure it counts, it was in Hollywood when I was there writing the movie script for my book. It was sort of an experiment for me and I think a career move for them," Doug said, slipping into the deeper, more distant mood that the ladies were beginning to understand. Kim and Ashley looked at each other but nether broke the moment of silence. Doug faltered as he arranged his thoughts. "I always wondered... I think dating two girls might be the key, it would give them someone to talk to. The last girl I dated, she actually asked me out, she loved the creative mind, or so she said, but she didn't understand it. When I'm writing, actually typing, you can disturb me as much as you want, I'd even prefer it. Don't because that's how I make my money, but that's the labor end of writing. The creative end is the fantasies and they can't be disturbed; if they are they might or might not come back. The fantasies are the important part of writing, at least my style of writing, and they happen when I'm working on the house, or building cabinetry, or walking in the woods, or hitting shags in the field, or just staring into space. So this last girl, I'd ask her not to disturb me for a while and go off and do my thing, then pretty soon she would come up dressed to kill and doused in perfume. Then she would accidentally bump into me somehow. She wanted me thinking about her when I needed to be off in never-never land "working," and she won, she put my mind on her 'til I kicked her out." Both Kim and Ashley laughed at the way he said it, but they were also both taking notes on the rest of what he was saying.

"It sounds like a lonely world," Kim said, looking at him closely.

Doug looked at her and thought long and hard before answering. He decided to take a chance, "There's a thin line between crazy and brilliant sometimes. I used to be lost in a fantasy world, barely able to deal with society. I was a high-functioning psych patient, then I took a pill and all of a sudden I still had my fantasy world but I had control over it. So I wrote a book, made lots of money, and now I'm a creative genius. Truth is I'm the same person. The only difference is that today I have a little more control. The loneliness didn't come till I started taking medication to make the fantasies go away." He paused for a moment to see how they would react to that statement. To his relief, both ladies cocked their heads slightly and deepened their gaze. "For a long time the fantasies had been an escape for me from a rather dismal reality, a cause and escape might be a better way of saying it. When I first started taking medication and got control of my thoughts my reality didn't change, it was still dismal. Without the fantasies to mask reality, reality sucked. When coming in from out of the fog, reality is one hell of a place to land," The last line he said almost to himself, it was a line he had used many times. "Now that I'm living in a rather pleasant reality and I have control over my thoughts the fantasies are a pleasant pastime and a very lucrative profession. When you buy my book you're paying me to share just the shadow of what I've lived in my mind, only an outline that I was able to get on paper. The whole thing would take volumes."

"Do the fantasies still takeover sometimes?" Kim asked with the concern indicative of a nurse.

"Have you ever heard the song "Just Breathe?" They both had so Doug continued, "There's a line in there, "two AM and I'm writing this song, if I get it all down on paper it's no longer inside of me, threatening the life it belongs to," or something like that, anyway. Whoever wrote that knew something. It really hit home. I still have fantasies that try to take over sometimes, but now I fight them. For me one of the best ways is to write them down. Telling them to someone else can also work sometimes, but it's easier and more effective to write it down."

"It's easier to write it than to just tell it? Seems like it would be easier to tell it," commented Ashley.

"Yeah, it sounds strange, but when I'm that deep it's really hard to communicate. And if I do manage to tell someone whatever wild story I'm trying to get rid of, they generally want to hear more of it, or get scared and freak out, or they ask a lot of questions that would take forever to explain. It's easier just to write it down," Doug replied.

"Sounds like a book of short stories to me," Ashley said only half-jokingly, the English teacher showing through.

"Imitating my publisher will get you nowhere," Doug said in a mockingly confrontational voice as he started maneuvering the boat into Grand Haven Harbor.

Chapter 2

He was surprised at how worried he was that they wouldn't show up. After the fun day they had spent on the water, Doug had invited the ladies to dinner at his house. He had told them a little about his troubled life, maybe too much, nothing that bad, or maybe it was just that there was worse to tell. It wasn't uncommon for him to make a date and have the lady cancel or not show up. Doug was a minor celebrity and while his life story had never been published in the tabloids his life had been thoroughly researched by them, and his story was readily available on the internet. Kim and Ashley seemed like the type that would go back to their hotel room and Google him. It was only fair, he had goggled them. Always the optimist he had already started a fire and had a large cauldron hanging from a tripod almost ready to boil. He threw the Ham bone he had bought in the caldron. When they arrived he would show them around his 28 acre compound, if they showed up that was.

As soon as Kim and Ashley had returned to their hotel room they did Goggle Doug Hines, for Ashley it wasn't the first time. Ashley had researched the writer before discussing his book in class. With that and what Doug had told them that afternoon nothing they found on the internet surprised or alarmed them enough to change their plans.

"If he's as good of a cabinetmaker as he is a writer this could be one of those incredible log homes," Kim said.

"It's a Timber frame home," Ashley corrected her. "What's the difference?" Kim asked.

"I don't know, but I know that people who do get mad when you confuse the two," Ashley explained.

They discussed how much fun they had had that afternoon and that they were both looking forward to the evening. What would come of it they would just have to wait and see? Like most people who visited Doug's compound they got lost on the way so Doug was relieved when they called for directions. The closest town only had 260 residents, mostly farmers, it was said that you could lead a New Orleans style funeral procession through the main drag and it wouldn't slow down traffic. From town the directions to his house got a little rural.

As soon as the ladies emerged from the trees that hid the house from the gravel road they knew it was worth the effort. Entering a six acre clearing they found the compound was still a work in progress. The older barn to their left seemed to be in good shape, what they correctly guessed was Doug's shop on the right was new and appeared to be finished. Directly ahead and sitting on a small rise overlooking a wide section of one of the many inland waterways that fed Lake Michigan was the house. Doug had told the Girls that it was a comfortably sized home. He said that big houses were a testimony of ones ego and a haven for loneliness and depression. Using the compound approach he would be able to expand as needed or desired, yet keep a cozy feel to the entire project. Driving up to the house the ladies liked the simple two story timber frame home with its steeply pitched roof. The roof was accented with twin dormer windows on each side but still had several tarps protecting the openings that would someday become fireplace chimneys. The house had several windows on the ground floor that looked out on a covered porch which ran the entire length of the house. It had the look that Doug had described, an unassuming West Michigan country home. With the open area of land surrounding the house and its additional buildings all overlooking the waterway it was easy to see that although it was a work in progress it would be well worth the effort.

"You found it," yelled Doug as he walked up to the house from the fire pit near the workshop. "I said it was a little off the beaten path."

"Off the beaten path!" Kim yelled back. "You're road isn't even on my GPS."

"Not by accident," Doug boasted as he gave Ashley a hug and kiss next to the passenger side door. "Cuts down on groupies," he added as he met Kim's embrace.

"This is really nice," Ashley pronounced. "The grounds look like a golf course."

"It used to be a sod farm but the soil had too much sand in it and the rolls of sod broke apart when they tried to lay them out, before that it was a hay field," Doug explained.

"How did you find it?" Kim asked.

"It belonged to a Mennonite family, most of their kids decided to leave the order and they were downsizing. A friend from my woodworking days had a friend who had a friend, I bought it on sight. I have the clearing," Doug told them pointing as he talked, "the woods out to the road and about a hundred yards of woods on either side. Not to mention about a quarter mile of river frontage."

"You can't keep your boat on the river?" Ashley asked.

"Can and will as soon as I build a dock. Lake Michigan is about seven miles away and there's a lock about three miles downriver. Come in the house let me show you around," He answered offering them each an arm.

"Does the river ever flood?" asked Kim.

"Not very often," Doug explained as they climbed the four steps onto the porch. Turning around he added, "If you look you can tell that all the buildings are on slight raises that keep them above flood stage, but really the last flood was 25 years ago and they've done some additional work upstream to prevent it from happening again. You're safe it's not like trying to control the Mississippi."

"What's that going to be?" Ashley asked, pointing to an area of the clearing that was being worked.

"Bunkers for the first green," Doug answered opening the front door.

As they entered the house the ladies gasp. It was a reaction Doug had often heard and never grew tired of. Even though the flooring wasn't installed, the walls still unstained, the fireplace unfinished, and the general mess of construction everywhere, the effect was still stunning. Guests walked into a formal entrance hall highlighted with a large American Walnut arch leading into the great room. Through the arch was the focal point of the house, a wall of windows that reached from the floor to the ceiling and was divided by an unfinished stone fireplace. The high roof the ladies had noticed driving up formed a T to the back of the house making the wall of windows and the great room seem enormous. Through the windows was a view of the river and the wooded bank on the other side. Walking in Doug explained that the arch was scavenged from a 120 year old mansion that some yuppies had converted into apartments and some of his friends who had done the work managed to scrounge for him. As they passed through the arch they entered the great room and looked around at the loft they had just passed under. The loft had a walk way on either side overlooking the large great room. Noticing the ladies gaze Doug explained that on each side of the upper floors were rooms, a bedroom and working office on one side and the master bedroom on the other. A sitting area located over the entry hall finished off the upstairs. On the first floor to the left was the garage which opened to the side of the house and an open area to the back of the house that faced the river, it would eventually be the kitchen and breakfast nook and had plenty of windows to take advantage of the river view. To the right on the main floor were two more rooms, the room to the front of the house was going to be used as a media room and Doug's permanent office would overlook the water at the back of the house. It was a long way from finished but still impressive.

"It looks like you've got a lot of work to do. How long will it take to finish?" Kim asked.

"Till I'm too old to work or I die is the general plan," Doug answered. "At this point I'm working to get it livable so that I can move in. Then I'll slow down and start doing custom work. I should have it presentable and move in by fall if all goes well."

"It's incredible as it is," Ashley said enthusiastically as the ladies started exploring. Opening the only door that had been hung they found the garage. They were both glad to see that Doug had a new truck and not just the auto auction special he had been driving around that afternoon. The rest of the lower floor had more unconnected pipes and wires than finished areas. Other than the view it was hard to imagine how it would look when finished. "I don't think that I would have the patients to wait. I'd have the contractors finish it as soon as possible."

"Most people would," Doug agreed. "I've spent most of my life building beautiful projects that I only saw finished if I had to package them for shipping, and that's when I saw the finished project at all. You're used to seeing finished projects, but this is what I'm used to. I see the finished project in this. Come upstairs and I'll show you the drawings. Can either of you read plans?"

Climbing the makeshift stairway to the loft the ladies first wanted to see the master bedroom. Again the view through the wall of windows was spectacular and with the upper decks finished they were able to step out the French doors and onto the bedroom's balcony with its spectacular view of the river. Returning inside the ladies saw that large bedroom space was empty and the master bath was the same unconnected pipes and wires they had seen in the kitchen. "I think this would be my first priority, this and the kitchen," Kim said as she checked out the two walk in closets.

"I have a friend who is one of the best tile guys in West Michigan. He's going to help me with the master shower as soon as I finish installing the walls and plumbing," Doug explained as he showed them how the large walk in shower would be laid out.

"Where does the tub go?" Ashley asked.

"Under the front window, but I haven't decided if I want a prefab multiuser spa type, or one of those old cast iron tubs," Doug said prompting the ladies for ideas.

"Multiuser spa," said Ashley.

"Two of the cast iron tubs side by side," Kim suggested.

"Or a built in tub with a tile deck flush with the rim of the tub for candles and flowers, maybe a TV and stereo built into the wall," Doug said, his hands painting a picture for the ladies.

"Yeah," Ashley responded, "that's what I want." "Loose the TV," Kim said.

Moving to the opposite side of the loft area they entered what Doug called his working office, it would eventually be used as a bedroom. This time it wasn't the view that caught the ladies eyes but the most beautiful raised panel desk they had ever seen. The desk had nine inlaid panels on each side and twenty four across the back. Brass hardware on the eight drawers accented the rich dark satin finish. The desk top had a deep satin finish and a Tiffany style banker's lamp sitting on top that finished the desk to perfection. "You didn't build this did you?" Kim gasps, much to Doug's delight. "It's a work of art."

Reaching into a file in the desk's deep bottom drawer, Doug produced a stack of drawings he had drawn for the desk. "It took 195 individual pieces to make the desk, each one designed to interlock together," Doug explained as he showed the ladies the drawing and pointed to the corresponding pieces of the desk. Kim and Ashley tried to look impressed at the drawings but Doug could tell that the ladies had no idea what they were looking at. Putting away the drawings he pulled out three small pieces of wood that he had run through the mitering process but that hadn't made the final cut for use in the desk, he and showed how detailed each piece was. Again his efforts were met with enthusiastic blank stares and smiles. That's OK, Doug thought, Kim had called his desk a work of art, that's all he cared about. He put the desk plans away and moving to his drafting table. He opened a drawing pad that he was using to plan the layout of the compound. With the ladies close at his sides he showed them the plans for the nine hole golf course he was building. The course only had three large greens but by tearing the greens and using three different colored flags on each, then shooting at them from three different directions it made it a nine hole course, sort of. Kim had learned to play golf with her brothers as a child and liked the game. Ashley had never played till she met Kim and had only gone out a few times. Still they approved of the plan whole heartedly. They responded to his plans for sculpting the land to build the high banked turns for the snowmobile race course with a little less enthusiasm.

"Have you ever thought of getting horses?" Ashley asked.

Flipping through the pages Doug told her that there wasn't much he didn't have a plan for. "Personally, I don't like riding anything that doesn't have handlebars, but eventually I do want some kind of animals." He showed them a plan that included a horse barn and two adjoining paddocks. The larger paddock was two and a half acres with a half-acre in the pines. The second was a smaller riding area next to the barn. "Eventually I'm probably going to build this, but unless someone really wants to take care of the horses it probably won't be for a while." Catching his drift Ashley snuggled in and said she'd think about the job. "Of course if nobody wants to take care of the horses I'll probably get some camels."

"Camels," They both said in surprise.

"Well that or lama, I haven't decided," Doug said.

"If not horses go with the lama," Ashley recommended.

"Can camels live this far north?" Kim asked.

"Yeah, I should probably check on that before I get them, I'm pretty sure they crossed the Alps with Hannibal and his elephants, didn't they? But seriously how many people do you know who have Camels?" Doug asks. The ladies couldn't argue with that kind of logic.

"How about a goat," Ashley prodded. "Don't get a goat," Kim countered.

"No goats are cool," Doug argued. "Have you ever gotten into a head butting competition with a goat?"

"A what?" exclaimed Kim? "Doesn't
it hurt?" Ashley asked.

"They try to back up and get a running start and if you let
them they can knock you out, but as long as you keep your head in
contact with theirs it's just a pushing match," Doug explained.

"I think we're starting to zero in on the problem," Kim told
Ashley.

"See these long thin scars on the back of my hand," Doug
showed them. "There from bull fighting."

"You fought a bull," both ladies asked in amazement.

"Well not really," Doug admitted. "I climbed into a paddock
with a bull and threw dirt clods at him till he got mad, then I
lost my nerve. The scars are from the barbed wire fence trying to
get out."

With a throaty laughing and a shake of her head Kim asked,
"By any chance were you drinking back then?"

"Well, yeah," Doug admitted. "It might have been something a
little stronger than that."

"You should have put that in your book," Ashley said shaking
her head and looking at Kim.

"I wasn't drinking when I rode across country, or when I wrote
the book," Doug told them. "I fought the bull back in college."

"Have you ever gone cow tipping?" Ashley asked. "I used to love
doing that."

"I've never done it, but I've heard that it's fun," Doug told her.
Kim just walked away. Doug and Ashley followed discussing the
lesser known points of animal care.

Returning to the loft's sitting area overlooking the great room,
Kim stood look over the railing. She agreed with Doug's plan, "You got
it right, it's big enough to be awe inspiring yet it doesn't have that
hotel lobby feel that some of these homes have."

From the loft Doug pointed out where he planned to put the
dining room table and various pieces of furniture. "It's going to be
beautiful," Ashley commented. "High ceilings have never felt
intimate to me though."

"I agree that's why the media room will be so important." Doug explained "I'm not going to do it like a modern theater room, more like a pillows on the floor family room. It has a stone fireplace and I'll build another fireplace on top of it in the master bedroom. The foundation is set, but I haven't started on them yet." After returning to the main floor Doug led the ladies out the back of the house through the French doors, then over some scaffolding, around some piles of construction debris, to finally to the garage at side of the house where his four seat Polaris side by side was parked. After climbing in he drove them along the bank of the river and showed them where he planned to have the pier built. To date he had not secured the permits to dredge and mark the area so that it would be deep enough to safely operate anything that required more than a few feet of water. As they drove into the hardwood forest on the east side of his property he explained that the hardwoods were the older of the two forested areas he had. The pine woods on the west side had been clear cut and reforested about 15 years ago, the hardwood forest, though not old growth, were much older and had grown naturally. Doing a large U turn in the trees they remerged from the woods next to an old lean-to that had once been used to store hay, now it stored four large logs. "Have you ever seen the History Channel show Ax Men when they recover old growth log from the swamp?" Doug asked.

Kim and Ashley looked at each other, "We know what you're talking about, but we never really watched it," Kim said looking at the logs. "Are those old growth logs?" she asked.

"Two of them are. They were recovered from Lake Superior. The other two are from the woods we just drove through. They need to dry some more before I have them cut. I've got a guy who is going the run them through a kind of CAT scan and give me a computer read out on what's going on inside them. Then I load that information onto a program I have, along with the plans for what I want to build, and it computes exactly how to mill the logs. Then all need to do is feed all that information into a computerized mill and you've got exactly what you need to build you're project. Assuming you don't screw up too much that is," Doug explained.

"That's cool," Ashley said genuinely impressed. "Do you know what you're going to build with them?"

"I'm hoping the two old growth logs will produce enough for the formal dining room set, maybe even the table," Doug said. "I haven't got any plans for the other two yet, maybe bookcases for my office or just miscellaneous pieces of furniture. I need to check on dinner," He told them as he continued driving to the now dying fire. "So what's on the menu?" Ashley beamed, admiring the old four gallon pot hanging from the tripod. The ladies both laughed when Doug picked up a three foot long ladle that looked more like a movie prop than anything anybody would actually use. When Doug used it to lift the meaty, foot long Ham shank from the caldron the ladies laughter turned to surprise.

"It's going to be a cool evening so I thought a bowl of Ham, Potato and Cabbage soup would taste good," He answered. "I need to go over to the shop and mix up some flat bread to go with it." Then with an equally comical size pair of tongs he picked up three flat stones and set them in the fire. "Gotta get the grills nice and hot," he added.

"We're going to cook the bread right on those rocks?" Kim asked with a smile. "I've heard of that, but I've never seen it done before."

"That's the plan," Doug answered as he built the fire back up. "It will take the potatoes about a half an hour to cook, you girl's getting hungry yet?"

"You're the boss," Kim said totally enjoying the evening.

"I want to finish the tour," Ashley announced. "This compound of yours really cool."

Next he took them to his shop. The shop was in a new timber frame building matching the main house but designed similar to a horse barn. It too had a high pitched roof to protect against the weight of the winter snow, accented with dormer windows to match the main house. Instead of stalls with horse's noses sticking out, the barn was lined with windows on both sides and barn style double doors on the ends. As they entered they could tell the building was divided down the middle with a stairway, one side was set up as Doug's woodworking shop and the other side had two rooms that were currently being used for storage. Doug explained that one of the rooms would probably become a finishing room for his woodworking projects and that the other would be set up to do glass blowing and pottery.

"How long have you been doing glass blowing?" Ashley asked, finally excited about one of Doug's hobbies.

"I'm hoping to get started in about a year," Doug answered. "But I have everything I need when I do. What I really need is someone who knows how to do pottery so I can have as much homemade stuff as possible," he probed.

"I took a couple of pottery classes as electives in college," Kim said.

Doug pointed to a box, "There's your kiln," he said. After looking around a little they headed upstairs to the studio apartment Doug was living in till the house was ready. Meager might be an understatement considering what else he had shown them, a few pieces of furniture, a piece of plywood for a desk, a queen size bed set up on cinder blocks, and a small kitchenette. It was large room with eight dormer windows and hardwood floors. The floors were partially covered with several randomly placed mismatching rugs. Perhaps the most notable feature was the stacks of woodworking magazines piled next to a leather chair.

"Nice to see you're a guy," Kim told him. Doug shrugged then moving to the kitchenette, he and Kim started mixing the dough for the flat bread while Ashley checked out the handmade quilt on the bed.

"Do you want to see the barn?" Doug asked as they left the shop with the flat bread dough, a picnic basket, and two furniture rugs to be used as ground covers around the fire. They decided to just look inside and they were glad they did when Doug told them on the way that the fifty year old barn was the product of a traditional

Amish barn raising. Once inside the ladies were amazed that the large barn could have been built in one day. Doug pointed out some features they were sure would have impressed someone who knew what he was talking about but did little for them. For the most part it was a barn with a tractor, several tools, and a bunch of wood stacked inside. Kim did notice a car in the corner with a cover over it that she guessed was another project Doug would get around to working on some day. Soon they returned to the fire where Doug began cutting up the potatoes while Kim and Ashley took a short walk.

"And you didn't want to come," Ashley prodded Kim. "This place is incredible, I think Doug is too."

"Yeah, I gotta admit he's got it going on here, I think Doug's pretty special too," Kim confessed. "But what are we doing, three days into our cross country adventure and were going to fall for the first guy we meet?"

"I know, I know, but he is kinda an adventure in himself. Besides we might learn something He's got enough projects going on maybe we can get in on one of them," Ashley countered.

"Too many," Kim observed, "he seems to be in over his head. A lot of those boxes weren't even opened."

"True, but if you think about it he pretty much won the lottery, he earned it writing that book, but he still got a lot of money all at once," Ashley pointed out. "From what I've seen all the stuff he's bought he is capable of using. I've heard of a lot of people being a lot less responsible in that situation."

"Well that's true. I kinda wish he had that glass blowing oven set up," Kim thought out loud. "I wonder if he cooks breakfast over an open fire."

"My guess is that he can, he has, and it would probably be pretty good," Ashley laughed.

When they returned to the fire Doug was pulling the flat stones out of the coals. He showed them how to make a bed of hot coals to rest the rock on and keep it hot. Grabbing a hand full of dough they soon each had a piece of flat bread baking on their rock.

The flat bread turned out to be edible at best, but the Ham and Cabbage soup was incredible. Soon the three of them were sitting on the moving blankets and watching the fire. Doug inadvertently brought up the topic he was hoping to avoid when he ask the ladies about their volunteer work sandbagging during a recent flood of the Mississippi river.

"You Googled us," Kim accused in feigned indignation.

"That's terrible," Ashley added. "I fell so cheap."

"Of course I Googled you, but it's OK, I couldn't find any sign of gold digging, no restraining orders, neither of you has even had a prostitution charge, I was impressed. Didn't you Google me?" he countered,

The ladies looked at each other. "Yeah, it was quite a read," Kim answered looking intently at Doug. "You've had an unusual life."

"Unfortunately it's been more unusual than it should have been." Doug had learned that changing the topic from his problems to the problems with mental health treatment in general was an effective way to avoid talking about his past life. "Some of the worst problems I faced were actually caused by the misdiagnoses of the psychiatrists and the meds they gave me. I'm a recovering alcoholic and I did some drugs back in the day, enough to know what I'm talking about anyway. I swear the drugs available on the streets can't hold a candle to the stuff the psychiatrists are handing out. Once you've done psychotropic drugs the street stuff is about like putting your forehead on the end of a baseball bat and spinning around till you get dizzy for a few minutes. Granted it takes psychotropic drugs two or three months to really take over, but once they do they take control of your life to the point that you can't remember what you used to be like. They're not like taking drugs anymore, they're the new normal, and the new normal is way out there."

"To hear them tell it all you have to do is take a pill and your life is all rainbows and spring flowers. That's the way it is on those commercials anyway," Ashley said empathetically.

"I know there's a pretty high relapse rate in psychology, is misdiagnosis a big problem as well?" Kim asked.

"You don't really relapse into mental illness, except addiction that is, for the most part it never goes away," Doug corrected. "For a small handful of people they do take a pill and usually receive a little counseling and life is better. But they need to get the right pill to the right person and the right counselor for the right client, that's where the system is falling apart. In my case and in over 70% of all cases they're giving the wrong person the wrong pill and often the wrong counselor. In my case it happened several different times and for several years. As far as you're advertising goes wait till the new DSM5 is released."

"I've heard they have some real problems with the psychology section in DSM5," Kim agreed. "How's it going to affect advertising?"

"The big two," Doug began, realizing he had awoken the nurse in Kim, Ashley was admiring the view, "Disruptive Mood Dysregulation Disorder, formerly known as temper tantrums."

"I thought temper tantrums were caused by bad parenting," Ashley commented, the teacher's interest being aroused.

"Sometimes," Doug acknowledged, "the kid throws a tantrum at a store and eventually the parent gives in and buys the kid a candy bar or whatever the kid was going off about, thus guaranteeing that the next time the kid wants something they will throw an even bigger tantrum. Kids throw tantrums when they want something, when they don't get their way, when they don't feel well, all kinds of reasons. Don't get me wrong, some kids who throw tantrums might have underlying psych issues that need treatment. But 20 ago when I first took psychology in college, they said tantrums were a part of the growing experience, learning your place and developing social and coping skills for later life. When DSM5 is released all you have to do is take the kid to a psychiatrist and get him a pill to deal with it. What do you think the chances are that that won't be abused?" Doug asked.

"So that means in twenty years we'll have an entire population of Pop Stars running around." Ashley joked.

"That or the pharmaceutical companies will come up with a drug for adults with temper tantrum issues," Kim added.

"But the fun's not over yet. Remember grieving?" Doug asked sarcastically. "That terrible feeling you get when you lose a loved one, a pet, or a job. In the olden days people went through the grieving process, denial, anger, bargaining, depression, and acceptance. Not only did people have to go through it, but for something as devastating as say the loss of a child, they had to go through it multiple times. Good news now we have Major Depressive Disorder. Now all you have to do is go to your psychiatrist and take a pill. The question is just exactly how this affects the overall recovery process that the grieving process provides. Didn't taking drugs to keep from dealing with emotions used to be referred to as stuffing your emotions or self-medicating?"

"I've heard about that one from my hospital," Kim said. "I think there are even some mental health providers that are going to stop using the DSM5 because of the changes. They do seem to favor the pharmaceutical companies and go against traditional wisdom."

"Well, traditional wisdom also includes creationism and a flat earth. Personally I don't have a problem challenging traditional wisdom sometimes," Doug countered. "It will be interesting to see how long it takes from the time the DSM5 goes into effect till the pharmaceutical companies start advertising the cures for the changes it makes." It was refreshing for Doug to discuss psychology with Kim. She took a very practical down to earth approach that was free from the emotions and stereotypes that discussing the topic often brought on. Ashley displayed more of the emotions that generally got in the way when mental illness issues are raised and it was clear to both Doug and Kim that Ashley was ready to change the topic. With the three of them sitting under the stars on the moving blankets they had brought from the shop, Doug pulled out his last trick for the evening, an IPad and three laser pointers. Soon they were lying back trying to identify the constellations with the help of Google Sky. If the night air had been a few degrees warmer

Doug probably would have cooked them breakfast over an open fire, but it was still spring and to cool for a sleep out. Eventually they made their way back to Doug's studio apartment over the shop.

Chapter 3

Doug woke early the next morning and watched the ladies sleep for a short while. He hated the awkwardness of the first morning, and the uncertainty of the ladies plans made this one even more uncomfortable. Quietly he slipping out of bed and went to the kitchenette where he put some water on for tea. Reaching into the refrigerator to find something for breakfast he was startled by Kim's gentle hand on his back "Good morning," She said, amused by his reaction, "Did you forget about us?"

"No, I defiantly did not forget you," he whispered, giving her a little kiss. "Can I interest you in something on a bagel?" he asked, getting the left over ham from last night's soup, some eggs and cheese out of the refrigerator.

"I usually just have a yogurt for breakfast," Kim told him. "That won't hold you over if you plan on working till lunch," Doug said giving her an inquisitive look. Kim understood the question and answered by looking over at Ashley who was still sleeping, then giving Doug a smile and a shrug. "Coffee or tea?" Doug asked, understanding the answer. The two of them drank their tea and talked for twenty minutes or so while Doug ate his breakfast sandwich. When he finished he reached for his shoes and told Kim he was going to check on some things in the house.

"We'll be over soon," Kim told him as he left. After waking

Ashley and giving her a full report on her conversation with Doug the ladies discussed their plans.

"I would like to stay for a few days and see what happens," Ashley said plainly.

Kim had always been amazed at how simple and unencumbered Ashley always is. "I agree he's seems like a great guy but if he's so great why is he still single?" Kim knew her argument would be easily challenged, she wasn't entirely sure why she putting up an argument at all. It was that old voice that always seemed to get in the way, that voice that was put in her head a long time ago, that voice that Ashley didn't seem to hear.

"Simple," Ashley stated, realizing that Kim's heart was ready to stay but that her head was telling her to her proceed with caution, "he didn't really start dating till two or three years ago, and he didn't have any real money till two years ago. Add to that the whirlwind that he must have been on after the book started to sell, and the simple fact that he just might not have found anyone yet, it's not that hard to see."

"I know, I know," Kim conceded, "so what are we going to do, help him build his house?"

"You think he'll let us?" Ashley said excitedly.

When they got to the house Doug was getting things ready to add a few layers of rock to the fireplace. He nervously gave Ashley a kiss but his spirits picked up when she asked what project they were going to work on this morning. "We're going to add a few layers to the chimney, but we need to pick out some rocks from the pile first. Do either of you know how to drive a Bobcat?" He asked them.

"What's a Bobcat?" Kim asked.

"I thought it would be Ashley who would volunteer," Doug said in mock surprise as he led the ladies out the back door. They climbed into the side by side and headed to the barn. Once inside he showed Kim the bobcat and reluctantly she climbed in. After giving her a very quick lesson on how to drive it he reached into cockpit and started the engine. "Try not to knock the door posts down on the way out. It would probably collapse the barn," he yelled back to her as he and Ashley made their way back to the side by side. To Doug's amazement, and Ashley's great pleasure, Kim drove the bobcat out of the barn like an experienced pro, or at least not like a bumbling amateur. In the four by four Ashley badgered Doug the entire way to the rock pile which was located near the pine woods. Looking back to watch Kim following in the bobcat it was obvious that she was not only getting the hang of driving it, she was also teaching herself how to use the scoop attachment on the front. When they arrived at the rock pile Doug showed the ladies what rocks to look for in terms color and size to match what he had already used in building the fireplace. The rocks were round and between 6" and 10" in diameter and while the ladies could move them around enough to search for the ones they wanted, Doug had to lift them into the Bobcat's scoop. With the rocks gathered and loaded they headed back to the house, Doug and Ashley in the side by side and Kim in the Bobcat. Kim was feeling confident with her driving skills by the time they got to the back of the house but when Doug instructed her to put the scoop inside the open French doors she lost her nerve.

"It's OK you've got the hang of it," Doug said reassuringly standing beside the Bobcat. "Just raise the scoop so that it's about a foot above the floor line, then center it between the doors. Then all you have to do is drive slowly forward till the scoop is inside the house and lower it to the floor." Kim tried to protest but with Doug's calm voice and Ashley's encouragement she slowly moved the Bobcat's scoop into position and drove it into the house and lowered it to the floor. Climbing out of the cockpit Kim was ecstatic and both Doug and Ashley gave her congratulatory hugs.

"I can't believe you did that!" Ashley yelled excitedly. "I could never have done that. I would have been a nervous wreck."

"I was actually more nervous driving it out of the barn," Kim told her as they followed Doug inside. "It all kind of lined up and felt right. It was still kind of scary pressing the accelerator though." With the scoop full of rocks now just feet from the fireplace, Doug had Kim start rolling the rocks into a metal bucket he had tied to a rope and was using to lift the rocks to the top of the scaffolding. He and Ashley then climbed up the ladder. The fireplace was already about fourteen feet high and Doug was happy to have someone at the bottom to load the rocks so that he didn't have to climb down with every load. While he and Kim worked on getting the rocks to the top of the scaffolding, Ashley began mixing the mortar by pulling an inch of the dry mix into the water at a time and mixing it with the hoe like he had shown her. With the rocks on the scaffolding and the mortar mix ready, Kim climbed up and joined them. Doug showed them how to select the rocks by color and size to match what he had already done. The ladies enthusiastically went about their job of picking the next rock to be laid and eventually even got the hang of laying the mortar itself. The rocks were heavy and they let Doug lift them into place. In no time at all they had added three feet to the eight foot wide fireplace, six more feet and Doug would have to move the scaffolding outside to finish the chimney.

"That's about all we can do on the fireplace today," Doug told them. "The mortar needs to set or the weight of the rocks will kind of squash things out of place if we try to do too much at one time." By now it was lunch time and with Doug doing the heavy lifting for both ladies he had had about enough for one day. "If my neighbors are home and they let me use their pontoon boat, would you girls be interested in taking a tour of the river?" He asked. The ladies readily agreed and it was decided that Ashley and Kim would fix a lunch to take with them while Doug drove to his neighbors to pick up the pontoon boat. An hour later they were cruising up the river eating their lunch.

"I can't believe how narrow the river is. From your house it seems as wide as the Mississippi," Ashley commented as they left the lake like area that Doug's property bordered and entered the river.

"The land around here is pretty flat," Doug explained. "It will widen and narrow all the way to the spillway five miles upriver. At some points it's only about thirty feet wide, at others it's several hundred feet wide."

"How far up river can we go?" Kim asked, passing Doug the bag of chips.

"Only to the spillway, there isn't a lock up there we can use, only a fish ladder for the Salmon. Then we'll turn around and head back towards Lake Michigan. We go through one lock on the way and then stop and eat dinner at the marina at the mouth of the river. The mouth of the river is kind of a neat place to explore. There are a couple of shops and an antique store at the marina. I have to take it down there to fill the gas tanks anyway. Did you bring some warmer cloths for the ride home?" They assured him that they had done as he had instructed earlier and the three of them sat back enjoying the tour of Doug's river. The ladies were struck by the diversity of the houses they passed. Million dollar mansions next to what looked like hunting cabins and several well cared for farms that Doug told them belonged to members of the small Mennonite community that was in the area. It was a beautiful ride up and down the river, and an experience for the ladies to go through the lock at the lower spillway.

Following an afternoon of exploring the river and the small but well equipped marina at its mouth, they had what turned out to be a very good diner on the patio of the marinas restaurant. The three returned to the pontoon boat and started the ride home just as the sun was setting. Kim was awestruck by the beauty of the river in the fading light of day. The cool evening air causing a mist to rise from the river gave a surreal look to the path that lay before them. The sound of the engine and the voices of Ashley and Doug discussing works of literature added to the enchantment till she heard Doug say in a loud voice, "How dare you call me Lancelot, what did I ever do to you?"

"What do you have against Lancelot? He was beautiful," Ashley asked defensively.

"Beautiful on the outside maybe, inside he was a bumbling egomaniac," Doug countered. "And Guinevere was nothing to write home about either. She married Arthur to be Queen and cheated on him with the first tall, dark and handsome knight that came around. Now she's turning tricks at a road side brothel since Lancelot dumped her for the first pretty bar maid that smiled at him."

"What are you two talking about?" Kim asked in bewilderment.

"Doug's jealous of Lancelot," Ashley told her.

"Jealous?" Doug countered getting angry, then just as quickly calming down he said. "Well actually you're right, I am jealous of Lancelot's ability to deceive women and get anything he wants from them. If what you really want is your very own Lancelot I'll tell you how to find him. Go to the nearest County Clerk's office and ask for a list of dead beat dads, there you will find all the Lancelot's you want. Lancelot isn't even British, he's French."

"I Thought Lancelot was one of the heroes of the story?" Kim asked.

"He is kind of a bumbling fool," Ashley conceded, nodding to Kim.

"It's all part of the magic of the Arthurian Legend," Doug said answering Kim's question. "One of its twists and turns. In truth it was Lancelot's son, Sir Galahad, who was the bravest, the purest, the noblest, the most worthy of all the Knights of the Round Table," Doug told her.

"I've never heard of him," Kim said.

"He didn't need for you to know about him, but he would have known about you," Doug assured her.

"Sorry, I should have called you Sir Galahad," Ashley said already realizing her mistake. Doug wasn't about to let her get away with it.

"Galahad still lives, one cannot be Galahad, one can only aspire to be like him." he shot back at Ashley who was already nodding her head, acknowledging her mistake. Then turning to Kim he added, "Sir Perceval, Sir Bors, and Sir Galahad went on a quest to find the Holy Grail, and they found it, the cup of Christ from the last supper which brings eternal life. Sir Perceval and Sir Bors tried to return home and tell the knights of Camelot the location of the Grail but they were both killed on their way back. Sir Galahad was given the honor of guarding the Cup of Christ till the knights' return, but the knights have not returned and Galahad still waits, still guarding the Cup of Christ."

"What do you think about the theory that the Holy Grail is actually the womb?" Kim asked.

"Personally I like it, but that's the only thing I liked about The Da Vinci Code if that's what you're referring to," Kim nodded that it was so Doug continued, "I don't believe that Jesus had a daughter for starters. Personally, I'm even offended at the idea that he or any of that group would lie or cover up something like that. And the Catholics aren't trying to replace Mary Magdalene with Peter, they just ignore Mary Magdalene. What they are doing is moving Mother Mary to a pedestal of her own and replacing her in the family photo with Peter, or symbolically with themselves."

Kim tried to respond to Doug's comment but Ashley, knowing that The Da Vinci Code was a challenge to Kim's Catholic upbringing, quickly jumped in, "Do you think that the two new Sherlock Homes movies go against Sir Arthur Conan Doyle's original characters?"

"I went through my Sherlock Homes period in my mid-twenties. I read about ten or fifteen of the books." Doug began quickly, realizing that he had just dodged a bullet. "At the same time I watched a Sherlock Homes series on PBS with Basil Rathbone playing an older and saner Sherlock Homes than Robert Downey Jr. did. In my opinion Basil Rathbone was the best Sherlock Homes of all the actors that have ever played the part of Homes over the years. He and his bumbling sidekick Dr. Watson, I can't remember who played him, made the perfect pair for the bulk of the books. But, and just by chance, the last two Sherlock Homes books that I read were the two that the new movies are based on and they really didn't fit in with the rest of the stories. It was almost like Ian Fleming was ghost writing for Sir Arthur Conan Doyle. The last two books just didn't seem to fit. Even the PBS series, or British series on PBS, didn't do a good job with The Game of Shadows. It wasn't till I saw the Downey-Law portrayal of Homes and Watson that the last two books really came to life for me."

"I've heard other people say that. I never really got into the books, but I love the new movies," Ashley said. "Do you think they should make another?"

"If they do I hope that they write an entirely new screenplay for it," Doug told her. "I haven't read all the Homes books, but Downey and Law wouldn't fit the ones that I have read. That being said I do hope they make another. I really enjoyed the two movies that they made. And remember that the question mark Sir Arthur Conan Doyle ended his work with left the door open for a new story."

"I really liked the movies too. I didn't know that Sir Arthur Conan Doyle really ended his writings with a question mark, I thought that was Hollywood," Kim said, still a little on edge. "How's your movie going to be?"

"Boring I think," Doug answered trying to be comforting, "but then I thought the book would be boring, people seem to like it though. It's hard to make a movie about an introspective, solo bicycle journey. The movie spends a lot of time on the adventures I had, and just kind of touches on the philosophy, the book is just the opposite."

"Some books don't make good movies," Kim agreed. "Are they at least your adventures?"

"Sort of," Doug explained. "There are a lot of extras added in. It's almost like someone else's fantasy story when I watch it. Don't tell anyone I said that though."

"It might make a good fantasy adventure if they add the right stories," Kim said remembering the stories from Doug's book. Still a little upset from the Saint Peter comment she added, "Someone told me that Isengard from The Lord of the Rings was a reference to the Vatican. Is that true?"

"Some say that Suraman the white is the pope and that Isengard is the Vatican, others say its Hitler and the Nazi Party. If you ask me the timing for when Tolkien must have begun his fantasy, not just started his writings, make it the pope and the Vatican. Tolkien was an interesting man, by today's standards he would be a tree huger, Greenpeace type, dead set against industrialization. He was also an animal lover and would probably be a member of PETA nowadays, and yes, he was raised a Catholic but had problems with it as an adult," Doug explained.

"Do you think he had a psych issue?" Ashley asked, partially knowing the answer.

"Absolutely," Doug said emphatically. "He was in a very active trench during WWI and saw a lot of people killed. Back then he was diagnosed as shell shocked, today he would probably be diagnosed with PTSD. The thing is that his imagination was so powerful that some people, including myself, think that he created Middle Earth as a way to escape the flashbacks from the trenches of WWI. Today I'm a bestselling author, five years ago I was on anti-psychotics to stop my racing thoughts, I.E. my imagination. The anti-psychotics did help stop my imagination but they replaced them with psychotic thoughts and paranoia for the fun filled four years I was on them. There's a difference between imagination and dilution.

I can't help but wonder if Tolkien had been diagnosed with PTSD today, and some psychiatrist had heard him talk about this place he had created in his mind that he called middle earth, if he wouldn't have been put on anti-psychotics as well. If he had we could very easily have lost the Hobbit and The Lord of the Rings." "That would be a shame. Those are great books and good movies," Ashley said.

"It seems like they tried to make Tolkien's work into movies before but they couldn't do it without all the special effects," Kim added.

"There is an animated version that actually pretty good, but for the most part the earlier versions are pretty bad," Doug agreed.

"And some movies should never have been made even with special effects. Have you seen Hitch Hikers Guide to the Galaxy?" Ashley asked Doug.

Doug just groaned, "I walked out of the movie. The book was

so out there that it made it a classic, and the British radio show the book came from is supposed to be the about the same way. The movie was just stupid. They say that a lot of great old movies were lost when the only copies burned in some big Hollywood movie storage warehouse fire. I can't help thinking how much more we lost when Hollywood's library didn't burn as well."

The three of them continued discussing books and movies till they got the pontoon boat back to Doug's friends dock. After tying the pontoon boat up, Doug and the ladies loaded their things into the old truck Doug had driven over in that afternoon. He told the ladies that when he picked the boat up that afternoon the owner had invited them all to a dinner party the following Saturday. The ladies said they would have to talk about it and would get back to him. To Doug's delight the old truck started on only the second try. "Must still be warm from this afternoon," Doug said with a smile, Kim and Ashley just groaned and rolled their eyes.

Chapter 4

———

On the forth morning that the ladies woke in the woodshops loft apartment they were greeted with a surprise, Doug had left them a pen and ink drawing of the two of them sleeping in each other's arms as they slept. Judging by the cheese stain on one corner they assumed that he had done it while he ate his breakfast. Even with the cheese stain they loved the drawing and they loved the idea that even on a busy morning like this Doug's thoughts were still on them. Doug had gotten up early to get ready for the work crew that he had coming to lay the hardwood floors. He had laid several wood floors himself and had repaired and refinished several more. He found it to be back breaking work and with a knee that he had injured playing high school football he was more than willing to let someone else install the wood floors in is new home. The tile floors in the kitchen, laundry room, and the three bathrooms, and the slate floor in the hall he would do himself, or hopefully with Kim and Ashley's help. Kim and Ashley had planned to spend the day shopping in Grand Rapids and when they got to the house to thank Doug for the drawing it was obviously a wise decision. With twelve workers already laying the flooring the house was a beehive of activity, they gave Doug a quick thank you kiss for the drawing and a second goodbye kiss and left for the mall. As planned they stopped on the way home and bought something for the three of them to eat for dinner. Returning to the loft at around 4:00

they prepared the glazed chicken and put it in the refrigerator for later. The ladies then went to the house to see how the floors were coming. To their amazement and delight the work crews were just finishing with the upstairs floors and all of the first floor was finished with the exception of the elaborate geometric pattern that Doug and the floor crew's one true craftsman were still working on. It looked great and they had Doug give them a tour and share in their excitement. When they eventually reached the master bath the news just got even better.

"Jim called this afternoon," Doug told them after finishing the tour.

"Is that your tile guy?" Ashley asked as the three returned to the railing in the loft that overlooked the great room and its patterned hardwood floor.

"Yep, he said he had a cancellation next weekend and can help me with the tile shower if I can get the walls and plumbing ready," Doug told them.

"Can you get them ready?" Kim asked.

"I don't have much choice now, I told him to plan on coming over and getting it done," Doug answered. "But I might need some help to get it done in time."

"Ashley, at your service." Ashley said bowing low in true dwarf fashion.

"I think that can be arranged," Kim added, laughing at Ashley's gesture and giving Doug a hug.

The ladies left to put the glazed chicken into the oven to roast and put their purchases from the days shopping away. Doug joined them an hour later. After dinner the three of them took a second tour of the house and eventually headed out the back to take a walk by the river. Finding a nice spot to sit and watch the water they talked about the next projects for the house. The night air was cool so Doug gathered some driftwood that was handy and started a small fire on the shore. Even with all the work that had been done on the house to talk about; and not entirely to Ashley's liking, Kim and Doug soon returned to their discussion of psychology.

"It's been about twenty years since the government changed the requirements for counselors and like most things the politicians fix it went straight downhill," Doug explained. "It used to be that experience counted, at least in alcohol counseling, that's all I was involved in back then. Most of the counselors that I ran into had a college degree in something, and at least two years of sobriety. Then they made it so you needed a college degree in psychology or social work and effectively took personal experience out of counseling. Some people went back to school and stayed in counseling but most of them just moved on. One of the best alcohol counselors I had was a pharmacist who liked sampling the meds before he gave them to his customers. When the law changed he had a choice of going back to school for two years and stay in counseling, or going back to being a pharmacist and earning about twice as much money. Naturally he chose to go back to being a pharmacist. Now days the thought of going into counseling really isn't even seen as an option by most people in recovery. I tried to get the degree but that's kind of the exception anymore," Doug explained.

"Isn't one alcoholic helping another one of key components of AA?" Kim asked.

"Not so much in the treatment centers, not with the staff anyway, education trumps experience," Doug told her. "The worst part is that all these people think that to be accepted they need to be alcoholic, or have some kind of addiction or mental health issue that they've overcome. They're constantly trying to relate with stories that just don't work. I heard one counselor lecture on depression, he said that one time he was walking through Walmart with his family and the thought hit him that it just wasn't worth it, all the work just to buy his family crap from Walmart, life just wasn't worth it. So having experienced this moment of doubt he now claims to understand clinical depression. I had another counselor when I was dealing with panic attacks tell me that he was walking up to the door to pick up a blind date and felt nervous, so now he understands panic attacks."

"I can see that the panic attack one is lame, but isn't questioning life part of depression?" Km asked.

"Of course, and being nervous picking up a blind date is part of panic, an unbelievably small part. They're bad comparisons to clinical depression and panic attacks," Doug told her. "A lot of the real disorders are life changing, all-consuming over exaggerations of real life normal healthy emotions. If you hear the diagnostic keys for a lot of psychological disorders you will very possibly diagnose yourself with the disorder, or at least relate to a lot of keys."

"That's true, I hear them talking on TV about obsessive compulsive disorder, or some mood disorder, and I wonder if I suffer from it," Ashley agreed.

"The truth is you should relate to them," Doug assured her, "and the more of them you relate to the more of Gods given emotions you have conscious contact with. A lot of mental issues are normal emotions taken to the extreme. Others are creations of the mind and even if you can relate to them it isn't always that bad. A lot of it's just having a healthy imagination till it takes over and becomes life altering."

"That all makes sense, but if we do have contact with these emotions why shouldn't we try to relate to people who are having problems?" Kim asked.

"It's offensive for one thing," Doug shot back. "About the same time I wrote my book and started making money the stock market and the housing market crashed and the depression or recession or whatever you want to call it hit. So say you lost your job and had one of those bad mortgages and your house is in foreclosure, you're thousands of dollars in credit card debt and you don't know where you were going to live next, or even how you're going to eat. Then I come along and tell you that I understand exactly how you feel because I had just passed the four million dollar mark and the very next day the stock market dropped over two hundred points and I only had three million seven hundred thousand dollars left. How would that make you feel?"

"I guess I can see your point," Kim agreed.

"And the most amazing thing is that people get mad at you when you don't accept their stupid attempts to relate. Most of the attempts are offensive, but to keep the peace you just have to sit there and take it, that or fight just about everyone," Doug said in exasperation. "In all fairness it isn't bad to empathize with people, we could probably use more of it in this world, but when someone needs to talk, shut up and listen."

Both ladies laughed and looked at each other a little nervously, both having been at times interrupted when they needed to talk, and both at times guilty of interrupting others. "Yeah, I can see that one," Ashley admitted sheepishly.

"Another problem is that people don't stop at relating, they move on to advising, and that's where they get into trouble. If you get nervous walking up to the door to pick up a blind date then stop, take a few deep breaths, give yourself some positive affirmations, and go knock on the door. That just doesn't work if you suffer from panic attacks, it takes a little more than a few deep breaths, it takes a lot more." The ladies both nodded in understanding so Doug went on, "Now imagine the counselor you've been spilling you're guts out to for the last several weeks, the counselor who's been saying that they have been where you are and that they understand and can help. Then this counselor tells you that what you need to do to cure your panic attacks and social phobia is to throw a dinner party, and I had a counselor tell me exactly that. All of a sudden you realize that they haven't been where you are, that they don't understand what you're going through, and that you have been wasting your time working with them. You could have gotten that kind of advice from your mother, or anybody else you might meet. So you walk out the door and just look up wondering what you're going to do next."

"So what do you do next?" Ashley asked a little uncomfortably.

"If you still have the strength and the will to go on, you start over," Doug sighed, remembering the old days. "When I was dealing with panic attacks I went to a couple of counselors that were no help at all. Then I took about a year and a half off and just adjusted my lifestyle to try to prevent the attacks. With social phobias leading to the attacks that pretty much meant locking myself in my apartment for a year and a half. In my case when I did come back out it wasn't with guns blazing, which seems to be happening more and more these days, I went back to another counselor. Fortunately, I eventually got one who was trained in Cognitive-Behavioral therapy and specifically Gradual Exposure Therapy and I was able to get the help I needed. By the way this guy wasn't suffering from anything, and wasn't being treated for anything, and wasn't recovering from anything, he was just a counselor, a good one, and an expensive one. I didn't get to finish the therapy with him because I couldn't afford it, but he taught me enough that I was able to finish the exposure therapy on my own. I had learned about Gradual Exposure Therapy in college years before, but you really need a guide who has helped others with it and who knows the way and the tricks to do it right. Once I found someone who knew how to prepare me for it, it was still hard to actually do, but it was pretty quick, and the way he taught it, it was pretty simple."

"Is Gradual Exposure Therapy the same as Systematic Desensitization?" asked Kim.

"Yeah, same thing," Doug said.

"Why didn't you go to someone who did Gradual Exposure Therapy from the start?" Ashley asked.

"Because counseling is for the most part is being done pot luck. You walk in the door and they assign you a counselor, and most counselors don't say what they specialize in, or they say they specialize in everything," Kim answered.

"Exactly, they're not certified in specific procedures like nurses or teachers, they're just certified in counseling. A lot of certifications are available, but they are not required. Imagine you get a promotion at work," Doug said expanding on Kim's comment, "but the new job requires you to move to a corner office on the sixth floor. You have a phobia about riding in elevators, or even more common a fear of heights that causes anxiety or panic attacks. You quietly go to a counselor so that nobody knows you're doing it, and the counselor start asking you about your potty training, or maybe your mother made you stand on a chair to get dressed every Sunday before church so now you have a fear of heights. Either way with years of talk therapy you might or might not overcome your fear of heights or elevators. Talk therapy is important in dealing with a lot of issues, and it can help a lot of people, but in this case you probably won't get the promotion because they probably won't hold the job open for long enough for you to go through that type of treatment. I would rather go to someone who has experience and training in Gradual Exposure Therapy to help me deal with my phobia. That way I can take a more direct approach at relieving the panic attacks that come from my fear of heights, or my elevator issue. So the question is how do you find the right person for you?" Doug asked shrugging his shoulders. "The counselors aren't licensed in the specific types of treatment they offer. Most of the PhD's in psychology don't advertise their specialties outside of the academic world. If they did require specialized licensing in psychology, like they do in other areas of medicine, then the client could choose the type of treatment that they want. Any move to specialization in therapy and away from the one size fits all, or pot luck therapy as Kim called it, would enable the client to find the help they need and find it in the style they want. Right now the major criteria they recommend for finding the right counselor is to find one you like. Personally I would rather have one who knows how to get the job done than one I like. I didn't go in to treatment looking for a friend. I went in looking for answers. I really don't want to spend the rest of my life exploring my inner soul with one of them.

"I took some psych classes in college and it seemed to me that they have enough different disciplines that they could specialize," Kim said.

"Actually at the university level they do specialize in social, clinical, sports, biological, developmental, educational, humanistic, evolutionary, industrial, cognitive, and several more. Then in the clinical setting students are trained in psychoanalysis or cognitive-behaviorism, and a few others. Then some of the clinical specialties have specific treatments that have been developed to treat specific disorders. The problem is that none of that matters to the client when finding a counselor or a psychologist because in the clinical setting its one size fits all. Imagine going to a doctor for heart palpitations and finding out after you've been seeing them for a while that they are actually trained in podiatry, or worse in psychiatry and not cardiology. There are more than enough different disciplines in psychology for them to specialize, and its past time they should be doing it," Doug explained to them in a rambling tone. "And after all of that when you actually get into treatment you have two choices, spend a ton of money or settle for talk therapy."

"It sounds to me like you're biased against talk therapy," Ashley observed.

"Not biased against just tired of, and wondering if one of the other styles would be more effective," Doug countered. "Currently even the counselors who were originally trained in other disciplines are just using talk therapy. It's pretty much all that's out there for the average person. It's not that talk therapy isn't needed; it's more like we need to rebuild the engine and get it working on more than one cylinder. Other treatment approaches are out there but they're hard to find and usually expensive. What usually happens is that you keep going to different counselors but you keep getting the same type of treatment, and you end up starting from the beginning with every one of them. There's no standardization, no book marks along the way, no finishing point."

"Didn't Einstein say that the definition of insanity is trying the same thing over and over and expecting different results?" Kim asked. "If what you're saying about all counselors using only one type of therapy is true, then going to more than one counselor is insane."

"Well, first of all it's never insane to keep trying to get better," Doug corrected. "As far as Einstein is concerned, you actually hear that a lot in alcohol and drug treatment. The thing is that even though AA and NA are only effective about thirty percent of the time, in reality they are the only proven options available. In psychology there are several options available, with research and treatment plans already in place, but the system is so stagnant that in most cases they are not being used and your only option available is talk therapy. If the average client wants to try a different approach, or a different style of treatment, then I wish them luck in finding it."

"If some of the other treatment options are better in certain situations, why are the counselors using talk therapy so much?" Ashley asked.

"It's cheap, it's easy, it's in style, and you don't have to get out of your chair to do it would be my guess. I really don't know, but with all the counselors I've been to, only one did anything but talk therapy. The worst part is that it's very easy with psychoanalysis to get into someone's head, so with a very basic understanding of psychoanalysis the counselors are able to break the clients down. Building the client back up is a lot harder, and a lot of counselors stop at breaking people down. Most of them say that the emotional release of talking about something is the answer. That's not right, that just gets you an exposed problem. You need to wrap the issue up, try to find some type of closure, then file it away and put safeguards around it, both to try to keep it in place and to manage it when it does surface again. You don't just talk about it and it's gone, and you don't just stuff it, you need to learn how to manage it so that it doesn't interfere with your life. I hear it all the time, people saying they love their therapist. I didn't go in to therapy to pay someone to be my friend or to have someone's shoulder to cry on, and I go to have someone I could bitch and moan to. I went into therapy because I had a problem that was negatively affecting my life and I wanted to deal with it. The therapists I had that actually helped me I can honestly say I didn't love, at least not at the time, I do love them and thank them now."

"But some people do go into counseling to have someone

to bitch and moan to or to have a shoulder to cry on," Ashley pointed out.

"True, and for some people that's what they need," Doug agreed. "As for me, well, one time I went to a McDonald's drive thru and ordered my food, on the way to the window to pay for it I had a panic attack and froze, I couldn't get to the window, I couldn't face the Mcployee, so I drove away. When the attacks were at their worst I couldn't walk out my door and get the mail for fear of someone seeing me, or having to talk to someone."

"I find that hard to believe," Kim laughed.

"I got better," he said in his Monty Python voice, "Anyway, I had a serious disabling problem and I wanted help. So let's say the mental health care givers, be they counselors, doctors, social workers, or whatever, not only give the disorders they are licensed to treat, but also provide the level of function they work with. So for my social phobia and panic attacks I could look for a counselor who specializes in behavioral psychology and is certified in the use of Gradual Exposure Therapy, specializes in phobias, and works with level one or level two clients. I would be a level two. A level one client would be in need of light therapy and they might or might not require medication. Level one therapy would be designed to help high functioning clients deal with everyday problems. Level two would be a client with a disorder that negatively affects the client's life and that possibly requires medication. Level two clients would probably require a planned counseling approach with specific goals so that the client could return to a high functioning state. Level three would be for clients with serious mental disorders that require an extensive treatment plan that could include enrollment in federal disability programs and possibly assisted living. Level three clients would be for severely handicapped clients who have very little chance of returning to a high functioning state. If we had a system like that in place and available to the public, anyone could look up what I needed and get the help I want without having to go pot luck on counselors till I happen to find the right person."

"How would you look it up?" Ashley asked. "I wouldn't know what to look for."

"An hour on Wikipedia would do it for most people," Doug answered. "Over time it would be like other areas of medicine. How do you know to go to a podiatrist if you have a foot problem?"

"Some type of gatekeeper would be helpful to get people where they need to go as well," Kim added.

"That does exist, in the mental health system they are usually called assessment counselors. The problem with that is that from my experience the assessment counselors work for the providers and are extremely biased, or they work for the insurance companies and the clients are sent to whoever is cheapest," Doug explained. "And if most of the treatment options are exactly the same, then what does it really matter? Let's go back to our recently promoted acrophobia sufferer."

"Acrophobia," Ashley said. "Fear

of heights," Kim told her.

"So our acrophobia sufferer doesn't get the help she needs and has to turn down the promotion. Now who do they give the job to, Bob, well Bob is a great guy, most of the time, and he does good work, most of the time, but there is something about Bob, something just not right, some of the time," Doug began. "A lot of people call them Shadow Syndromes, not really bad enough that anyone suspects a mental illness is behind it, but enough to cause problems. Remember Bob had two divorces, and he has alienated some of the other workers. Bob seems sort of moody at times and sometimes his work isn't up to par and it's turned in late, then other times it's on time but wordy and scattered. What nobody realizes is that Bob might be suffering from a very slight mental illness in this case possibly bi-polar. The disorder isn't life altering enough, or apparent enough, that Bob ever seeks help. If Bob does seek help then there are several scenarios that could happen. Woody Hayes, the legendary Ohio State Football Coach used to say that he didn't like passing the ball because when you do one of three things will happen and two of them are bad. So Bob goes to a psychiatrist and walks out with a diagnosis and a prescription, unfortunately with the current ineptitude of psychiatrists and their seeming refusal to use psychological testing to help them make their diagnosis, it's a coin toss whether Bob got the right diagnosis and the right prescription from his half hour assessment. I know, that's what happened to me. Second Bob could go to a counselor and spend two years reviewing all the mistakes his mother made raising him, and in case you haven't figured it out, all parents make mistakes. Third Bob could go to a clinical psychologist and with luck be given a psychological test like the MMPI and the hour long semi-structured interview that goes along with the test. What we really need is more psych tests, and more accurate ones, but that's one of the problems with the ivory tower research psychologists. So Bob gets a diagnosis from a psychologist, then Bob has to go to a psychiatrist who might or might not agree with the psychologist. Then, depending on Bob's insurance, the psychiatrist will probably send Bob to a counselor, not that the psychologist or the psychiatrist is done with him mind you. Bob has just entered the fun filled world of the mental health system. May God help him, he will need it," Doug concluded.

"That can't be the way it really happens," Kim challenged.

"It's amazing how many people know that the mental health care system is a mess, but when you tell them what its really like inside they all seem to say exactly that, it can't be that bad. Why do you think most people know that the mental health care system is in bad shape? It's because that is exactly what it's like. Worse, that's what it's like at its best, it goes downhill from there. Remember that nearly seventy percent of people who seek treatment return in one year for more treatment or a new diagnosis. Just ask anyone you know who is in the system or has dealt with the system how many different drugs they have been on. And yes they are telling you the truth," Doug countered. "Of course part of that is because they are going to the wrong treatment facility and they're getting the wrong level of treatment. I should never have ended up in a level three facility, the only reason I did was that the disabling problems

I was facing that were caused by the drugs I was being prescribed for a disorder I didn't even have."

"You should write a book telling your story," Ashley said. "Well,"

Doug said sheepishly, "That might not be too far off, but that's another story."

"And that stories for another night," Ashley said, quickly standing up. "I'm going to head in," She added.

"Hang on," Doug said as he started kicking the embers of their small fire into the river, "I want to look at the floors one more time before I turn in."

"Me too," Kim agreed, getting up to join them.

Chapter 5

At first the ladies were in shock when Doug told them how they needed to dress for the dinner party the doctor and his wife were throwing. Doctor Brett Bissman and his wife Tammy lived two houses up river from Doug, about three quarters of a mile. The ladies had met them a couple times including their first night together when they returned the pontoon boat, since then they had all become friends. It wasn't till Doug explained that the dinner party was part of a murder mystery that they would play act during the evening that the ladies understood. As soon as Doug told them about the game they both tore into the character profile and suggested script for their characters that came with the game. With three days warning Ashley, the tipsy floozy, and Doug and Kim, the hard driving industrialists and his high society snob of a wife, would be ready. As the ladies designed their costumes, Doug dug his convertible out from the back of the barn where he had stored it for the winter. As soon as the ladies saw the car they both wanted to kill him. After being driven around in one of Doug's trucks for the last week and a half they were shocked to find that he had a two year old Audi SR5 convertible that he just 'hadn't bothered' to get out for the summer yet. While Doug got things ready to wash and wax the car, Kim, who liked muscle cars, got the keys and she and Ashley took it for a test drive.

"Nice car," Kim said two hours later as she tossed the keys back to Doug. "When'd you get this?"

"Glad you like it," Doug replied with a smile. "Got it when they were making the movie about my book. Since it was about a cross country bicycle ride we shot a lot of it on location. This is the car they gave me to use during the shoot. When it came time to turn it back in, the dealer offered it to me for $45,000, so I bought it."

"How much was it originally?" Ashley asked. "Around

90 the way its set up," Doug answered.

Kim shook her head, "We're in the wrong business," she said to Ashley.

What Doug didn't tell them was that part of the reason he had not taken the Audi out of the barn was that it had bucket seats. The only vehicle that any of them owned with a bench front seat that they could all sit together on was the old auto auction special that he had been driving them around in. The two hours that the ladies had spent test driving his Audi, he had spent looking through used car ads to see if he could find a cool car with a bench style front seat. The prospects didn't look good.

When the night of the party finally came Ashley, who as a high school English teacher had directed several school plays, played her part of the tipsy floozy to perfection. Doug, the usually laid back woodworker, struggled with the part of the hard driving industrialist till Ashley suggested he play the part like an angry psych patient trying to change the system, after that his character improved. Kim's portrayal of the high society snob was done so well that everyone was glad when around 10:00 she was exposed as the killer. It seems the man she was having an affair with was cheating on her. As drinks were served on the Bissman's patio overlooking the river it was generally agreed that it was a good murder mystery but not the best the group had played. It became apparent to Ashley and Kim that although it was not an official monthly party, the group had met for several other roll playing parties in the past. The ladies were somewhat relieved to see that Doug was able to interact with others without going into one of his speeches. For Doug's part he was grateful for the home improvement craze of the last decade, it always seemed to come up in the conversation and it was his strong suet, money talk bored him. Doug, always hyper aware in social settings, had seen the ladies interact in social groups before and knew they would be perfectly comfortable in this setting. All in all it was a fun evening and they all said goodnight planning on doing it again as soon as one of them found another game worth playing.

It was a pleasant evening in West Michigan and with the top down and the ladies sitting together in the passenger seat of the Audi, mellow from the wine and the conversation of the evening, Doug decided to take the long way home and drove them all into the night. Soon the ladies began making out in the passenger seat and Doug found the shortest route home. "I need to find a hot car with a bench seat in front," Doug said to no one in particular. A thought the ladies quickly picked up on.

Chapter 6

After spending a rather dismal morning doing odd jobs inside the house, Doug, Ashley and Kim sat in the great room eating lunch and watching the rain fall outside the wall of windows. The ladies had been looking forward to spending the day working on the cabinets for the master bathroom but Doug had changed the plan due to the effect of humidity on woodworking. Everything they had done that morning needed to be done, but the endless list of odd jobs and the rain had them all feeling a little blue. During lunch Ashley told Doug about a friend of her and Kim that had recently relapsed on crack cocaine after several years of being clean. The friend lost his job and was in the midst of a divorce because of it. It was troubling to both the ladies "How could someone throw away their lives like that?" they both asked.

"Relapse into addiction is hard to explain to normees," Doug struggled to begin. "There are way too many variables for simple answers, including the individuals themselves. There is something called a relapse track though. If you can outline your own relapse track you might be able, or someone close to you might be able to identify your particular relapse signs and stop the relapse process before you actually use."

"Sounds complicated, is that what NA is all about?" Ashley asked urging him on.

"Yeah, well actually no, the NA and AA twelve steps are more about getting rid of the garbage that people accumulate in life and learning new ways to keep from accumulating more. Relapse track is more an aftermarket thing that's usually done in counseling or with a really good sponsor." Doug said thoughtfully. "Any idea why he relapsed?"

"His wife thinks he met a girl in a meeting that he used to party with and that they hooked up," Kim told him. "Is that what they call thirteen stepping?"

"Traditionally thirteen stepping is when someone uses the program as a pickup angle, using the program as a way to get into someone's head so they can get in there pants later." Doug explained. "If he knew her before the meeting then it was probably something else. If she was new to the program he might have been legitimately trying to help her and it backfired on him, backfired on both of them really. That's why you always take someone with you on twelve step calls. Twelve stepping is helping someone; thirteen stepping is helping yourself to someone. Of course it goes both ways, especially with drugs, she could have been broke and came looking for him to get a fix. Anymore, because of the way the court system uses AA and NA meetings in sentencing people, it's very possible that she wasn't there for recovery at all."

"Why would the court system be using the programs?" Ashley asked. "I thought the programs were independent."

"They used to be, and they're supposed to be, but the courts don't respect their privacy," Doug told her. "The courts make the assumption that anyone who gets arrested for a drug or alcohol related offence is an addict or an alcoholic, that's just not true."

"It sounds like a pretty good assumption to me," Kim challenged.

"They say that ten percent of the people who try alcohol will get addicted, the percentage for drugs is a little higher and some drugs are worse than others, but the percentage is still well below fifty percent. Granted, by the time a person gets into the court system the addiction percentage goes way up, but it's still not even close to one hundred percent," Doug began. "Did you know that it's not uncommon for people in NA to run into their old drug dealer in a meeting, thanks to the courts? The dealers are sent to treatment by their lawyers when they get arrested in the hope of getting them a reduced sentence. Then the courts make the dealers go to meetings to get these papers signed that the courts hand out to prove they went to the meetings."

"Are the dealers addicts?" Kim asked. " I've heard they usually try to keep from using their own product, but then other times I hear about them using too much of the drugs and getting in trouble with the suppliers."

"A lot of them are addicted to the money," Doug explained. "And some of the low level foot soldiers are addicts, but if you want to make it in that business, and it is a business, they better not be addicts. If they are then they usually do end up in trouble with their suppliers for using too much of the drugs and coming up short on the money. That or they make mistakes and get arrested. The thing is that you don't have to be a user to get arrested, but in the eyes of the court you're still an addict."

"Do the dealers deal in the meetings?" Ashley asked.

"It's been known to happen, but because some people in recovery will narc on them if they catch them dealing at the meetings it's probably safer to deal at your school or at your hospital," Doug said turning to Kim. "There are some meetings where almost everyone is there to get court papers signed. There are other meetings where only a small percentage of the people need to get the paper signed. You can probably guess which meeting is more concerned with recovery. In the old days, before the courts got involved, it was pretty easy to see if someone was there for alternative reasons like dealing or thirteen stepping. Anymore, with some of the meetings having more active users than recovering people, it gets harder to spot the phonies and it's all thanks to the courts," Doug explained. "I thought you had to be clean and sober to go to the meetings," Kim said.

"No, not at all, if you're high or drunk and cause a scene then you will be asked to leave. The theory is that by attending the meetings when you are high or drunk there is the hope that something that you hear during the meeting will stick with you and you will eventually find recovery. And to be honest a lot of people do find recovery in just that way," Doug told her. "You are encouraged to come regardless, but if you're using then you are asked to just sit and listen, that's not the problem. The problem is all the people that go to meetings that have no intention of getting clean or sober, and before and after the actual meeting make that fact clear to anyone who will listen. Sometimes they talk a person who is at the meetings for the right reasons, and is trying to get their lives back on track, to go back into active addiction. That's not just the dealer's either, it can be as simple as a user asking a legitimate newcomer or even an established member to go out and burn one with them. You have to realize that it's not uncommon to meet someone you used to party with in a meeting. The courts say that they get people into recovery by forcing them to attend the meeting, and that is true, they do get some people into recovery. What they don't say is how many people they get to relapse using the same forced attendance of people who don't want to be there," Doug explained.

"So what's the answer?" Kim asked.

"Who knows," Doug said shrugging his shoulders. "The best one I've seen is what some call drug court. Drug court is sort of a cross between outpatient therapy and probation. The people ordered to go get both alcohol and drug counseling in a therapy group or meeting type setting with a court appointed therapist. They are also forced to submit to drug and alcohol testing with consequences if they fail the test. Then if they are serious about recovery they can go to outside meetings as well, but the outside meetings aren't mandatory. Right now the outside meetings are mandatory in most drug courts, and their attendance is monitored with the sheets they need to get signed."

"It makes a lot more sense for the courts to keep their charges under their own control and away from the recovering people, especially if the convicts don't want anything to do with recovery in the first place," Kim agreed. "It seems like it would be better for the recovery programs as a whole, both the drug courts and the AA, NA programs really."

"The courts definitely shouldn't be doing anything that would lead to the relapse of someone they have no authority over, or anybody else for that matter," Ashley added.

"So next time a judge comes up for election ask them what the acceptable ratio is for getting one of their charges into recovery, versus the number of relapses caused by their current use of the AA and NA programs in sentencing," Doug suggested. "If they say that there is no evidence that there are any relapses caused by forcing active alcohol and drug users, and active dealers into AA and NA meetings, then they are correct, there isn't any definitive proof that I am aware of, but that's just because nobody has done the research yet, it's not because it's not happening."

"I would never have thought of it, but now that you say it I can't believe there aren't any relapses because of it," Kim said.

"Another thing people don't really understand about relapse with drugs is just how hard the dealers work to keep their customers," Doug continued. "For a midlevel dealer, not the kid standing on the corner, or the people actually transporting the drugs, but the dealer with the 911 service and maybe a house or two where the drugs are sold and used. The busiest day of the month is the day welfare checks are handed out. The dealers need to get the money before the landlord, or the grocery store, or the bank if the person has any loans. They also need to keep records on when their customers get their pay checks, are they paid every week or every two weeks. They need to keep track of people's retirement checks or when they get annuity payments so they can get there first."

"They really work that hard at it?" Kim asked in amazement. "If they want to make the big money they better track that stuff," Doug answered. "I was in a treatment center, and this was a pure alcohol and drug treatment center with no mental health connections so it was over ten years ago. Anyway my roommate was a midlevel drug dealer who got busted for possession with intent to sell and was doing the treatment center on the advice of his lawyer. According to him he only did crack once or twice a year, didn't drink, and only occasionally smoked pot, and personally I believe he was telling me the truth, he was telling the counselors a different story. The thing was the guy was smart, he could have gotten a college degree in anything he wanted, but he wanted it now so he sold crack. I sort of led him on and made him think that I agreed with him both to keep the peace and to keep him talking. He thought he was some kind of saint because one of the welfare mothers he sold rugs to, and occasionally used for sex, had a son. The son, of course, had nothing since his mom spent every penny she could get on crack. So one Christmas he bought the kid a pair of sneakers."

"And that made him a saint?" Kim laughed shaking her head in disgust.

"Yeah, I don't think his guy's standards were very high, just his clients," Doug said agreeing with Kim's disgust. "Anyway this guy was making seven thousand dollars a week and was 26 years old. He had two crack houses he ran, and a stable of crack ho's he used for personal pleasure and for profit. He also used the crack ho's to get people who were trying to quit back on the drugs. He would give the girls to his clients who were trying get clean, or had just gotten out of treatment, along with some crack to trick them back into active addiction and keep his money coming in."

"That's terrible," Kim said.

"So the dealers know when someone is trying to get clean or is going to treatment." Ashley added.

"Of course, so do some of the bartenders," Doug added. "Treatment centers used to give you a coin, a token when you completed the program with the idea that you keep it in your pocket as a reminder. There's a bar in Grand Rapids with a big jar on the counter and if you drop your treatment token in the jar then your first drink is free."

"It's amazing anyone recovers," Ashley said shaking her head.

"There's a reason I go out to lunch every Thursday without you, there's a reason I play on an AA, NA golf league even though they play on the worst course in GR," Doug started.

"There's a reason you left us twice now to take a phone call," Ashley added with an approving smile.

"And there's a reason I'll probably blow you off a third and fourth time as well. I don't even go to that many meetings anymore, I stay sober by staying in touch and getting involved with the people I grew up with, grew up with in the program that is. Getting involved in AA is the key to early recovery. Today, the key for me is getting involved in life outside the meetings and keeping in touch with the people I've met in AA," Doug said solemnly.

"So that ninety meetings in ninety days is intended to get people involved in AA, and make the program a part of their lives," Kim said.

"Sort of," Doug said, "ninety in ninety is intended to make yourself part of the program, once you internalize the program you start expanding your horizons back into the real world. Then by taking the program with you as you grow it becomes a part of your everyday life," Doug thought for a minute then added. "You have to understand the addictive mind, you don't just stop in after work and have a drink, you go to work thinking about the drink you are going to have after work. By lunch time you have already ordered the drink, in your mind, a hundred times. When you're trying to recover you have to give recovery that same kind of priority, at least at first. That's the reason for the ninety in ninety."

"So as the urge to use fades away with time, the time you need to spend focusing on recovery lessons, and that's the time you use to move on with your life," Ashley half asked and half stated.

"Exactly, if you get it right," Doug told her, "Some people move on with life to fast, so when the urge to use eventually overtakes them, and it will, they start using again. Others move on completely and leave the program behind and when, and again when not if, the urge to use overtakes them they have no defenses left because they left them all behind. Others don't move on at all and they get stuck, most of them just end up switching addictions or go on a dry drunk. A lot of times that's where the Big Book thumpers and Bible thumpers come from. Yeah you memorized it buddy, now try applying it to your life," he said mockingly to an imaginary thumper as he watched Ashley start gathering up what remained of their lunch. She stopped short when she heard Kim's next question.

"So what's your relapse track?" Kim asked.

"First of all never ask a person in recovery, or in treatment for other issues for that matter, what you want to know, ask them what they need you to know. Everybody's different, and everybody works a different program. The treatment programs differ in their approaches and in the lingo they use. Asking your specific questions is hit or miss at best and it's more likely to piss the person off than it is to get you an answer. Remember the TV shows are staged, in real life you need to use a little more tact. All that said I do use the term relapse track, and relapse track is a part of the program I work so, I'm glad you asked. Do 'ya think I maybe over planed the house a bit?" Doug asked jokingly as he pointed out various projects around the room. Then getting very serious he added, "Planning grandiose projects is a way I use to escape reality, so when I started planning this house and the compound my AA friends confronted me on it. As it turned out I had the money, and the land, and was working with a contractor and an architect. After they found out that I was really going to build this place they started to encourage me. I was grateful that they recognized that it might be a problem and tried to step in though," Doug said in sincerity.

"But you over plan everything," Ashley pointed out.

Getting up and looking at the list of things he wanted to get done Doug explained, "Grandiose, unrealistic, and most important, addictively. If I'm being unrealistic and withdrawn it means I'm back into my active addiction cycle and in time will return to my favorite addiction, alcohol. If I'm planning something that is realistic, and that I do intend to do, then leave me alone I'm working. The key is in the understanding of the addictive mind and the individual's personal behavior patterns and how they play out. The problem is that everybody is different."

"Then we'll just have to get to know you better," Kim added with a smile.

Doug's relationship with the free spirited and fun loving Ashley had become warm and nurturing. His relationship with the more conservative Kim was becoming playful and Doug decided it was a good time to have some fun with her as they started back to work. "If you think about it," Doug probed Kim. "Addiction might even explain some the pedophile problems in the Catholic Church. When most people think about addiction they think about addiction to vices like gambling, sex, or drugs, but addiction to behaviors that are traditionally thought of as good are in truth just as detrimental, and follow the same addiction track. One of the characteristics of addiction is that when addiction starts, emotional growth stops. One of the many reasons underage drinking and drug use is such a problem is that when the addict quits using later in life, many are still emotionally in their teens. Members of the clergy who are in fact religious addicts, and have been since an early age, are in reality emotionally stuck in their teens. That's true even though many of them are older now and are taking on leadership roles in the church or mentor-ship roles with the kids who turn to them. Take a 14 year old religious addict who is starting to get ostracized by his peers at school for his fanaticism, and an older adult priest whose emotional age is arrested at around the age of 14 due to his religious addiction and peer problems, and put them in the same room. The true 14 year old and the emotionally arrested 14 year old both find a kindred soul for possibly the first time in their lives, and society thinks this is going to produce positive results. Would it yield positive results if it was an adult with a sex addiction rather than a religion addiction, how about eating addiction, drugs or alcohol, texting, video gaming, power, money, or any of a thousand other things that can become an addiction? I'm not saying that religion is bad. I'm saying that religion is a problem when the passion is based on an addiction to a theory, or an escape from reality, rather than a pursuit of true spiritual growth. In the case of one of the oldest human endeavors that can become a problem, which in my mind is the misuse of religion, society and psychology are not stepping in for fear of angering the group, rather than trying the help the addicts the group produces."

"Priests aren't all pedophiles, and all pedophiles aren't priests, if you haven't figured that out yet," Kim barked defensively.

"You do know what's behind the problems in the Catholic Church don't you?" Doug asked, pleased with Kim's indignation.

Kim and Ashley looked at each other for a minute then reluctantly Kim asked. "What?"

"There are no knights left, the musketeers have all gone away." he answered.

The ladies looked at him in disbelief. In shock, ire, and in unison, they both said, "What?"

"Think about it, for centuries if the priests got out of line the knights would set them straight, and if the knights got out of line it was the priests who reeled them in. Later it was the musketeers, some say that even some of their own, the Knights Templar, had a hand in keeping the priests in balance. If the knights had found out about this sex scandal stuff it would have been over in a matter of days, instead it's been going on for decades with new cover-ups being uncovered every two or three years." He gave this time to sink in then continued, "The problem is the knights were too crazy for a civilized society so a couple hundred years ago they, and the musketeers, and the rest of the high societies professional hard-asses assimilated into society with its laws and courts and the rest of society's more melancholy ways. The priests were finally free to run amuck. The priest and the knights had yin-yang thing going on. Now the priests have no yin for their yang and their yang's are getting them in trouble." The ladies heads both dropped in laughter. That was it that was all they could take. Gathering the picnic basket and the furniture pad they had been sitting on they headed for the kitchen.

"Back to work," Ashley announced looking at Doug and shaking her head.

"Was it something I said?" Doug asked in mock confusion as

he began gathering some tools. "You can still sleep tight there are some knights left."

"Anyone we know?" Kim challenged.

"Yeah, so who do you think is America's greatest knight?" Doug asked, "I'll give you a hint, if she had reached for her sword they would have cut her down, that's what they wanted."

Kim and Ashley both stopped, turned, and looked at Doug, surprised by the question.

Doug stood tall and faced the ladies, "Rosa Parks," he said and turned to go back to work.

Chapter 7

The ladies had learned both from watching him work and from personal experience that Doug had incredible hands. Strong enough to toss around lumber like it was linen, yet skilled enough to sand intricately carved woodwork to perfection without damaging the design. They also had learned that the lonely years had made Doug a deep thinker and slow storyteller, when left to ponder and explore his inner thoughts. These were skills the ladies enjoyed and they came up with a plan to take advantage of both. They waited till the first rainy night and set their plan in motion. Using the new carpentry skills they had been learning, they built a stable four foot wide by eight foot long table about two feet off the floor in the extra bedroom upstairs. They then covered the table with some freshly washed moving blankets Doug used to protect the furniture he builds when he moves it. They then worked on setting up mood lighting with candles and low wattage bulbs that they strategically placed around the walls of the room. The final step was to lightly coat the blankets with a Jasmine scent. The Jasmine would work well with the vanilla scent they would use on their bodies later that night. They knew that Doug's meeting with his accountant would be over a little too early to create the perfect mood so they had arranged to meet him for diner and if necessary a little shopping to get them home around dusk. With their stage set they left to meet Doug for dinner.

The trio arrived home around 8:30 and the ladies set their plan into motion. Kim told Doug to wait 15 minutes then meet them in the empty bedroom. The ladies then hurried to the room and put the finishing touches on their plan. After lighting the candles and making sure the lighting was soft and low they undressed. The vanilla scented massage oil Ashley had chosen and the jasmine scent Kim would use were selected to give a nice glow to their skin in the light of the candles, not to oily not to dry. After applying the massage oil they climbed onto the table they had built and assumed the pose they hoped to hold for some time. Soon Doug walked in and looked at the ladies who were perched naked on their stage, posing, staying still as statues on their hands and knees. They were both facing the center but not each other, both at a slight angle and still able to see each other out of the corner of their eyes. Doug looked around the room, at the candles, the stage, at the girls. The ladies had even placed a fountain in the corner for sound. Doug had seen this before, he had done it before, he knew what they wanted and the sound of the water in the fountain gave him an idea.

"He was a junky," Doug began, slowly walking around the walls of the room, stopping occasionally to adjust a candle or light, all the while ignoring the stage and the ladies perched upon it. "A leather clad member of a motorcycle gang, till he got busted for selling LSD and sent to prison for 20 years. It was one of those weird stories you hear about sometimes. After six years in prison he decided to turn his life over to God and within a week he was given shock probation. Even weirder, he kept his promise. When I met him several years later he was a Catholic priest with two parishes, a horse racing track and an alcohol and drug treatment center. I heard him speak at the treatment center and he was good, he made sense to me, so I scheduled an hour of private consultation with him. We talked about a lot of things during that hour, at some point I said I was thinking about reading the Bible. He laughed and said wait five years till you get your head together and you might have a chance of understanding it. He said I needed to stop worrying about existential things that I can't yet understand, and try to find peace in the here and now. Then he changed my life by giving me a book titled, Questions to a Zen Master. He told me that faith in an existential being and the practice of calming one's mind through meditation are not mutually exclusive. I would like to say I read the book and applied the teachings to my life and that I lived happily ever after, but I didn't. I did read the book and I liked it, I even read a few more books on Zen, and a couple by the Dali Lama. It would be five years till I applied any of it though."

Up till now Doug had been slowly walking around the walls of the room, looking over the scene and ignoring the ladies. Upon finishing this thought he moved to the stage and the ladies perched upon it. The scent of vanilla and Jasmine and the faint aroma of hazelnut from some of the candles all added to the feast that lay before him. As he walked around the table he used one finger to gently trace the curves of the ladies bodies as he passed, barely touching their skin, occasionally he stopped to slowly outline the curves and contours of one of their bodies, or to adjust their hair. He registered the ladies reaction to his touch by the increase of their breathing and the involuntary sounds that came from deep in their throats. Neither Kim nor Ashley moved as he traced the lines of their soft bodies, not a twitch nor a head bob. Doug was impressed, but soon he would move to more sensitive areas.

"It was soon after I turned thirty. I had four operations in eighteen months, three knee and one back, laminectomy," The last word he said into Kim's ear. He then began tracing her ear with his gentle touch. It was the beginning of a journey that would take them both to distant shores. "I spent six months lying on my back. It was a year before I could walk 100 yards. Then when I finally could walk I found that I couldn't go anywhere. Agoraphobia they call it, fear of the marketplace. I would stand at the door to go out and get the mail and freeze, unable to turn the doorknob, unable to go out, afraid to be seen. It was then that I learned about the power of meditation. The ability to calm one's mind by bringing back images and feelings one has learned and practiced in private, and call on them in situations that are troubling, or sometimes just to relax for a minute or two."

Doug now stopped walking around the stage and concentrated on Kim's body, admiring the radiance of her oiled skin in the soft glow of the candles. He adjusted her hair before slowly tracing her face, shoulders, and spine, never really touching her yet very much in contact. He moved to her hips and inner thighs before finally reaching her most sensitive area. As she moaned in response to his gentle touch he continued, "I found my favorite spot in the world not by my travels, or work, or my home, but in my mind, with the help of a recovering acid head turned priest and a book of Zen. I'm sure Ashley remembers the book Siddhartha, we all had to read it in school. After a life of success and failures, Siddhartha found peace as a ferry boat worker sitting by a river with an old man, watching the water flow by. The combined knowledge of all people, places, and things contained within the water as it passed. But what happens to the water after it passes the ferry crossing?" he asked. "It slowly and calmly travels down its banks till it reaches a cliff, a cliff a thousand feet high. The water falls over the edge and begins its long decent. As the water falls it separates into smaller and smaller parts till it finally becomes a droplet, all alone on its journey. As the droplet falls it encounters other droplets, and it collides with the rocks that are hidden in its path. The droplet is at the mercy of the ever changing winds, ever moving faster and faster as it makes its chaotic decent." By this time Kim's breathing was labored, often coming in gasps but she held her body as stiff as a board. The feelings within her that were being produced by Doug's gentle touch were starting to overwhelm her. She was still aware of Doug's calm voice, but could no longer register the meaning of the words. Without warning Doug's hands moved from between her legs and again began tracing the lines of her body. He continued his story, "Suddenly, as if a hand reached in and rescued the droplet, I was transported to a cliff overlooking the falls. From this distance I could see the beauty of the falls I had just been in. How calm the falling water looked from this distance, how peaceful and serene it all seemed. How chaotic the falls seemed when I was in them, how tranquil they seem from a distance. As I looked around the cliff where I had been delivered, I found that I was surrounded by lush gardens filled with flowers of every color. Birds and butterflies made their way from tree to tree and flower to flower. An old friend stopped by and sat with me for a moment, but just for a moment, just long enough for me to say something to him that I had needed to say. I felt a great calm enter my soul." By this time Doug hands had returned to Kim's vagina and he could tell that she wouldn't last much longer. Building his voice, Doug continued, "Soon I was returned to the falls, the rush of the water and the blowing winds sending the droplet back into the frenzied rush, its fate uncertain, its destiny inevitable." Kim gasp as the orgasm that had been building inside of her engulfed her. Turning her head slightly to look at as Doug he finished his story. "In time the droplet completed its journey rejoining the other droplets in the pool of water at the bottom of the falls. Again becoming one with all, was it a dream, it had all passed so quickly."

After kissing Kim's cheek and forehead Doug turned his attention to Ashley. He moved her from her hands and knees and had her lay on her back, her arms and legs spread slightly. He then moved Kim so that she was sitting on her knees with her calves framing Ashley's head but not touching. He then instructed them to gaze into each other's eyes. Like with Kim, Doug's hands began their journey by gently adjusting Ashley's hair, he then started tracing the contours of her body.

"It was a time of innocents and persecution," he began. "In the small Puritan community in 1692 the harvest had been brought in, but not without problems. In order to store the rye for the long winter it needed to be dried in the sun, but the rains had fallen and soaked the rye that the villagers had laid out. They turned the rye and laid it out to dry a second time, again the rains came. The villagers turned the rye and set it out to dry for a third time, and again the rains fell. This time as they tuned the rye they found that a fungus had started to form on it, they all knew that this part of their harvest was ruined. Discarding the moldy rye they spread the next batch from their harvest out dry, and prayed for better weather. But not all the villagers saw the fungus as a problem. For the poor it was an opportunity. Among them was the poor black slave woman named Tituba who lived on the outskirts of town. Tituba saw the fungus infected rye as a free source of food for the winter. What she didn't know was that this fungus was special, this fungus wasn't like other years, this fungus had a bi-product, this fungus produced a chemical compound commonly known as LSD." Ashley had heard this story before but Doug was a good storyteller and she liked his choice, more importantly she loved his hands. One of Doug's hands had already found its target but the results were not what he was looking for. Ashley's breathing was heavy and she was responding to his touch. She was still holding still to allow the sensation to surge through her, but she was still in control. Looking at her face Doug could tell she was not struggling with the sensation. Instead she was enjoying the feeling and listening to his story, not at all what he was looking for. Moving back to her shoulders he continued his story, "Nine year old Betty Parris and eleven year old Abigail Williams were the first to show signs of the strange affliction that was would soon take over the children of Salem. Strange behaviors both in action and in tongue. Actions never before seen, chants in a tongue never before heard, and worse, they even disrupted a church service, could it be the Devil at work? Had the girls visited that strange black slave woman at the edge of town? The woman who was known to tell children stories of sexual encounters with Demons. Soon more young girls were showing signs of this affliction, something had to be done," Doug could tell he still didn't have the control over Ashley that he wanted so he quickly finished his tale of the Salem Witch Trials. Like he had done with Kim his hands returned to gently tracing the lines of Ashley's body, he would try her inner thighs again later. Keeping in the same time frame but changing direction he began again.

"From the Priests to the Knights, America has had a rich history.

A factual history might be another story. Listen my children and you shall hear, of the midnight ride of Paul Revere, one if by land, and two if by sea, and I on the opposite shore shall be, ready to ride and sound the alarm. And he did sound the alarm, sort of, and he is an American Knight, but probably not as a result of this night. After receiving word of the British plans Revere and a man by the name of Dawes began their ride, soon they were joined by a doctor named Prescott, and all rode to sound the alarm. After warning a few people the three were stopped by a mounted British patrol, and from the sound of it got into a little rugby style scrum on horseback." At this point Doug's hands went from gentle to firm and his voice became strong and proud "Revere was knocked from his horse by a British officer and injured his ankle, and no he did not tell the British that the British were coming as some would tell it, but he was held prisoner for the rest of the night. Prescott and Dawes were able to escape and continue sounding the alarm, but only Prescott made it to Concord. So who really lit the signal fires that night? The true answer is that probably a lot of people did. Who lit the most signal fires, who earned their place among the great Knights in American history? A 16 year old girl."

He wasn't playing fair, thought Ashley, realizing he was going to double up by putting pride over stimulation. That's not fair she thought, she said nothing and she didn't move it was a game she would be more than happy to loose.

"She was the daughter of one of the Minutemen's commanding officers, a young girl of grit." Doug said in a proud voice, his hands moving ever closer to Ashley vagina, "Imagine the men she saw as she did her choirs, men coming in to meet with her father to make plans for the freedom of her country. Men that in the 1770's she would have served food and drinks to. Men she would have listened to late at night as she lay in bed. As a girl of grit herself, she would have known these men. She would have seen them for who they were. She would have known who her father would need by his side to stop the British. After receiving the warning at her father's farm, she and her 18 year old sister mounted their horses and headed into the Massachusetts night to make sure their father's men would hear the alarm. By morning she had ridden forty miles lighting fires for her father and her country. Forty miles, sidesaddle, must have been one hell of a horse," Doug said now confident that he had Ashley under his control. He knew she couldn't hold out for long, a few stories of the Minuteman's harassment of the advancing British troops on the road from Boston to Concord, and their stand on the North Bridge was all that Ashley could take. As she recovered from her orgasm Doug climbed onto the stage the ladies had built, letting them know that it was his turn and that this planking crap was over.

Over the two decades that Doug had worked as a cabinet maker he had trained many people. From the temps, to the builder assistants, to the people he had mentored, just as he had been mentored so many years ago. He found training Kim and Ashley to be a pleasure. Their enthusiasm combined with the intangible choice of wanting to do a project right, and not just getting a project done. It all came crashing down, as did the stage that the ladies had built when Doug's weight was added. After the initial shock all three of them broke into laughter.

"For your next lesson," Doug began, "we'll be looking into the proper use of lateral supports."

"No, no, no," yelled Ashley laughingly, "That's not part of my lesson plan for tonight."

"We've had enough schooling for one night," added Kim. "I really think that its important," insisted Doug.

"You talk too much," Kim said, getting serious and moving closer.

"Well I think that's pretty much universally..." was as far as he got.

Chapter 8

———

The next morning Kim and Ashley found themselves building a box. When Doug told them what he needed them to do they thought that it was in response to the fallen stage of the night before and put up a protest. It turned out that because Doug's friend from his days as a professional woodworker was coming to tile the master shower, Doug was pressed to get some work done. The box the ladies had been assigned to build was going to be a built in tile bench in the shower with a knee high faucet featuring a spray head on a long hose. In order to make it the right height Doug had told them to figure out how high they would want it to shave their legs. So far things weren't going to well.

"You're not done yet!" Doug exclaimed, holding back a laugh, "We're under the gun, I have more projects I need you to do if we're going to get that shower done this weekend."

"I think we've got the right height but our box isn't quit square," said Ashley.

"It isn't quite stable either," Kim added as she grabbed the poorly constructed box and wobbling it.

"It'll get stable when we put on the wallboard, but you're right, that might have a little too much play." He told them as he took out his tape measure and showed the ladies that it was also the wrong size.

"That can't be, we did it just like you said, measure twice and cut once, right?" Ashley said, totally exasperated.

In truth it was exactly what Doug had expected, and had wanted from them. "When you measured twice did you use your tape measure both times?" he asked.

"Are we supposed to use two different measuring devises too?" Ashley said now getting thoroughly frustrated.

"Hang on," Kim said grabbing Ashley and looking at Doug, "I think he's up to something."

"Well if you mean one of the measuring devices is a mechanical pencil and a drafting ruler, then yes," he answered enjoying their frustration, then looking at them both he added, "You only measure for the cut once, that's the second measurement. The first measurement is a measure of your soul. Let me show you what I mean." The ladies followed excitedly, this was the kind of training they wanted. Doug walked them over to a drafting table he had in the shop and pulled out a half inch thick stack of drawings he had done for the kitchen cabinets that he had been working on for the last couple of weeks, "I design my projects as well as build them, but even when I was doing this professionally, and being handed plans for a projects that someone else had drawn, the first thing I did was make my own drawings." Spreading the stack of drawings out on the table, and then spreading out the drawings he had done for the overall project he began explaining the difference, "These are the project drawings. They make the assumption that every piece of wood you use has been milled to perfect dimensions, and in a pro shop that is possible. In the real world none of the wood you will work with is even close." At this point he handed each of them a piece of the Walnut that he conveniently had at hand, and a 6" precision ruler. These are pieces of 1" x 4" Walnut stock directly from the mill. That means they should measure ¾" x 3 1/2", so what are you holding?" After years of training people Doug was relieved to see them both measure the wood with the rulers that he had handed them and didn't tell him that they were holding a piece of wood.

"It's slightly under what it should be," Kim said.

"Mine is slightly over," Ashley added. "So we have to adjust the measurement of every cut for the piece of wood we are cutting?"

"And that's one of the reasons I use these individual piece drawings," he said pulling out one drawing from the stack that was covered in scribbled numbers, "It gives me a place to do all the calculations. There's more to it than that though, if you look at how complicated some of these pieces are, like this one with a dado running along one side and mortise tongs on each end. It's only a six inch piece of 1 x 2, but I have to run it through ten setups to make it so that it will fit into the project. By doing the drawing I can make all those cuts in my mind before I even get into the shop, and that saves a lot of time from being wasted and a lot of wood from going into the scrap pile."

"I can see doing that for what you're doing, but we're just working with 2x4's, and making a simple box. You're not going to tell me you go to all that trouble for that?" Kim challenged.

"First, yes," Doug responded reaching for a yellow legal pad and showing them page after page of drawings and figures. "I might not do it on a drafting table, but I use the same procedure for every cut regardless of what it's to be used for. Second, it's not just a box made out of 2 x 4's, its 'you're box' made out of 2 x 4's." The ladies nodded, understanding the difference. "Third, if it's so simple then why is your first attempt in the scrap box?" Moving back to where the ladies had made their first attempt Doug walked them through the procedure of making the first of the two measurements. Soon the ladies had their second measurement done, a simple mark 14 ¾" (L) on the 2X4. He had given them basic instructions on how to use the chop saw earlier, and they had each made a few cuts. This time he showed them how to use a chop saw, "The saying is, measure twice, cut once, but I teach, measure twice, cut twice. The first cut is like the first measurement, it's mostly mental but instead of double checking the numbers, you double check for safety and make sure your head is in the game." He showed them how to bring the blade down on the wood and check how it met the cut marks they had drawn. He explained that the blades width was 1/8" and that for an exact cut they would have to line up the cut mark with the inside of the blade on the mark. He told them it was better to be long than short, and showed them how to "bump off" 1/32" at a time by bumping the 2 x 4 into the lowered blade when stopped, then holding the wood in place while bringing the rotating blade down again.

"Do we have this much to learn about with all of the tools?" Ashley asked.

"I'm starting you off with one of the simple ones," Doug told her. "All this does is cut. Wait till we get to sandpaper." When all the 2 x 4 pieces were cut he started over on how to use a cordless drill. He had shown them how to use it earlier, but like the chop saw, this time he showed them the right way. He demonstrated the proper way to use a counter sink bit, and showed them that when the screw goes into a second piece of wood after passing through a first piece it typically raised the second piece in relation to the first. He showed them how to account for the offset and how to back the screw out and bring it back in to get a tighter joint. Soon the ladies had a 2 x 4 box that they were actually proud of. They wanted to keep going with their lesson but Doug really did need to get the plumbing and wallboard installed by the weekend and just didn't have the time, so with all his prefab work done the three of them moved to the house along with the ladies well-built box.

While the ladies had been working Doug had noticed that Kim was a quick study, she had learned how to use the power tools and ruler with ease. Ashley, who Doug felt was the true artist between them, had struggled with both the ruler and with the power tools. In the end Doug felt that Kim's projects would be well constructed, but lacking true flair. Ashley's projects, if she ever finished, would be creative, one of a kind pieces. "If I set up the pottery wheel would you be interested in making a few things?" Doug asked Kim as he drove them to the house in the side by side. Turning to Ashley he added, "We should probably use some of those glazes before they dry up." Both the ladies picked up on what he was doing, and they both liked the fact that he was working with them as individuals. When they got all the prefab parts into the master bathroom Doug began installing the plumbing that he had been working on in the shop. He gave the ladies a few choices of odd jobs that he thought they could manage but they decided to watch and help him instead.

"Last night you talked about spirituality with a story from you're readings on Buddhism. Are you a Buddhist?" Kim asked. "Not a good one," Doug answered. "I'm also a Christian, but I'm not a good Christian either."

"I didn't know you could be both," Kim said in a mocking voice. "Some religions do conflict, but Christianity and Buddhism don't. Even the religions that in theory do conflict can all be used in conjunction, if you view religion as religion and God as God," Doug responded. "Take what you need and leave the rest."

"Well said, I've been trying to explain that to her for years," Ashley told him.

"The thing is that when I needed help from a higher source I didn't find that help in the Bible, I found it in a book about Zen," Doug offered.

"But didn't you say that a Catholic priest gave you that book?" Kim asked in a defiant voice.

"Even the devil has his day," Doug said with a smile, as he lit the acetylene torch and began soldering the copper pipes in place. "Case in point is all of the television doctors. They present themselves as one of the supper Doctors of the mental health profession. They can diagnosis any client, with any problem, and diagnose them correctly in a few minutes. Then they make millions of dollars by exploiting the client's problems on television. Then they make themselves look like a saints by giving the person they just exploited a few thousand dollars' worth of therapy. The thing is that the therapy they do set the client up with is specifically tailored for that client's problems, and it is being done by mental health providers that at least claim to specialize in the exact areas that the client needs."

"So they are providing exactly what you feel should be provided," Kim said.

"Exactly," Doug agree, "Well they're claiming to provide it any way. The thing is that if you call a counseling group and tell them that you have adult attention deficit disorder they will assign you to a counselor who specializes in adult attention deficit disorder. What they don't tell you is that the same counselor specializes in bipolar disorder, obsessive compulsive disorder, phobias, addiction, eating disorders, depression, and any other of life's little problems. In other words the counselor specializes in counseling. It's very possible that every client that the counselor will see on any given day is there for a different reason. That's what I mean when I say that mental health treatment is one size fits all."

"It does seem that a little specialization could improve the quality of the service they are giving," Kim agreed. "Granted every client is different, but the various disorders do have characteristic issues that are generally associated with them. I know that I get better as nurse in the cardiac ICU with every patient that I work with."

"So what you want is something like the general practitioner that I have in medicine," Ashley suggested. "The doctor I see on a regular basis and who handles the small things herself, but if I have any bigger problems she refers me to a specialist?"

"Right, and in theory they do have that in mental health, but it's usually done by an intake counselor not a doctor," Doug explained. "Then the intake counselor assigns you to a counselor, or to a psychiatrist, or a psychologist, or sometimes even a priest. At least that's what they do in theory. In truth the intake counselor is working for the mental health provider, and the person who they actually refer you to is more dependent on whom they work for, or possibly who they think you will get along with, or worse they assign you to whoever is next on their list of counselors in need of clients. That's a perfectly legitimate way to assign you a counselor in a system where every counselor specializes in everything. It's the best system for the mental health care provider. Unfortunately that's not the best system for the client. Like Kim said, if one counselor worked exclusively with one or two disorders, then repetition and experience would give them a better understanding of the issues a client faces who suffers from that particular disorder. It would also go a long way in providing researchers with real world data on specific treatments for specific disorders that might help them improve and standardize clinical procedures, and measure their effectiveness."

"Are there enough clients with any given disorder to make specialization possible?" Ashley asked.

"In the larger markets yes, in smaller markets the counselors would need to get certified in counseling multiple disorders to make a living," Doug said.

"That's true in nursing, or any form of medicine. You will almost always get more specialized treatment in bigger cities, that's just common sense," Kim added.

"If specialization is needed, and the system is in as bad of shape as you claim, then why isn't anything being done about it?" asked Ashley.

"Several reasons," Doug began. "First, mental health has a built in code of silence. A lot of the people who are receiving treatment just don't want to talk about it. Politicians don't want to talk about it, the general public doesn't want to talk about it, unless it's behind the crazy persons back anyway. If you took your car in to get the radiator fixed and it came back with a problem in the fuel injection system, then you left it there to have the fuel injection system fixed and it came back with a problem with the air conditioning, you would be furious and you would tell everybody you knew not to take their cars to that service station. If you get a wrong diagnosis from a psychiatrist, you quietly go to a different psychiatrist, or just deal with the problem alone. Remember that about 70 percent of the people receiving treatment return in the first year."

"Yeah, I guess that's probably true," Ashley agreed. "I think this piece of wallboard is done."

Doug looked up from the box of wires that that he needed to

install to make the 16 head, computer operated shower assembly work. Running the copper pipes to the 16 shower heads was easy, he was used to assembling various projects, but all these wires had him stymied. By the time he and Ashley had carried the next piece of wallboard into the shower and put enough screws in it to hold it in place, Kim, who was used to all the wires in the ICU, ask him how to drill holes in the studs. As he showed her how to drill the holes and install the conduit he continued, "Second is all the feuds in the system.

Psychologists are feuding with psychologists. Cognitive psychologists are feuding with the environmental psychologists, psychoanalytical approach verses behavioral approach. It's a big bottle neck of egos and feuds and nothing much has changed for the client in a hundred years, except for advances in medication that is. If it wasn't life or death for so many people it would be more fun than the WWF. Third, the education counselors get is still theoretical. To get your teaching certificate you had to observe several hours of classes and then do your student teaching. Nursing requires hands on experience as well. The degrees needed to become a licensed counselor are available from almost every online university, and a lot of the people entering the field are middle age."

"That doesn't seem all that bad, life experience is the best teacher," Kim challenged.

"Kinda depends on if it's been a life of success or failure and why. For a lot of people entering the field the only practical experience they have is a life time of watching daytime television," Doug responded. "Forth, well, in you school when the kids start getting out of control the principal has all the teachers tighten up on the rules for a while till the faculty regains the control."

"It's a pain," Ashley coughed.

"And in the ICU the head nurse occasionally has you go through all the cotton swabs and check for expiration dates," Doug added.

"Yeah," Kim agreed. "It's a way to get one on track and focused. All well run companies do that."

"Exactly, get rid of the waste, get back to fundamentals and refocus on the objectives, a time to get everything moving in the same direction, a fresh start. In a huge, multi-level system like mental health care that's incredibly important to do from time to time. The problem is that it's congress that does it. Congress doesn't know that much about it and they really don't want to deal with it." "So what you're talking about is similar to the bullying legislation that was in front of congress not long ago," Kim suggested. "Exactly," Doug agreed, "and while not much came from the federal government because of it, a lot of the states passed legislation designed to stop bullying in school, workplaces, even cyberbullying. The mental health system is way overdue for that kind of shakeup. It's even worse since the last shakeup got stopped in its tracks thanks to President Georgie Bush."

"What did he do?" Ashley asked.

"Proposed mandatory psychological testing for all Americans," Doug said shaking his head. Both ladies stopped what they were doing and looked at him in shock. "Can you imagine how much money the pharmaceutical companies would have made if that went through? They'd be trading computer companies and oil companies like penny stocks."

"So what happened?" asked Kim.

"Congress shut it down and rightfully so," Doug laughed. "It was one of the few things that republicans and democrats agreed on. Unfortunately it also stopped the last adjustment period for the mental health system."

"So a shakeup really is past due," Kim said thoughtfully.

"Just look at the research that's being done. Psychologists are out catching butterflies and the results are being used more on late night monologs and morning radio than they are in the clinical setting. Then there are the researchers who can't get along because of the petty squabbles, and egotistical head cases that just need to be given their walking papers. Just getting control of how the tax payer funded research is being used could take care of a lot of problems. They can work together and work for the client or find someone else to fund your research."

"So how does one ignite a government shakeup?" Ashley asked.

"I don't know," Doug said. "But if you were looking for it you would have seen a serious attempt to start a debate on the mental health system following the Sandy Hook shootings, but the gun control people overtook it. Unfortunately a rampage is about what it takes to make it an issue."

"There has got to be an easier way than that," Kim argued. "So how much are you paying us for all this work we're doing?" Ashley jokingly asked him.

"How about a trip to Los Angeles and a world movie premiere," Doug answered to the ladies surprise.

"As long as it's not that boring movie they made from your book," Kim shot back.

Doug had expected to spend three days getting the shower ready for the tile, but with the ladies help, and Kim's gadget savvy rescue, they were able to test the computerized shower controls before dinner. Tired from the day's work, they decided to finish the wallboard in the morning. Too tired to cook they drove to the Lake Michigan shore and had fish and chips on the pier near Grand Haven.

Chapter 9

Even with Kim and Ashley's help it took most of the morning to dig the pottery wheel and kiln out from the pile of boxes in the extra room in Doug's shop. By early afternoon they had the room cleared out and the pottery wheel in operation. Doug threw together a work bench for Ashley to use as a glazing station for Kim's creations.

"It's been a while since I've made any pottery, I hope I can remember how," Kim said.

"You'll remember," Ashley said encouragingly. "I love the pottery we still have that you made in college."

"If it's not too early to make a request, I need three or four semi deep bowls with large rims that I can use to cook on an open fire," Doug hinted as he sorted through some wires trying to remember which one was set up for the kiln and wishing he was better at marking things.

"So what are we going to make?" Ashley asked him.

"How about Fajitas," Doug suggested. "One bowl to cook the steak, one for chicken, and another one for the onions and peppers."

"And a flat griddle for the tortillas," Ashley suggested, then looking at Doug she added, "The rocks really don't cut it." "Coming right up," Kim chimed in enthusiastically. Getting her hands in the clay for the first time in years felt good. She squeezed the clay between her fingers, softening it for the pottery wheel. But it was the feeling of belonging, of being a part of the compound and the life that Doug was building that felt even better. Could this be the home she had been searching for so long? Ashley was as happy as she had ever seen her, which was saying a lot since Ashley always seemed happy. She watched her lovingly setting up her glazing station on the bench that Doug had built her. Doug was connecting wires and starting to feed them out a hole he had drilled in the wall. Kim had seen men working on their home improvement project before, her ex-husband, her father and brothers. They would try to wire things, or build things, or fix things, but it had never turned out exactly like they had planned. She felt confident that whatever Doug had in mind was not only exactly how it would turn out, it would work, and work well. She plopped the clump of clay she had been working onto the bat and putting her foot on the pottery wheel's foot pump started the top spinning.

"I'm going to the barn and get a couple of bags of quickcrete to make a foundation for the kiln," Doug announced to no one in particular.

As soon as Doug had left, Ashley moved behind Kim. Put her arms around her to do a little Ghost, she whispered into Kim's ear, "I could really learn to love this."

"I think I already have," Kim responded leaning back into Ashley's embrace.

Later that night after they had finished their dinner of fajitas and were sitting around the fire, Ashley said, "One of my students told me that if you take a piece of garden hose and stuff it into a piece of copper pipe, it will turn the fire different colors."

"That's true," Doug told her, "but it's better left to the idiots from the Jackass movies. It's toxic and makes the fire stink. The worst part is that the colors you do get from it are small and not very impressive, it's a waste of time."

"I've been trying to figure out who you remind me of," Kim laughed. "The cast of Jackass, you'd fit right in."

"I think he's more the Forest Gump type," offered Ashley. "No, I want to work with the cast of Ghost Busters," Doug announced. "Actual I want to work with Ray and Leon. True they're a little out there, but what they're going after is a little bit out there as well. They're dealing with something that nobody can see and few believe in, but that "something" is very real for the people who do see it, and do live it. Somebody has got to go in and try to help those people. Ray and Leon applied valid scientific theory, backed up by experimentation to reach their conclusions."

"Valid?" Kim asked with a mocking smirk.

"Well, valid by Hollywood standards anyway," Doug acknowledged. "They did get Beakman's character right, he started off doing some off the wall experiment in a university that had more to do with chasing skirts than helping anyone. For the rest of the movie his contribution was off the wall theories, which in his case proved to be right. Now look at Psychologies most famous and revered figure, Sigmoid Freud. In his professional career he had about 7 or 8 clients, all female, and from most accounts had sex with every one of them. He reportedly at least tried cocaine, probably had a full blown addiction to it. With very little clinical experience he sat around thinking up wild theories that, unlike Beakman's, have for the most part been disproved. Yet, Freud is still one of the fathers of modern Psychology."

"It sounds to me like they need a new father," Ashley suggested.

"That's what I used to think," Doug quickly responded. "When I did finally get the right prescription I didn't start writing, I went back to college in psychology. I left after one year because they weren't teaching anything that would be of any use in the trenches that I had just come from. It was all this theoretical crap, it seemed like we were learning more about the names of the Psychologists who were coming up with the theories than how the theories applied to the real world. They never once discussed treatment in a clinical setting."

"If you were only there for a year you probably didn't get that far," Kim pointed out.

"Probably true," Doug agreed. "I also went back to soon; I needed more time to get my head together. But two things happened that last semester that were more than I could handle. First, they kept talking about research that was pointless, interesting sometimes, but pointless. My personal favorite was a million plus dollar research study that involved students and professors from multiple universities and definitively proved once and for all that a higher percentage of teenage boys, in comparison to teenage girls, mow the lawn, and that a higher percentage of teenage girls, as compared to teenage boys, wash the dishes. They wrapped it all up under the fancy title of Gender Role Expectations."

"You've got to be kidding?" Ashley shot back.

"Where did you get that, sounds like something Leno would come up with?" Kim added.

"Leno doesn't come up with the studies, he and the morning radio shows get all kinds of material from Psychology research. The thing is that you might as well laugh at it since most of it is funded by your tax dollars. But no, I didn't make it up, I got that one from a 400 level college psychology class. I also pissed of the professor when I pointed out that the teenage suicide rate had just gone up again, and asked him how the results of the study, or having us learn the names of the Psychologists that led the study, were going to lower it." The ladies both cringed and gasp at the challenge, seeing their reaction Doug added, "You gotta go back to college in your forties, it's completely different than when you were younger. Trust me the professors are no longer gods, they're more like idealistic clowns with no contact to the real world."

Leaning into Ashley, Kim said, "We should try that in twenty years," Ashley readily agreed.

Trying to ignore them Doug went on, "When I first went to college back when I was eighteen, I took a few psych classes as electives and had one really good professor. One day someone ask him what his research was about, he said he was teaching spiders to dance."

"What!" both ladies challenged.

"Yeah, you've heard of Pavlov's Dog, ring a bell, present food, the dog salivates, do it enough times and all you have to do is ring the bell and the dog salivates, even if there is no food present." The ladies nodded they had both heard of Pavlov's dog so Doug went on, "So this professor I had was trying to prove which spiders could be trained, and which couldn't. His PhD work and fifteen or so years later his continuing research involved putting a spider on one side of a cage and a food source on the other side. Between the spider and the food was a metal plate hooked up to an electrical charge. The metal plate was only on the bottom of the cage, so the spider could take a more indirect route on the sides of the cage to get to the food if it wanted. So, the unsuspecting spider goes after the food the first time and gets a shock from the electrically charged plate, that's the dancing part," Doug gave the ladies plenty of time and a short demonstration to help them understand this important point, even though it probably wasn't needed. "Then by repeating the process over and over he would prove which species of spiders would eventually learn to avoid the metal plate, and which species walked over it and get shocked every time."

The ladies shook their heads in a combination of amusement and discussed, "And we're paying for that," Kim said in disgust.

Doug jumped on Kim's rhetorical comment, "Yeah, no, well actually yes, but not through the normal grants. This research was being funded by none other than the United States Military," Doug announced standing tall and saluting. Both Kim and Ashley laughed when they heard this. "Back then we all thought teaching spiders how to dance was funny, and judging from morning radio and late night TV, a lot of people still think some of the psychology research is funny. The problem is when you need help, or a friend, or family member needs help, and you find out there is very little in the way of testing to help the psychiatrists and psychologists make their diagnosis, then the fun research and the money spent on it isn't so funny."

"It's not funny to begin with, not if you really think about it anyway," Ashley agreed.

"Another fun fact about psychology research comes from a study done in 2010 that proved that 97% of psychology research findings positively supported the original hypothesis of the researcher. A little too high for comfort, unless of course you've already written the paper on your theory that your research is designed to prove or disprove," Doug offered for thought.

"So it's like Christian research, or tobacco funded research on smoking, they're just setting up experiments that prove what they want to prove?" Ashley asked.

"Who knows, but it sure looks bad. It's called publication bias. Have you ever heard of WEIRD research?" Doug asked.

"Yeah, but don't most people just call it psych research?" Kim joked.

"Close, WEIRD stands for Western, Educated, Industrialized, Rich, Democratic. Most psychology research, somewhere between 60% and 90%, is done in colleges and universities, and the test subjects are often the students. The problem is that college students only reflect about fifteen percent of the population," Doug told them. "When I was in school the first time I even got extra credit in my psychology class for volunteering for one of their psychology research experiments. Not exactly a random sampling. So I ask you, if the researchers are going in with publication bias and using only WEIRD test subjects, then how valid are the results?"

"So in fact your dancing spider professor was breaking new ground by using reliable test subjects," Kim kidded. Doug grinned and raised his eyebrows; as much as he didn't want to he had to give her that one.

"What needs to be done?" Ashley asked, knowing they were going to find out anyway.

"Glad you asked," Doug started. "What would you think of offering a proactive approach to mental health? Take the guess work out and replace it with a series of standardized tests people can take periodically throughout their lives. Some, if not all, of the most reliable psychological test are done using statistics. There's already several out there, multiple choice questionnaires like the MMPI for diagnosing mental health disorders, honesty tests some employers use. In others tests you put pictures in order to tell a story. I even took one where I they had me play with blocks. They then compare your answers to tens of thousands or even millions of other people's responses."

"You mean like the Rorschach Inkblot Test?" Ashley asked.

"Yeah, actually Rorschach was developed in the late forties and used a lot in the 50's, the Korean War era, but it lost favor with almost everyone but Hollywood in the 60's. There are a few people who still use it though, mostly at the high price Christian recruitment centers. That's where I took one," Doug explained.

"Did you see vaginas or butterflies?" Ashley asked.

"When I took the test the first ink blot she showed me had a perfect silhouette of a Two Toed Sloth," Doug answered to the amusement of both the ladies, "From then on all I could see in them was animals."

"You were probably looking for them," Ashley offered.

"No doubt," Doug agreed, "I even commented to the women giving the test that I was trying to see other things but all I could see were animals. She told me just to keep going. The thing is that I've seen the ink blots in other places and I see different things in them every time. It turns out that if the examiner can make a reliable diagnosis during a half hour semi-structured interview then it doesn't matter if they are showing you ink blots or pictures from their latest vacation. It's the skill of the person giving the test that counts. If that person doesn't have the skill and training to make the proper diagnosis, then the ink blot test is a waste of time and money. If they do have the skill to make a diagnosis then the ink blots test, the actual ink blots and what you see in them, is arbitrary. A good examiner will get the same results with or without them."

"You said they call these places Christian recruitment centers?" Ashley asked.

"Yeah, well that's what the clients call them," Doug explained. "They're the private psych hospitals that cater more to the lost souls, board housewives, and the normal day to day problems people face in life rather than the deeper psych issues requiring medical intervention and long term solutions like pharmaceuticals. Not that life's little issues can't become major life altering problems," He added quickly. "There's definitely a place for these facilities, and they help a lot of people. The problem is if you need be diagnosed and treated for a severe mental disorder and you go to one of these 28 day time out centers, you're probably not going to get the care and the diagnosis you need. The flip side is that if what you really need is just some time to get your head back together, someone to talk to, some life skills training, some role playing to help find new ways of dealing with life, stuff like that, and you go to a down and dirty psych hospital, then there is a very good chance you will wind up with a diagnosis and a bottle of medication you very possibly don't need.

Right now it isn't required that the treatment centers tell prospective clients what level of care is being offered. I don't think there's even a scale being used, at least not one available to the clients, it goes back to the one size fits all approach to treatment." "People really call them as Christian recruitment centers?" Kim asked.

"Yeah, the people who've been around do, the retreads call them that," Doug replied.

"Are they really that different?" Ashley asked

"Night and day," Doug told her. "At the full price houses and the state run places you mostly just sit. The people you get to know the best are the orderlies who are in the rooms all the time, and the volunteers that come in once or twice a week. The staff pretty much stays hidden and calls you in a couple times a week, more often at the full price houses than the state run hospitals, but you still don't see them very much. At the Christian recruitment centers it's more like an adult summer camp where the counselors are always around and you're constantly doing something. Endless games, granted the games are designed to work on important issues like assertiveness training, self-esteem, communication skills, stuff like that, but it did remind me of summer camp. And again, for some people that is exactly what they need. For a lot of people just getting off their lazy ass would do a lot to improve their quality of life. Then there are the meetings, some topics deal with life issues, others, well to be honest some of them really are recruitment centers," Doug replied.

"How do they refer to the hardcore places?" Ashley asked.

"Mostly by the food," the ladies laughed at Doug's answer, he kind of shrugged and said, "It might sound funny but that is the number one thing you're going to hear the retreads talk about, that the beds. They talk about the amazingly long list of different drugs they've been prescribed over the years. You can also go to the internet chat rooms for that, drugs are about all they talk about on those. The problem is that there are too many retreads. The percentage of people who return to treatment is around 70%, suicide rates are up, school and workplace shootings are up, anorexia and bohemia numbers are up, and the system hasn't changed in decades. Think about the thousands of G I's that came home from Vietnam with PTSD, now we have thousands coming back from the Middle East wars with PTSD, and from the sound of it the ones from the middle East aren't getting any better diagnosis's and treatment than the Nam bunch. It seems to me that if there had been a mature, let's work together and solve this attitude after Nam, and with the number of potential test subjects coming out of that war, they could have come up with better diagnostic tests and better treatment options for the Middle East vets."

"So the Afghan and Iraq vets could be getting better help if the researchers had done their jobs," Kim thought out loud.

"It's impossible to say what could have been. I can tell you which species of spiders can be trained to go around a shock pad, and which ones keep on dancing. The Nam vets were coming home about the same time the psych professor was a PhD candidate and was starting to teach the spiders how to dance, and he was doing it using military funding. The Nam vets were having all kinds of trouble readjusting and pretty much being told to just suck it up," Doug offered.

"And at the same time the military was training spiders to dance," Ashley said solemnly.

"That's awful," Kim barked in anger. "So why won't the researchers work together?"

"And that brings us to how I pissed off my second professor that semester," Doug said with a smile.

"Cool you went two for two," Ashley chirped, turning to Kim she added, "We have got to take a class with him."

"Or we could have him audit one your classes," Kim responded jokingly, giving Ashley a little head butt.

"I don't think so," Ashley replied, acknowledging Kim's head butt with a kiss. Looking back at Doug she said, "So what did you do to your other professor?"

After watching the ladies playful exchange Doug was deep in thought, but he wasn't thinking about what they had been talking about. Seeing the hunger in his gaze the ladies countered with inquisitive looks, it was still too early and too nice a night, they would make him wait. Doug reached for another log and with a few adjustments he found it a place on the gently burning fire.

"This professor was asking for his," Doug began. "He was on some panel involved with the new DSM4 several years back, Diagnostics and Statistics Manuel fourth edition," He said looking at the ladies. They both nodded that they knew what it was, "So he was pretty much blasting all the contributing researchers, both personally and there research. Talking about how petty they were in trying to get their work in the DSM. Then he said it, he asked the class, why do you think research psychologists do what they do? Then he added, I'll give you a hint, it's not for the money. After a few people guessed he said, we do it for the recognition of our peers. So like an idiot I yelled out, what about the client? We had two midterms and a final in that class and I got an A on all three and a B for the final grade."

"How did you do in the other class?" Ashley asked laughing, "Got an A, but he was just a PHD candidate, this guy was a full professor," Doug told her. "Anyway, he wasn't the only person who was pissed at that little exchange. I was already feed up with all this theory crap, how boys mow lawns and girls wash dishes. I just couldn't believe all the nonsense they were teaching us. I was there to make my way back into the trenches and try to help some people, and I've got a professor that's bragging to the class about playing grab ass with the other researchers instead of providing the research support from the ivory tower to the clinical world like they should be doing.

Kim and Ashley looked at each other; they had to admit he might be right on this one, "Granted it was a stupid thing to say, for both of you, but," Kim said, "all professors have giant egos. All doctors for that matter, you should meet the cardiologists I work with."

"Well I don't know about all doctors," challenged Doug, "Some are OK."

"Don't bet on it," Kim coughed out.

"Regardless of their egos, a psychology researcher should be working for the client," Ashley offered in compromise.

"Well, maybe not all, they should be figuring out everyday life issues," Doug conceded, "And there is a lot of good client centered work being done in psychology, but it's not enough. Psych research is the last medical discipline that still leans heavily on the ancient Greek Philosophers method of sitting around figuring out the universe. Freud is still a founding father of modern psychology, or in his case let's get stoned and postulate some answers psychology. What we need is a post-modern psychology. One where the research focus is on helping the client and aiding in the recovery process, not just research designed to seek knowledge just for the sake of knowledge. And definitely not research designed to amuse late night audiences. Personally I think they've had enough fun for a while, but if they need to do this totally off the wall research then let them pay for it. Until the numbers, suicide rates, going postal, the revolving door type statistics drop, all government funded research should have clinical applications. The news interviewed a psychologist after the Virginia Tech shootings who said it's impossible to predict violent behavior. I yelled at the TV that just because you haven't figured out how to predict violent behavior yet, doesn't make it impossible," Doug said angrily.

"They're always saying that the warning signs where there, after the fact," Kim added.

"Yeah, they do a great job of predicting a predisposition of violent behavior after the fact," Doug agreed. "They can also predict if a prospective employee is going to steal from the company with a short multiple choice tests. They had that Virginia Tech shooter, they had some short stories that alarmed one of his professors and the system had him in a treatment facility. If they had accurate tests to predict violent behavior, accurate tests to aid in diagnosing mental disorders or just used the ones they do have, and semi structured procedures for counseling, they might have stopped the Virginia Tech massacre. What about the thousands of client who don't pick up a gun, couldn't they be better helped with more reliable testing and treatment procedures. Let's face it most of the people in the field of mental health, regardless of what degrees they have or what title they hold, don't have the "IT" factor, or the crystal ball that they all seem to think they have to see into a client's inner soul. There might be some of these super shrinks out there who really have the gift of looking inside another person and correctly diagnosing them, but if there really are any around they're few and far between, and with every passing year it's getting worse."

"They had the Sandy Hook shooter too," Ashley said.

"They had one of the Boston bombing brothers as well," Kim added.

"What we need is a national debate on mental health reform. We just had one on bullying recently. After Sandy Hook both the gun control people and the mental health people both tried to get one started, but the gun control took it, again," Doug said as he sat down next to Ashley.

"Does that mean the media is more interested in gun control?" Kim asked.

"Rock, roll, and rant," Doug whispered as he began nibbling on Ashley's neck.

Chapter 10

After three days of practice Kim felt confident, though not entirely excited. Doug had bought Ashley a fishing pole as well, but after untangling the fourth birds nest from her reel he had decided not to push her on practicing. For both ladies the idea of getting up at 5:30 in the morning to spend half the day in Doug's row boat wasn't high on their lists of fun ways to spend a day, but Doug was excited and they had promised him that they would give it a try. So long before sunrise they were in the auto action truck heading for the bait shop for minnows.

"Explain to me again why I spent three days practicing casting if we are going to use live bait," Kim asked.

"For a proper fish stew we need more than one kind of fish," Doug told her. "The minnows are for crappie, the worms for perch, the corn for trout, and the lures for bass."

"Have you ever heard of hotdogs," Ashley asked sarcastically, "I hear there catching on."

"Yes, but there aren't any musky in the river," Doug answered.

The ladies opinion of fishing began to change when they got to the bait shop. Like many bait shops in the region this one was owned by a retired couple in their seventies and the ladies were instantly taken by the love and fellowship they found.

As soon as they walked in Doug handed the minnow bucket to the old man who was standing by the aerator tanks. Soon he and the old man were discussing the recent action fishermen in the region were seeing. As they were discussing what size minnows were getting the most action, two teenagers who were checking out the wall of lures joined in the conversation.

The ladies walked up to the counter where they were greeted by the old man's wife, Betty. After exchanging pleasantries, and a much needed cup of coffee, they found themselves answering a barrage of questions about themselves. It turned out that Doug was a regular at the bait shop, and the ladies presence in town had not gone unnoticed, and Betty was just the one to get the inside scoop. The ladies enjoyed giving her their stories almost as much as they liked getting a handle on the local gossip. After what the ladies thought was a short thirty minutes they were all back in the old truck and heading back to the river.

The sun was just rising as they got underway with Kim sitting on the plastic seat in the bow of the old wooden rowboat, Doug sat on the bench in the back operating the small trolling motor, and Ashley reclining crossways in the middle of the boat on a bed of cushions. As planned Ashley had brought a book and was just planning on watching. Soon Doug had them up river about a quarter of a mile. Along the way he had been showing them how to read the water surface to get an idea of what was happening below the surface. He could tell the crappies were biting by the frenzied action of the minnows near the surface so he found a shaded spot and he and Kim prepared their lines.

Both ladies had a little moral episode when he showed Kim how to put the hook through the minnow's side just below the midline stripe, and just behind the dorsal fin, so that the minnow would not only live but be able to swim. He explained that the minnow would tell her when a crappie was checking it out by trying to swim away. The minnows swimming would in turn move the bobber against the current, and that movement would tell her when to get ready to reel in the fish when it took the bait. He also explained that crappie swim in school, so when you catch one crappie it means that there are others near. In the boat they would try to follow the school, but when fishing from the shore you had to catch the fish when they were there, then wait till another school swam.

To Kim and Ashley's surprise it happened just as he had told them. Soon Kim saw the bobber moving against the current. Just as Doug had instructed her she took in the slack in her line. Then the bobber started plunging a few inches under the water, it took all her self-restraint to keep from pulling on the line. Soon the bobber disappeared completely and she reeled in a modest sized crappie. Both of the ladies made so much noise in their excitement that Doug wondered if they had scared the school away, but soon he had a fish on his line and Kim was already getting some action with her second minnow. Ashley even managed to catch two crappies after Doug baited her hook. Soon they had eleven crappies and after Doug picked six that he would use in his fish stew he released the rest.

"Next," he told them, "we need some bass."

By now the ladies were fully into the adventure. Doug took them up river about a mile and turned the boat to face downstream. He then set the trolling motor on its slowest speed and turned it so that it almost held the boat steady against the current, they started to slowly drift down the shore. Doug tied a spinner on his line and began casting towards the shore, Kim tied one of the quarter ounce yellow jigs she had been practicing with on hers and tried her luck. Doug had told her to look for logs, brush, and inlets, and to cast her lure into them. He also explained that the bass will rarely strike on the first cast, so when she sees a good spot to cast into it ten times in a row. The bass fishing didn't go as well as the crappie, but in two hours they had three eleven inch largemouth bass in the basket, enough for the stew. Factoring in Kim's lost lures Doug calculated they cost about three dollars a pound, but by this time they all agreed it was worth it.

Next he drove the boat upriver to the spillway. Having fished the river several times with the help of his fish finder, he knew that the water coming over the spillway had formed several deep holes about one hundred yards below the spillway, and that the holes were loaded with trout. They were especially productive when the water was low and the trout congregated in the deeper holes, but even with the water high, like it was today, they were still usually good for a few fish. Because the water was high and the current strong he was able to talk Ashley into fishing the holes by telling her that he would need both hands to keep the boat steady and in position. In truth the motor was operated by a foot control. This time he had the ladies remove the bobber and attach a half once sinker six inches above the hook. Then he showed them how to bait the hooks with canned corn. He showed them on the fish finder that the water was four feet deep, and the holes they were fishing were about ten feet deep. He had them lower their lines to six and eight feet and wait for a bite. It didn't take long till Ashley was reeling in the first of the ten inch trout. Soon Kim joined in with one of her own. Within an hour they had each caught seven nice rainbow trout. This time Doug picked the four best and added them to his basket before releasing the rest.

Next Doug drove them back to the wide area of the river that his compound overlooked. Along the way he showed them how to attach a one ounce weight to the end of their lines, and a four inch line with a hook six inches above it. He explained that perch were bottom feeders and that they would let the sinker drop all the way to the bottom, then bring in the slack. By doing this the hook would be floating about two to three inches off the river bottom with a big juicy worm on it. He also told them that although perch weren't usually found in rivers, since they preferred calmer water, they could be found in some of the wider sections of his river where the water didn't flow as strong. Soon he had them over a calm section that he knew averaged about eight feet in depth. This time all three of them fished for the perch with Kim and Ashley having the advantage since Ashley wasn't about to put a worm on a hook, or as it turned out take a fish off of one. The perch were small, averaging only about six inches or seven inches, but they were plentiful, soon had the eight perch he needed for his stew. By this time the ladies were totally enthralled with fishing, but after spending six hours in the row boat they were ready to get back to shore as soon as Doug told them that his shopping list was complete.

"I can't believe how much fun that was," Ashley said on the way in. "I could never see what people liked about fishing, it had always seemed boring to me."

"It is kinda boring if the fish aren't biting," Doug admitted, "But it still beats sitting at home."

"I don't know," Kim said, "I went fishing with my brothers a couple of times and all I wanted to do was get home. But they didn't catch anything. There's more to it than I realized."

"Yeah, I guess you need to know what you're doing to catch anything," Ashley added with a smile.

"True, it also helps when you've fish an area as much as I've fished this river," Doug explained, "I took you to all my hot spots, normally I try different areas and might or might not have this kind of luck."

As soon as they got the boat pulled onto shore, and most of the gear loaded into the side by side, the ladies headed to the big house as they now called it. Doug had managed to get the large spa style tub hooked up, though not exactly built in, and the ladies were anxious to soak away the six hours in the boat. When Doug finished filleting the fish and putting the gear up, he drove into Grand Haven and bought a half pound of scallops and two dozen mussels for the stew. Then he stopped by a bakery and bought a loaf of sourdough bread. By the time he got home the ladies had the side by side loaded with everything they would need for dinner around the campfire.

"We didn't know if you would want the three gallon caldron or the one and a half gallon one, so we packed both," Ashley told him.

"The smaller one," He told them as he put his purchases in the side by side's bed, "Go ahead and get the fire started, I'm going to take a quick shower and I'll meet you up there."

"Do you want us to get the pot set up," Kim asked, referring to the one inch steel rebar Doug had liberated from a multi-level parking garage construction site and was now using as a tripod.

"If you want," he told her, "but I'll probably be up there before you get the fire ready." He was amazed at how well the ladies were adjusting to the country life, and decided to take a long shower just to see how far they could get setting up the fire. When he finally made it to the fire ring a half hour later, the ladies had the tripod in place over a roaring fire.

"We didn't know how much water you needed so we just filled the pot half way," Kim said as he approached.

"That should be just about perfect," he told her. "There's a jar of spices I premix for fish stew in the basket, add about a half a cup to the water while I get the fish cut up." He had learned from experience that when using fresh caught fish most people wanted to know which fish was which when they eat it, so he cut the fish fillets in different geometric patterns so he would be able to identify them when the ladies asked. With the fish they had caught that morning, and the scallops and mussels he had bought in town, there was enough fish stew to feed a small army, but between the three of them they managed to make a sizable dent in the pot. With dinner done and the dishes put away, they again found themselves sitting on the moving blankets watching the fire.

"You said that the psychologists were getting worse with every passing year, why?" Kim asked.

"It's because we have a winner in the centuries old feud between Psychiatry and Psychology. By popular demand the psychologists have won. The only problem is the psychiatrists have been able to delay their own extinction with the help of the political power of the AMA," Doug explained. "You see if given the choice most people who know how the system works would go to a psychologist for testing, treatment, and counseling. The only thing they can't get from the psychologist is a prescription for psychotropic drugs, if they need them. If you go to a psychiatrist you will get a diagnosis, that's pretty much guaranteed, and in almost every case psychotropic drugs will be required, even if they're not. If you need psychotropic drugs and you want counseling, you have to go to a psychiatrist and to a counselor. A lot of insurance plans today only cover six or twelve psych visits a year, and if you're on one of those it's very likely that the psychiatrist will use them for monthly medication reviews, and you won't be able to see a counselor at all, unless you pay for it yourself. Twice there has been a bill in congress that would have given the psychologist the prescription pad so they can prescribe psychotropic drugs, but the AMA has been able to block it from even coming up for a vote both times." "It seems like people should have the choice of who they can see," Ashley said looking at Kim.

"It makes sense, they're giving limited use of the prescription pad to Doctors assistants, Dr. Nurses, Nurse Practitioners, and even some Pharmacist can write scripts these days," Kim agreed.

"If you think about it psychiatrists spend an average of ten years studying psychology to get their PhD." Doug elaborated. "Psychiatrists spend four years in premed, four years studying medicine, two years as an intern practicing medicine, then in a lot of cases just two years practicing psychiatry during their residency, then they're licensed psychiatrists. A psychologist general spends an hour, fifty minute hour anyway, with their client. A psychiatrist generally spends fifteen minutes to a half an hour with their client, and psychiatrists charge more than double what psychiatrists do."

"Is the psychiatrist that much better than the psychologist?" Ashley asked.

"No, they're that much worse," Doug shot back. "Remember that twice congress has considered giving the psychologists the prescription pad but the AMA has blocked it both times. Also believe me when I tell you that most people if given the choice would see the psychologist rather than a psychiatrist. So if the psychologists ever get the prescription pad it will spell the death of psychiatry, or at the very least bring about a big drop in there number of clients. Now the final piece, this has been going on for the last twenty years, and it's well known in medical schools and intern programs. So the effect of the AMA keeping psychiatry on life support for so long is that any kid who spends over a decade in school and training to become a medical doctor isn't going to risk their future by going into a dying field, not by choice anyway. So let me ask you, what do you think is happening to the quality of psychiatrists?"

"Anybody that's any good is choosing to go into other fields. So the overall quality is going down," Ashley said.

"That's a terrible way to talk about overseas medical school students," Doug said sarcastically.

"In my hospital most of the psychiatry residents are foreign, or they're kind of nerdy," Kim added.

"Kind of nerdy," Doug repeated, "Strait A's in class and no common sense or social skills outside of class. The nerds and foreign born kids, for whom English is a second language, are diagnosing psych patients in fifteen to thirty minutes, generally with no testing of any kind, and the percentage of clients returning to treatment facilities is around 70%. Worse, with each passing year the percentage of older psychiatrists who actually entered the field because they wanted to goes down as they retire. So the longer they keep psychiatry on life support, the worse it gets for the clients."

"And it's the client who suffers from the overall decline," Ashley said shaking her head.

"And follow up visits with the psychiatrist are rarely more than fifteen minutes, so if they do get the wrong diagnosis it unlikely that they will catch it," Doug continued. "Compare that to a psychologist who spends ten years studying mental disorders, and sees the client for one hour sessions. Then if counseling is needed it is usually the psychologist who does the counseling. Psychiatrists never do the counseling. So a client who goes to counseling with a psychologist once a week will spend four hours a month with the psychologist. A client who goes to counseling once a week through a psychiatrist will see the psychiatrist for a fifteen minute medication review once a month."

"I have heard that if you walk into a psychiatrist's office, you have already been diagnosed with a mental illness," Kim added.

"With one exception, the psychiatrists themselves don't have to be tested for mental health issues to get licensed. There were a lot of times when I met with a psychiatrist that I wandered if I was the healthy one in the room," Doug said shaking his head. "Of course anymore you don't even have to walk into a psychiatrist's office to get diagnosed; you can do it by Email."

"Telepsychiatry, I've been hearing about that," Kim acknowledged.

"So you don't even have to see a doctor to get a diagnosis and a prescription?" Ashley asked in disbelief.

"It gets better," Doug told her, "There is a shortage of psychiatrists, especially in the field of child psychiatry, so you can get your kid diagnosed and on medication by Email, or over the phone. Apparently psychiatrists have gotten so good at diagnosing mental disorders that they don't have to see the patient at all. That or they are just so into the money that they found a way to make more of it in their spare time."

"I can't even imagine putting my child on psychotropic drugs by Email," Ashley said in horror.

"But they still won't give the psychologists the prescription pad, even when they admit that they are overstretched. That's just irresponsible," Kim added. "Psychiatrists aren't that much better trained than psychologists."

"Let me guess," Joked Ashley, "The reason there is a shortage of child psychologists is that the nerds and the foreign students going into psychiatry don't care if they mess up an adult's life with their incompetence, but messing with the children's lives is still off limits, even for them."

"Wow, you really are getting a feel for how the system operates," Doug told her.

"I just can't believe this is true, it's to messed up," Ashley sighed.

"The system is in trouble. So who do people turn to for answers on how to fix it?" Doug asked. "The

doctors," Kim agreed.

"All I want is to be able to get psychological testing, along with an interview session, before they start giving me a lot of powerful drugs, a second opinion, preferably done with a standardized test.

Unfortunately second opinions in mental health are not popular with psychiatrists, and many insurance companies handle mental health issues differently than other medical issues. Co-payments are generally higher, and they often give the clients a limited number of visits. Add to that the fact that with most of the treatment facilities you don't know what kind of treatment is provided till you get started. So if you want to change treatment styles, you will probably end up paying for it yourself. The facility could offer medical, psychological, or religious based treatment, and they don't have to tell you which before you sign in."

"Religious, is that kind of like the place Michele Bachmann's husband runs?" Ashley asked. "Those pray away the gay type treatments."

"I really don't know what that's all about, but I have heard them questioning Senator Bachmann if it is pray away the pain, or the gay type treatment. But just think about it, if she can't tell the media what type of treatment is being offered, and the media covering a presidential candidate can't find out, then just how is the individual seeking treatment supposed to find out?" Doug asked.

"You're right, that's just plain wrong," Kim agreed.

"So if one of you enter a pray away the pain style treatment center for some issues that you are dealing with, let's say fear of heights, or depression. At the treatment center they find out you're bi-sexual and they start that pray away the gay treatment. You decide to leave because that's not what you came in for. If you signed up for 28 days, like most of those places have you do, in order to get out you will have to leave AMA, against medical advice, which means that most insurance plans won't cover the time you've already been there and you will have to pay for treatment that you didn't want out of our own pocket."

"Does that really happen?" Ashley asked.

"It's a big problem with the Cristian recruitment centers, but all these places lock you down. They search you and your belongings and they confiscate anything that can be used as a weapon. A lot of them even take your shoe laces so you don't hang yourself with them. All makes sense since some of the people in the center are probably dealing with suicidal thoughts. Even if you checked yourself in they make it hard for you to leave, and the courts and the police are on their side. And if you have insurance, well, let's just say they want the money," Doug told her. "In the end, once you sign in you're probably in for the duration."

"And again because of the stigma attached to mental health the public will support the facility," Kim added.

"Public, courts, family, friends, you would be amazed at how much influence these places have once you sign the intake papers. And you originally checked in because of a fear of heights," Doug added.

"And if you check in with insurance your screwed," Ashley said.

"Granted that's an extreme example," Doug told them, "but if you have a phobia and want Gradual Exposure Therapy, which is generally done in a facility that uses Cognitive-Behavioral based treatment, and you find out after you get started that the facility uses Psychoanalytical treatment, or talk therapy, you're probably stuck accepting whatever they are providing. Since the treatment facilities don't have to advertise the style of treatment they use, or even tell you if you ask, and since the system is so poorly regulated that most of them will say that they offer all of the different types of treatment, even though in reality they don't, you're stuck with whatever they give you. All the control is in the hands of the care givers, the client has no ability to decide what they want. Bachmann's husband's treatment facility is the perfect example, if the media can't find out what kind of treatment is being provided, then how is the prospective client supposed to find out?" "Michele Bachmann is just a nut job herself, she shouldn't be in politics," Kim added.

"Well the truth is that I'm just as much to blame for that as anyone," Doug responded.

"How's are you to blame?" both ladies asked.

"Well, when the old hippies from the great north woods elected Jessie "The Body" Ventura to be Governor of Minnesota, I was all for it, I thought it was great. At first I thought it was a joke, but from what I've heard he did a decent job as a Governor. The problem is that the old hippies enjoyed the attention that Ventura brought them so much that they tried to one up themselves and elected Michele Bachmann to the United States Senate. Of course all that did was proved that long term Marijuana use does cause severe brain damage," Doug said jokingly.

That was enough for the ladies, even though the night air was warmer than usual, so was the mist rolling in from the river. Kim and Ashley began gathering up their things and headed back to the small room above the workshop. As was becoming the norm, Doug stayed with the fire for a while before joining them.

Chapter 11

———

Kim's natural athletic abilities had made her a hit from the start, while Ashley outgoing personality had won everybody over. It wasn't that Doug had been worried, he had been playing volleyball with this group every weekend for several years, and he knew that the ladies would be instantly welcomed. What had started as a pick-up game on the beach years ago had transformed itself into a close group of friends that extended well beyond the white beaches of Grand Haven. As usual after a couple of games they all took a break and had a light brunch. This time it was Sandy's turn to bring it. Sandy, a high school biology teacher form Olive Hill, and Ashley had been swapping war stories from school most of the morning so it didn't surprise anyone when Ashley volunteered to help her set things out. The best part was that with two of the weaker links out, the next game would be the best of the morning, and on the beaches of West Michigan where volleyball is king, a good game was never taken lightly.

When the group finished the game they were all ready for the brunch that Sandy had brought. Sandy and Ashley were still talking about teaching as the group started fixing their plates. By this time the ladies were swapping funny versions of the horror stories teacher's face with their unruly kids.

"OK, try this one, the best prank ever pulled," Ashley challenged Sandy as the group approached. "Starting after lunch a group started unscrewing and removing every bell cover in the halls, so by the end of the day, when the final bell was supposed tom ring, there was nothing but silence."

"That took some planning," Ashley conceded.

"I used to think that teaching would be an incredibly rewarding job," one of the players commented. "I even looked into it when I was in college but back then it didn't pay anything. Any more it seems like all I hear is horror stories about how out of control the kids are and how the government messed everything up with all this testing."

"I've loved teaching from day one, and I still do," Ashley responded. "But I gotta admit that dealing with the testing is a pain. As far as the kids are concerned, I've always had discipline problems, but it does seem to be getting worse. At times it's even fun seeing what they come up with, but most of the time it's just a pain."

"That's true, some of the pranks were great, but any more it seems like I've seen them all. For a long time the kids made me feel young, but these days they, well, they just wear me out," Sandy added. "For me it's dealing with some of the parents that's the worst part. When I started I had my counters filled with every kind of animal I could find, iguanas, mice, snakes, anything I could get a cage for. Now I'm down to one aquarium with tropical fish because the parents keep complaining that they're distractions, or intimidating, or something's wrong with them, the kids used to love them."

"We get the same stuff in English. It seems that every book we read is offensive to someone," Ashley agreed. "It really does limit what I can do. The worst part is that it's the kids that suffer. The truth is that a lot of the books I have to use really are boring."

"Thirty years is a long time in the classroom," Sandy said. "I think they should try a 20/20 plan," Doug suggested.

"And what is a 20/20 plan?" Sandy asked with a smile, she was used to Doug's "ideas".

"Well, since you asked," Doug began, returning Sandy's smile.

"It's where the government and private industry work together to attract young kids to the teaching profession by splitting it into two careers. The college kids would sign up for the program, then instead of teaching for 30 years and retiring, they teach for twenty years. After they finish the teaching portion they move on to a twenty year stint with one of the participating companies."

"Companies are always trying to recruit out of schools," Ashley added.

"Of course, it's exactly the skill set that many companies are looking for. Communication skills, organizational skills, independent work in most classrooms, they are all skills that come up in an interview. Even when I was in school we lost some of our best teachers to corporate jobs," Doug said.

"So what are the advantages?" Brad who was one of the group's original members asked as he took a bite out of his sandwich.

"For the kids they work two jobs, when they finish them both they get two retirement checks, 2/3's of a teacher's pension, and a second check from whatever company they work for. For the school system they get young quality teachers, they save twenty years of retirement, insurance and benefit payments, when the kids are working their second job, and they only pay half of the benefits when the kids retire from their second job. They also save since the last ten years of the teacher's career are the most expensive due to raises. The companies also save half on the benefits after the kids retire. They also get twenty years to recruit the kids when they are teaching and they can train them during the summers and send product and procedure updates during the school year so that when the kids teaching commitment is over they can walk in the corporate door with years of knowledge and some experience," Doug concluded.

"So what corporations are going to get involved?" Sandy asked. "Most of the teachers I know who have left became sales reps, I don't want to be a sales rep."

"How about being the manager of a pet store?" Doug asked.

Sandy cocked her head and shrugged, "I could do that. So I

started teaching at 23 and am scheduled to retire at 53. With your 20/20 plan I work twenty years as a teacher, twenty as a pet store manager and retire at 63 with the same benefits but more money," She thought out loud.

"Exactly, of course how much money depends on who you work for during the second twenty, and how well you do with them. The rest of your benefits remain the same, it's just that the school and the company you work for split the cost after you retire," Doug explained.

"And the school system or the company picks up the entire cost of the persons benefits when the person is working for them, but they share the cost of the benefits when the kid retires," Bill added.

"Exactly," replied Doug. "Of course if the kids want to they can still go the traditional 30 years and out. This is a way to attract talent at the college level, reduce costs, and prevent teacher burnout all at the same time."

"Where do you come up with this stuff," Sandy's husband Chris asked as he handed out drinks from the cooler.

"Woodworking requires patients, skill, and a steady hand, but I have to admit that not all of it requires thought," Doug answered. "Give me a couple of months and I'll have Kim and Ashley doing the same thing."

"Don't you dare," quipped Sandy, "We've already got you to deal with, besides we like them," she added to the general approval of all.

Chapter 12

———

To celebrate their first month anniversary Doug bought the ladies each a mountain bike. He had several riding paths of varying lengths running through his property, he had even marked off a twelve mile loop that went through his Mennonite neighbors farm and into a wooded area that the Bissman's owned. Kim and Ashley had been using two of his older mountain bikes and had ridden with him on his morning rides at times. Kim was even going out by herself occasionally, and they all enjoyed taking evening rides together along the river bank. But the bikes they were using were old and too big for the ladies. The bikes Doug gave them were new and properly sized and colorful. Doug also gave them several colorful accessories, it turns out that the same outrageous colors that get sponsors recognized during the Tour de France, keeps cyclists from being mistaken for deer and shot in West Michigan. The gift was received with the same enthusiasm as the fancy watch that Doug kinda liked and would have to remember to wear when they got dressed to go out. Personally he couldn't see what was wrong with the 99 cent watches he liked to bid on through EBay. Doug had also made reservations at one of the finest restaurants in Grand Rapids, so after a short ride on the bikes all three jumped into the walk in shower in the new house. They still hadn't completely moved from the loft over the shop and into the house, but they were spending more and more time there. The official move would probably be when Doug hooked up the kitchen appliances. After a wonderful dinner and a so-so play, they headed home with Kim riding in the back seat and Ashley in the front. To both Doug and Kim's surprise it was Ashley who brought up the now all too familiar topic.

"Don't you think that people would protest if they had to take a psych test?" Ashley asked.

"Of course, you thought the mandatory immunization for HPV caused problems, just try to force people to take a psychological test and see what happens. Junior President Bush tried to make mental health testing mandatory for everyone and he got all kinds of organized resistance. Forcing people into a broken system that can do them more harm than good is just plain irresponsible. Even if we do get the mental health system working, mandatory testing would still be wrong and probably unconstitutional. For a free country our politicians seem to be using the word mandatory a lot," Doug stated. "When I say we should take a proactive approach to mental health, I'm not talking about mandatory testing. Think of it more like going to an optometrist to get your eyes checked. If you need glasses then you have to go every year or two and get a prescription for your glasses or contacts. If your eyesight is 20/20 without glasses, then it's still a good idea to see an optometrist every so often just to make sure your eyesight hasn't changed or there isn't some kind of problem with your eyes. My dad has Wet Macular Degeneration in his eyes and has to have a series of three shots in his eyeball every year or two. The problem is that Wet AMD has genetic links which make me susceptible to it, so I have to have my eyes checked every five years. And I do get them checked because I do not want anybody sticking a needle in my eye. Colonoscopies are another good example of something that I don't want to do but I do it anyway. If there is a problem I want to know about it. Having a random mental health checkup periodically throughout your life would be a way of staying on top of your game. Or I should say that it would be if they could accurately diagnose and treat mental health issues."

"With psychology having such a social stigma, and the horror stories coming out of treatment, it's hard to believe that anyone would take the test willingly," Kim argued.

"I don't think I would want to take one. There are some things I don't want to know," Ashley added.

"OK, let's go back to the optometrist analogy," Doug suggested. "Say someone has 20/40 vision and they never go to get their eyesight checked. 20/40 isn't that bad so they'll probably do just fine in life, other than a few extra dents on their car that is. If they do get glasses or contacts that give them 20/20 vision, then they will see things more clearly and save themselves some car repairs. Another person with 20/120 eyesight realistically doesn't have a choice but to get glasses or it will seriously affect their lives. Now look at mental health, excuse my misuse of terminology, say a person has 20/40 mental vision, or mental health, they have a few problems in life but with the current state of mental health care and the stigma and fear that goes along with seeking treatment they probably will never get any kind of a checkup, even though they would have clearer mental vision if they did. They would save themselves a few dents in their lives, like a divorce, or a lost promotion at work. That's assuming they get proper care. The person with 20/120 mental vision is probably already receiving care and is probably deeply embedded in the system, if not they are having all kinds of problems in life. In order to get the person with 20/40 mental vision the help that would improve the quality of their lives we need to get a safer more reliable mental health system in place. Even if we can get the mental health industry cleaned up with specialization in treatment, testing for diagnosis, advertised levels of care so people aren't just being thrown into a one size fits all system, and whatever else it needs, there is still the social stigma," Doug continued. "As far as the social stigma is concerned just remember that a few years back the idea of a group of men standing around a grill and discussing erectile dysfunction and the wonders of a little blue pill wasn't realistic either."

"There is still the social pressure. A lot of people laughed at

Charlie Sheen's meltdown, I didn't laugh, but it sort of made me uncomfortable," Kim added.

"Well that and all those daytime TV freak shows that are so popular, if you ask me they're doing more harm than good. They are good research sites for hypochondriacs though. Personally I think one of the worst offenders is Woody Allen poking fun at how messed up the system is. Changing the perception people have of psychology is important, but we need to fix the system first," Doug explained.

"Then he marries his adopted daughter," Ashley laughed. "Yeah,

he probably should have been listening to what his psychotherapist was saying to him and not how it would sound to an audience. It's not that what he was saying wasn't true, people do play around with psychotropic drugs and people do become addicted to therapy or become pawns to their therapists. The number one lawsuit in psychology isn't malpractice, its sexual abuse. And the movies aren't wrong about how they portray the academic world either. If anyone in one of those college based movies has sex with a professor, it's probably a psychology professor. When I went to college the first time, I took intro to psychology and intro to philosophy my freshman year. It wasn't till years later that it occurred to me that I learned theory and names in psychology, and I had a work book in philosophy that used mathematical type equations to prove truth and logic in arguments. There was more science in philosophy than there was in psychology. It just seems to me that psychology is a fun degree and that if a college's psychology researcher's get their research findings on the Tonight Show monolog it shows that it came from a fun university. It's a great degree for frat boys and sorority sisters."

"I can imagine some smooth talking a frat boy or a sorority sister who has a great time in college and after graduation comes to the realization that they've wasted their entire education. Thus is born a motivational speaker," Ashley said.

"Or a self-help guru," Kim laughed, then added, "Or a mental health counselor."

"Yeah, well now imagine having a life altering mental illness, suicidal thoughts, panic attacks, or hallucinations, and going to a sorority sister who couldn't find a husband that could support her so now she's your counselor," Doug said angrily. "And don't think it isn't happening every day."

"It does seem that some form of control, or as you keep saying it level of treatment options are needed," Kim agreed.

"I can't help thinking that with my bi-polar condition, and being classified as what's called "high functioning", that if I had been properly tested and diagnosed from the beginning I would never have seen one of the Christian recruitment centers, the softer treatment centers. I also would never have ended up in one of the hard core institutional mental hospitals. I would have fit in the middle since I do need medication, and I would have needed appropriate outpatient counseling for a year or so. If all that had been done early enough I would probably be a married architect with a nice house and a couple of kids. Also, if my case had been handled correctly, my entire treatment would have cost around 10,000 to 30,000 dollars in total. As it is I've been through the entire gamut of psych hospitals, and can I give you a personal analysis of about fifteen different psychotropic drugs designed to treat several different disorders that I don't suffer from. And it was all done at a total cost that is well into the hundreds of thousands of dollars range and probably approaching a million dollars by now," Doug said angrily.

"It seems like such a waste," Ashley softly said. "And it's not only the money but the human lives that are being thrown away."

Now think about the employers who should be taking the lead in mental health reform," Doug pressed on. "Mental health issues are costing them in insurance premiums, time off, employee problems, and productivity. Think what would happen if standardized testing and quality treatment, safe treatment that people feel comfortable seeking was available. What's the current divorce rate, about 50 percent," Doug said, answering his own question. "Some of that has to be caused by mild forms of mental disorders that could be treated. How about worker satisfaction, ever worked next to a depressed person? Absenteeism, if we could raise work place productivity by just 10 percent by offering quality, responsible mental health care, quality care that doesn't carry the social stigma; it would be the biggest gain to productivity in history. How about everyday life, how about a 10 percent increase in the quality of everyday life. And I am not suggesting we do it by going out and catching butterflies. I'm suggesting we do it by getting the research psychologists to stop going out catching butterflies, and stop playing grab ass with each other, and start holding them accountable for getting the job done that we have been paying them to do for the last hundred years. Take off the patch jackets and put on some lab coats, or if I'm right about statistics being the key to creating accurate tests to diagnosing mental disorders then get them to dust off their calculators."

"You would still need to break the social stigma of going to see a shrink. I don't see how you could ever do that," Ashley countered. Kim couldn't believe she said that, Ashley was pushing this conversation. Catching Ashley's eye Kim realized that she was doing it on purpose. She was trying to get Doug riled up. So Ashley wants something kinky tonight, Kim thought, that's fine count me in.

"Advertising level of care and specialization in treatment would go a long way in making mental health care less intimidating. Empowering the client so that they could make informed decisions and choose the treatment they want would take a lot of the fear of the unknown out of treatment. As far as the ivory tower we just need some maturity and applied science, or more likely statistics. If someone came to me asking who to go to for help, I would tell them to go to a psychologist and request an MMPI. The MMPI is one of the best statistical tests they have. The problem is that even if they do that, then where do you send them? A psychiatrist and a sorority sister type counselor? It system just doesn't work," Doug's voice changing to frustration. "We need more analytical tests, both broad based tests, and tests designed to pinpoint issues related to specific disorders for fine tuning medication and treatment needs. The problem is that it takes years complete, hundreds of researchers, working in dozens of research facilities, and thousands or even hundreds of thousands of test subjects to produce a reliable statistical test. Then when the work is done the only people who get their names in the text books are the lead researchers or the facility where the study began. In Freud's world of Id, Ego, and Superego, the superegos of the ivory tower can't handle it; they need the attention and the recognition, so they do these quick hit research projects just to see their names in print. Even worse, a lot of the universities support them by making two to three publications per year mandatory to get tenured."

"I have heard there's a lot of pressure on psychologist's to publish," Kim added.

"Quantity verses quality?" Ashley asked.

"It's not that there isn't any quality research being done in theoretical psychology or that there isn't any research being done to help in the clinical settings. What we need is a shift in the percentage of research away from theoretical and start focusing on clinical research. Do that and give the researchers who are doing the just plain stupid research their walking papers." Doug continued "Another problem is, do you remember Sybil? It was made into a movie but it was really a true story, well actually it was a total lie, but the psychologist claimed it was a true story."

"Sybil was fake?" Ashley said in surprise.

"It was all done with hypnosis, wasn't it?" Kim asked Doug.

"What little of it that was true probably was done by hypnotism; most of it was just made up. Anyway, the thing is that we have pockets of mental disorders in this country. Today what Sybil had is called Dissociative Identity Disorder which is very rare in the general population. Let's say that a city the size of Grand Rapids has three actual cases of Dissociative Identity Disorder which would be about average or maybe even a little high for a city that size. Then you go to a city the same size and all of a sudden you have thirty or forty cases of Dissociative Identity Disorder. Assuming it's not something in the water, you can bet that there is a psychologist or psychiatrist in that city who is fascinated by, or studying the disorder," Doug explained.

"So people are being intentionally misdiagnosed," Ashley said in horror.

"Not exactly, the psychologist or psychiatrist is just hyper conscious of a particular disorder and over reads the signs, that or some even lead the client into a disorder. That's what happened to the real Sybil through hypnotic suggestion. Remember when I said that if you read the diagnostic keys for many disorders you will very likely diagnose yourself with that disorder. Psychiatrists, psychologists, and counselors are all human, if they walk into a room with any preconceived ideas then that will affect your diagnosis," Doug explained.

"That's another very good reason to move to analytical testing," Kim agreed. "And not only are the doctors going in with preconceived ideas, but because of all the psychology based TV programs many of the clients are going in emphasizing certain diagnostic keys that they saw on those programs. So when the diagnosis is done entirely by question and answer the doctors can lead the client very easily, or the client can lead the doctors. We get that in nursing all the time."

"And the client has a mental disorder, so their answers are not always accurate to begin with. Even if they don't have a mental disorder, most people are a little nervous answering personal questions from a doctor. People don't always tell the truth, people get confused, or they get frustrated, or embarrassed, or don't think that something is important, and all of these can lead to a misdiagnosis and the fun filled adventures that being prescribed the wrong psychotropic drugs can bring," Doug said as he tuned into the driveway and up to their house. And none too soon for Ashley and Kim, after all it was their first months anniversary, and they had other plans for the evening.

Chapter 13

Doug managed to score three tickets to a White Sox vs. Ray's baseball game in Chicago just two rows behind the Sox dugout. None of them had any interest at all in baseball, but the seats were too good to turn down. With Kim and Doug looking over her shoulder, Ashley checked the internet to see how the Sox were doing this season, not to good, typical. She then typed Arizona Rays and to Doug's surprise got mad when he pointed out that rays, skates, and sharks live longer in water. After figuring out her mistake she searched the Tampa Bay Rays web page only to find that they were doing worse than the Sox. "Should be a good game," Kim said enthusiastically. Doug and Ashley agreed and Ashley checked Ticket Master to see if there was anything else they could do to make a vacation out of it. In twenty minutes they had theater tickets, hotel reservations, and two dinner reservations for a three day, two night trip to the Windy City. They had already run into the problem of not having a car other than Doug's Auto Auction truck that had a bench seat in the front where they all could ride. The ladies had heard that it was common for people in West Michigan to take limos to Chicago to spend the day shopping or to catch a show, and suggested they take a limo. Doug wanted to rent a car with a bench front seat so they would have more freedom when they were there. After booking the limo Ashley got up from the computer and Doug sat down and started searching the internet for a cool car with a bench front seat.

The limo picked them up on Friday morning as planned. Doug and the ladies enjoyed the view of the West Michigan shore as it passed by the windows of the luxurious ride. They talked about plans for the house and adventures left to be taken. At one point Doug pointed out a boat that was anchored a few hundred yards offshore and told the ladies that it was over a shallow ship wreck that he would feel safe taking them to, if they both promised not to even think about going inside the wreck.

"There aren't any dead bodies on board are there?" Ashley asked.

"No, it was a 180 foot cargo ship hauling coal to Michigan City, Indiana that got caught in an early freeze and was stuck in the ice for the winter. From what I've heard the crew just walked across the ice to get to shore," Doug assured her. "Then once the ice was thick enough they used horse drawn wagons to get the coal, and anything else that was salvageable off her. Then they just let her sink when the spring thaw came."

Soon they entered the more industrialized North Shores of Indiana and Illinois. As the view out the window changed so too did the conversation, "I voted for Obama for his first term as president, when I thought he was a true politician, but then I realized he was a priest so I didn't vote for him for a second term." Doug said in the limo on that Wednesday morning when the conversation turned to politics.

"What do you mean a priest?" Kim barked, "If anything he's too much a politician."

"Really," Agreed Ashley, "he's fighting everybody."

"Exactly," agreed Doug. "He's daring all comers to knock him off his pulpit because he has faith that he's right instead of working with others to figure out what is best. A politician, like a knight, jousts with their opponent, fighting for ground, the give and take of battle, ending in an armistice of some sort, possibly surrender, possibly compromise, possibly defeat. In congress today we don't have any jousting, no debate, and no chance for any kind of compromise. We have two sides who both know they are right and often can't even agree to talk to each other. The only give and take is a bunch of childish name calling."

"The childish name calling I'll agree with, and I'll even give you the lack of debate in Washington, but I still don't see Obama as priest," Kim argued.

"OK, let's try it this way." Doug pondered his next words, "A lot of people say we need to get religion out of politics, others say we need God in politics, the truth is that they are both right. Now let's move to your job in the ICU, or yours teaching," Doug said trying to get Ashley into the conversation. "In the ICU you have patients code, when that happens you, the doctor, and the other nurses come running to get into position. Most of the time it works just the way you've practiced it. Other times the timing is off and everything feels wrong. Then every once in a while everything clicks, you're in the zone, everybody is in sync and working as one, and you know that nothing could go wrong, you know the patient is going to make it. When that happens it's the greatest feeling in the world because God was holding the reins, you let him. In teaching and woodworking it's the same way, when it's right you can feel it, it's great I live for those moments. Unfortunately, at least in woodworking, sometime the pieces just don't want to fit and instead of working with them till they do fit, I find myself working against them, fighting them, eventually I'll get them together but the results aren't as good as when as when I'm in the zone and working with the wood. The results aren't as good as when I let God take the reins. Still with me," Doug asked.

"I think so," Ashley said now listening.

"I agree with all that in theory, but the fact is it's not possible, not with the government we have today," Kim challenged.

"Exactly, it's not just Obama, the republicans are just as head strong and convinced that their way is the only way as the democrats are. It's just that Obama is such a great example of a priest in Washington. He ran the first time promising change and

I thought he saw what was causing the stalemate and had a plan to get congress back debating issues instead of just taking sides on them. Turns out his only plan for change was to make himself the high priest of American Government. Religion has taken over government and we now have four high priests who are calling the shots. The only one who was elected is Obama, name the other four."

"If there not elected they can't be in charge," Kim argued. "Rush Limbaugh," Ashley said jokingly.

"That's two, Limbaugh and others like him that is, Oprah for one," Doug said holding up two fingers.

"No way," Kim shot back, then thinking she said, "If that's where you're going with this then three and four are the directors of the National Democratic and Republican Committees."

"And your Senator and Congressperson run back to their National Committee, or the media, to find out how they are supposed to vote instead of running back to their constituents like they're supposed to. What we have today is priest's running back to the high priests to get their orders. The American people have been taken out of the process, God has been taken out of the process, religion has taken over. We need to take religion out of Washington and put God back in," Doug concluded.

"I agree my congressman doesn't always vote the way his constituents want, but I still don't buy this priest thing. Actually I agree with everything you said except the priest," Kim said growing angry over what she saw as a stupid conversation.

"Facts and ideas need to be weighed on their own merits, not on your feelings about the person or group who are presenting them," Ashley told them.

"OK," Kim agreed, "I understand your point, but that's immaturity not religion."

"Its religion if you take it all the way to a seat in government," Doug countered. "Its religion if you follow a group regardless of the facts or even your own beliefs. Its religion if the politicians vote based on a belief system and not for each individual issue on its own merits. It's a religion if you support bills like Obamacare because you're a democrat, but you would oppose the exact same bill if it was presented by republicans."

"Fine, our politicians are immature, spoiled children, they're not saints, but they are definitely not priests," Kim said with finality.

"They're pretending to be saints," Doug pressed on. "We would be better off if they stopped pretending and started telling the truth. As voters we need to figure out what job we're electing them to do and allow for the background that a qualified individual would actually need to have in order to do that job. There is an old joke, sort of. An election is coming up and you have to vote for one of the candidates, but you haven't been paying attention to the issues, and don't know the candidates. All you do know is that politician A drinks two pints of liqueur a day, chain smokes, and cheats on his wife, politician B drinks one pint of liqueur a day, chain smokes, and cheats on his wife, politician C doesn't drink, doesn't smoke, and is faithful. Who do you vote for?" Doug asked.

"Politician C," Kim and Ashley said in unison.

"The reason it's not a joke is that it happened in the 1930's in three different countries. Politician A is Winston Churchill, politician B is Franklin Delano Roosevelt, and politician C is Adolf Hitler," Doug told them.

"I thought Hitler was a drug addict," Ashley said.

"Not till the 1940's," Doug said, "before that he was just insane."

"And they never proved that FDR had an affair," challenged Kim.

"They never proved that he had a physical relationship with his mistress," corrected Doug. "Anyway my point is that we need to get rid of these self-proclaimed altar boys we keep electing and get back to good old fashioned politicians. FDR was no saint, but he was a damned good politician and he saw this country through several of its darkest days. The ones we have today can't see out the window."

"Where do you get this stuff?" Ashley asked with a hint if irritation.

"I heard the Hitler thing in AA. The priest part came from

studying Psychologists practicing psychology,'" Doug answered. "Psychology has become a feuding set of religious doctrines based on the teachings of Freud, Skinner, Pavlov, Jung, Adler and several others. These demigods are being held up as profits by the groups that believe in their teachings. Any new theory or advance in treatment by one group is instantly ridiculed by members of the rival clans. The good of the client, much like the good of the politician's constituents, or the good of the masses in true religion, is second to the childish need to be seen as the holder of the ultimate truth.

"So psychology is a religious organization as well?" Kim asked with more than a hint of sarcasm.

"Exactly," Doug told her. "The only thing is that politics didn't become a totally dysfunctional religious quandary till the Clinton administration. Psychology has been divided into religious factions for more than a century. The great part is that a lot of the research psychologists want to start their own theological branch."

"Are we going to be in the sun at the game?" Ashley broke in, "I brought some sun screen just in case." This time Ashley was successful in changing the subject.

The three of them had a great time at the baseball game which the Sox won 5 to 2. The food and ambiance at the five stare restaurant lived up to the reviews it had received, but the play got mixed reviews with Ashley loving it and Doug getting bored which had Kim acting as a peacekeeper. The next afternoon the ladies went shopping as planned, but Doug skipped his tee time and bought a light blue 1967 Chevrolet Impala SS Convertible with a 396 C.I. 325 horsepower engine instead. The car was in perfect condition but it had been heavily modified from its original configuration and was of no interest to the serious collectors. That made it perfect for the day to day use that Doug wanted it for. It was cool looking, but not something he wouldn't need to worry about damaging. It had the bench front seat he was looking for but they would have to install a third set of seatbelts so he couldn't drive it home that day. Doug arranged for the seatbelts, a dash mounted GPS and an upgraded sound system to be added, and to have the car delivered to his home in about a week. He then went to meet the ladies for a late lunch and a tour of some of the Windy Cities Art Galleries as they had planned. He hadn't decided if he would tell the ladies about his new car yet or not. Having the kind of money to buy a 42,000 dollar car on impulse was still a bit uncomfortable for him, even if he had been thinking about buying a classic muscle car for over a year. All things considered the entire trip to Chicago was a great success. Still they were all happy when the limo returned them home a few days later.

Chapter 14

The next morning found them laying tile in the laundry room. Doug hadn't done much tile work but with the experience gained when he and the ladies had helped Jim tile the walk in shower in the master bedroom, and the step by step instructions Jim had given them on how to lay floors, they managed to do a pretty good job of it. Having finished the laundry room before lunch they decided to forge ahead and do the kitchen in the afternoon. They had worked out a system in the laundry and applied it to the kitchen. Kim spread the adhesive, Ashley placing the spacer stars, and Doug putting the tiles in place. They worked together like a well-oiled machine and in only three hours they were standing back and admiring their finished kitchen floor. Tomorrow they would tackle the slate hall, and get as far as they could with the bathrooms. Doug offered to take them out on the boat or to take them to dinner, but the ladies were tired and sore from the day's labor so it was decided to just build a fire and to sit and watch it under the stars. It was becoming routine but all three of them loved it. Later that night, with dinner done and the three of them sitting on the moving blankets watching the fire, Ashley could not believe what Kim was doing. The look she gave Kim was cold and disbelieving. She was the one who had been taken in by Doug's first book, not only by the adventures from his travels but by the deep thoughts from his adventures of the mind as well. Now they had him all to themselves and could explore that mind and all its deep caverns. A beautiful night sitting around a fire and this was what she wanted to talk about.

"I don't understand what you mean when you say you want psychiatric hospitals and counselors to advertise their level of care and their style of treatment?" Kim asked.

"Well actually I figured that out a long time ago when I went to my first psychiatric hospital. I was used to going to alcohol treatment centers by that time. The thing was that I was having trouble but I wasn't drinking so I tried a psych hospital in Grand Rapids. I didn't have insurance but I had 10,000 dollars that I got from an inheritance, so I decided to spend it in the hope of making a better life for myself. I was thirty at the time, all alone, not suicidal but just kinda dying inside. The only thing keeping me going was that my fantasy world was so strong that most of the time I just didn't feel the emotions, the loneliness and the depression, they just couldn't break through. When they did it would hurt so much that I just wanted them to go away, which most of the time meant relapsing into a bottle or into the fantasy world, I just couldn't handle reality.

"Sounds bad," Kim said.

"It was," said Doug, "that's why I checked myself into a psych hospital for the first time. But it turned out to be a Christian Recruitment Center. It was an adult day care more or less, not at all what I needed. We played games most of the time, granted they were games that worked on things like trust issues, assertiveness training, and communication skills, but they were still just life skill games that assumed the problems the client was facing were learned skills, not medical issues. We also did a lot of role playing to try different ways of dealing with specific situations. When we weren't playing games we were sitting in a lecture, that's the Christian recruitment part. Don't get me wrong there are a lot of people who can get a lot of help with this kind of treatment. A little time off from real life and some work on life skills for when they get out so that they can better deal with the problems of daily life. My problem was that I had a chemical issue in my brain that was preventing me from having a daily life. My 10,000 dollars only paid for about 22 days and when I left I did feel better for a week or two, but nothing had changed so in no time at all I was back to the same dysfunctional life I went in there to change. It's called a "treatment high" and lasts a couple of weeks after you get out of any of these centers, alcohol or psych. For the people who need that type of life skills training, hopefully get what they need and then apply what they learned to their lives and their lives get better as a result of going to this type of treatment. Unfortunately I needed a more medical diagnostic type approach than this place was set up to do, so when the treatment high ended nothing had changed."

"Didn't they give you any type of testing or have you assessed by a psychiatrist or psychologist?" Kim asked.

"This place didn't use psychologist only psychiatrists, most of these places go one way or the other and if they use psychiatrists they can charge more and the MD sounds better than the PhD. Remember that I said I took the Rorschach Ink Blot test in one of the hospitals, a test that for all practical purposes was proven invalid in the 1960's. I took it in the 90's at a Christian recruitment center. As far as the other tests they gave me I wish I could remember what they were so I could research them, I've never seen any of them since. It was also the only time I ever got a psychological test from a psychiatrist. Psychiatrists generally avoid them since most of the tests were created by psychologists, a clear violation of the feud. In this hospital it was almost like the whole medical end of it was for show. I didn't realize the significance then, but nobody even mentioned psychotropic drugs. I left rubber stamped sane, with no diagnosis or medication, which was the only time that ever happened. About three years later I went to another psych hospital with medical rather than spiritual based treatment and things were different. It was also a private hospital but I had insurance this time. This place used psychiatrist and not psychologists like the first one, but they didn't give me any psychological tests. They did get my file from the first hospital and told me that there was nothing in it

141

that was of any use to them since most of the tests hadn't even been graded. As far as the treatment they provided, it was more like an alcohol treatment center, classes, group and individual consoling, and no games. I also saw a psychiatrist who did give me a medical diagnosis. It was the wrong diagnosis and my first experience with psychotropic drugs other than antidepressants. They gave the first of many unnecessary psychotropic drugs and this one sent me on a four year trip through never-never land, but it was a diagnosis, or more likely a guess."

"What did they diagnose you with?" Kim asked.

"They said I was schizophrenic and put me on an anti-psychotic," answered Doug. "The problem is if you take anti-psychotic medications when you're not psychotic they tend to make you psychotic. Then when you go back for follow up appointments and tell the psychiatrist about you're new psychotic symptoms they tell you that they are on the right track and that they just need to increase the dosage of anti-psychotic medication they are giving you, which of course makes you even more psychotic. Congratulations, you've just jumped aboard one of the worst roller coaster rides life has to offer, all brought to you by the incompetence of psychiatric diagnosis's and their aversion to psychological testing."

"This can't be true, even if it did happen to you it just can't be the norm in that world," Ashley said angrily.

"Not only can it not be true but it's happening every day and nobody will listen to the clients. Let's face it, we're psych patients and they are doctors. It makes people mad that all these crazy patients are looking for someone to blame. People don't want to hear it, not from the clients anyway. Granted the system is screwed up, everybody knows that, but we can't turn to a bunch of crazy people to find out what's wrong with it. People think that they need to ask the doctors what needs to be done to fix the system, and the doctors say it's as good as it can get, or it's underfunded, or the clients won't take their meds, or that it's God will or someone else's fault, and nothing happens to change the system. The doctors aren't about to admit that the problem is in any way their fault.

Even if the psychiatrists, or the psychologists, can see that they are part of the problem, they aren't going to admit it. So year after year, decade after decade, nothing happens, the revolving door revolves, the kids kill themselves, the street people live on the street, the bulimics throw up, and the solders relive the horrors of war, and nothing changes," Doug said, his voice trailing off into despair.

"Is there any truth to the underfunding?" Kim asked.

"Good question, moving right along the third psychiatric hospital I was in. It was possibly the worst 28 days of my life, but I still managed to do it more than once. It was a state run facility that was ridiculously underfunded and understaffed. I met with a psychiatrist twice a week for fifteen minutes, which didn't do much good since he didn't speak English very well. Of all the counselors, nurses, orderlies, custodians, grounds keepers, this psychiatrist was the most incompetent person in the whole place. Fortunately it was near the end of the four years I spent under the spell of the anti-psychotics and I had started questioning things by then, I still didn't have any answers, but I had come to the conclusion that they didn't have any answers either. Anyway the only other person I saw at the state run hospital was a social worker who I also saw for about fifteen minutes twice a week and that was it, one hour a week total. They had a gym that you could go to for an hour each day if there was enough staff to take you and if you got your name on the list in time. They also had an art room that was pretty sad. It was staffed by a few 60's hippy types. They were supposed to have group therapy, at least it was scheduled twice a week, but in the four weeks that I was there it was only held once. Other than that you just sat. In order to survive you go into a type of sleep like trance, for normees the only thing I can compare it to is jet lag. Not really asleep but not awake either. A lot of people call it the Thorazine shuffle, but the truth is there is no Thorazine involved. Other than that all you have to look forward to is someone going off the deep end. I would sit and watch for hours, that's how I made it through, by watching and studying the other clients. Anyway, inevitably someone would wake up from their trance and you could just watch them gaining speed as the boredom overcame them, pretty soon they would go off the deep end and cause the staff problems and wind up in time out. Everyone who worked there, the orderlies that is, brought a book to read because they would have to sit outside the time out rooms, or in the day room, or anywhere else for that matter, there really isn't a whole lot of difference, they would sit and read till the person was quiet for a certain period of time then they would release them back into the general population." By this point Doug was just staring into space, just remembering all this seemed to make him numb. Ashley and Kim were anything but numb, more like horrified.

"How on earth did you end up in a place like that?" Ashley asked.

Coming out of his semi trance Doug looked up, with a strange smile that made the ladies back off a little and said, "Suicide attempt," then going back into his trance Doug rubbed his wrist and continued. "They say if you're thinking about suicide to call someone, and you should, but for me it wasn't a thought process at all, it was an emotion. It was like rage or lust, all consuming, there was no rational thought involved, there was no choice. The scar isn't long but its deep, a woodworker's knife. To this day I have no feeling in two of my fingers because of the nerve damage. I was sitting in my car when I did it, looking out at the water. It was strange, as soon as I had cut about an inch and a half I felt as calm as I had ever felt in my life, total peace. They say when you actually do it, you feel calm, and for me it was true. I sat in the car for about two hours with my arm on the arm rest looking back and forth from the lake to the blood dripping from my fingers, all the time reflecting on my life, all in perfect peace. When the sun came up I started the car and drove to the state hospital and they took me right in." With a strange laugh he added "I'm probably the only person on earth that ever tried to commit suicide with their seatbelt on."

Ashley was horrified and got up unable to listen to this, but

Kim, who as a nurse was more accustomed to hearing patient's horror stories asked, "Do you still think about committing suicide?"

"No, not since I stopped taking the anti-psychotics.," he answered. "Actually that's not true, just recently they gave me the drug Abilify and I started having suicidal thoughts again, so I stopped taking it and the thoughts went away."

"What made you finally stop taking the anti-psychotics?" Kim asked.

"Well that's the worst story of all. I'll tell you if you want but I guarantee you will wish you hadn't heard it," Doug told them.

Ashley and Kim looked at each other, "I want to hear it," said Kim.

"I don't," said Ashley getting up. "Anyone want anything from the house?" She asked in a cheerful but forced voice.

When she was gone Doug began, "It was when I took a year off from cabinetmaking and drove a semi coast to coast, over the road is what they call it. The hallucinations were taking over my thoughts because of the anti-psychotics, not the fantasies I was used to, I could have dealt with them, these were different. I didn't know what was real and what wasn't. Add to that a deep paranoia that also comes from taking Zyprexa. The paranoia made me think that just about everyone was out to get me, and for the first time in my life I was a threat to society. A threat to society driving an 80,000 pound truck. I was driving through Pennsylvania and totally out of my mind when I thought my own trucking company had sent semi's to harass me on the road. I got on the CB and said, bumper cars, to let them know that things were about to going to get ugly, and it would have, I was ready to have a little fun. Just as I was saying that I passed a sign for Hershey Medical Center and through the grace of God I pulled in. I parked my truck in the emergency room entrance, walked in and asked to see a mental health care specialist. After they had me move the truck they took me right upstairs. The next morning they told me that the hospital didn't accept my insurance and they gave me a choice of going to a hospital in Pennsylvania that did accept it, or taking a Gray

Hound bus home and checking into a hospital there. I took the bus home but didn't get in till almost dark so I got a hotel room. I also got a bottle of Jack Daniels. I hadn't had a drink in seven years but I went to the room and had three or four shots. Then I went to a convenient store two or three blocks away and got a couple of sandwiches, a bag of chips, and a large soda. On the way back to the hotel there were a half dozen police cars gathered in a parking lot, so I went over to see what was happening. Turns out it was the parking lot of a strip club and some of the patrons had gotten into a fight, but they left before the cops got there. Apparently I fit the description of one of the trouble makers so the cops started questioning me. Being psychotic and paranoid they apparently didn't like my answers so they took me to jail for the night. I keep trying to explain what had happened on the road, and in Hershey, but all they said was that I could deal with it in the morning. They locked me in a private cell and I was mad, and paranoid, and crazy, and wanted them to know it. So I decided to leave them a message, but I couldn't find anything to right with. I decided to do it in blood, so with my teeth I gnawed through a vein in my wrist and just as I got the blood flowing and was about to start writing, a turnkey saw what I was doing and I spent the rest of the night in shackles," with a smirk Doug continued. "The worst part about it is that the cops wrote it up as a suicide attempt, so now if I go back to the county lockup they won't give me a blanket. And they keep it cold in those jails, keeps the smell down." This last line was an attempt at humor but it failed miserably with Kim, it always does with normees, but it kills in treatment center day rooms. Since Kim didn't even realize that he was trying to be funny Doug just went on, "So the next day I checked into a psych hospital, but I didn't listen to a word they said. I just keep thinking that this isn't me, I don't do things like this, and how did I get this crazy." Kim noticed that as Doug was speaking his eyes were unseeing, he was staring into space, but his eyes were in constant motion as if he was looking for something he couldn't find. She could tell that even now he had no idea what had happened to him. In a faraway voice

Doug continued, "I left the hospital with the usual prescriptions for anti-psychotics and anti-depressants and took them for about another month or two, but the spell had been broken, I no longer trusted the doctors. I knew I had to figure it out on my own, but my mind was just mush, I couldn't put 2 and 2 together and come up with any rational answer. Finally, for some reason, I just threw the prescriptions out. It wasn't till the drugs wore off a couple of weeks later that I finally realized that they were treating the wrong disorder. It was the diagnosis that was wrong, and it was the drugs I was on that were causing the problems, at least the current set of problems. That's the thing about psychotropic drugs, they completely take over and you become a different person, you can't even remember what you used to be like, there not like street drugs. It wasn't that I didn't have problems, but what they were giving me was causing an entirely new set of problems. For four years I took what they told me to take, and they were the worst four years of my life, total insanity."

"Is it common for other people to be misdiagnosed or was this an isolated case? It just seems so hard to believe," Kim asked.

"It's very common, even most normees have heard horror stories about how bad it is, but what you said is exactly the problem, it's just too hard to believe, so people don't believe it," Doug said shaking his head. "Look at the numbers, 70 percent of people entering a psych hospital will return within a year. Think about this, if you take a multiple choice test with four possible answers, and you guess C on every question, you will get about the same percentage right as a hospital psychiatrist's correct diagnostic percentage. You can also talk to the clients, ask them what to do if you don't like your diagnosis, or you're medication. The most common answer will be change you're psychiatrist. I believe that the only reason I got a schizophrenic diagnosis in the first place was that the drug Zyprexa was the wonder drug of the day. Until the drug company lost two huge class action lawsuits they were handing Zyprexa out like it was candy."

"Isn't Zyprexa used to treat bi-polar disorder?" Kim asked.

"Yes, it was designed to treat psychotic disorders, but it is being used to treat Bi-polar disorder as well," Doug said. "But I wasn't diagnosed with bi-polar disorder till a couple of years after I stopped taking it and the other antipsychotic drugs I was being prescribed. And for about six months during those years I was on prescription amphetamines with an adult attention deficit disorder diagnosis. Now the hot drug is Abilify, so don't be surprised if you get a bi-polar diagnosis if go in today."

"Do you think there's some kind of payola going on?" Kim asked.

"No, it's too big a problem for that, somebody would let it slip," Doug said. "It's the ever declining competence of the psychiatrists and their refusal to use diagnostic tools developed by psychologists. It seems like the psychiatrists are guessing and the drug company sales reps are helping them make their guesses with free samples and advertising, but I don't think there's any money involved. Four years of my life was wasted because of the schizophrenic diagnosis, three more years because I went to a pray away the pain mental hospital and walked out cured, and before that I spent five years on anti-depressants that I got from psychiatrists in alcohol treatment centers and from the psychiatrist I saw in private practice for follow-ups. And by the way if you take anti-depressants when you're bi-polar, they tend to make you manic. But to be honest I don't mind that, manic is fun," Doug said the last part cheerfully. Seeing Ashley walking back to the fire he let the story end with that.

"You were right to leave it was pretty bad, but it explained a lot," Kim said to Ashley, who had returned from the house with pint of Blueberries and the makings of a crisp topping. Kim and Doug smiled at each other when instead of handing the ingredients to Doug she sat down and started preparing them herself. "What's this, are you getting domesticated on me?" Kim prodded.

"When in Rome," Ashley said with a smile.

Chapter 15

Kim and Ashley returned from their day shopping in Grand Rapids to find Doug already home and working out in the field beside the house. With the relationship growing they both found they were proud that Doug would abandon them on a Saturday to help the Mennonites that lived down the road. Granted it was just a chicken coop for an egg laying operation they were building and not the full Amish barn raising of legend, but it was still pretty cool. Even though the ladies had campaigned for the liberties and rights of same sex couples, they were also ladies of respect, and able to accepted that their presence at a gathering of Amish and Mennonites would be offensive to their religious beliefs, so they had willingly bowed out and went shopping. Still they liked the idea that their new boyfriend would be accepted in such a gathering, even if their presence would not. As they walked out to the field to say hello to Doug they liked what he was doing. He was using some of the wood left over from the construction of his house, and some he picked up at the chicken coop raising to build a small bonfire. A perfect idea seeing as the forecast was for showers the next two days. Doug welcomed them both home with a kiss and showed them the 4 gallon pot he was going to use to cook up a pot of Corned beef and Cabbage for dinner. Even though it was not one of their favorite meals, they were still excited by Doug's contagious enthusiasm, and they both loved the idea of a bonfire. With the West Michigan evenings still a little cool they headed into the house to change out of there nice cloths and into something warmer.

"Not to warm," Doug called after them, "The fire is going to be hot."

In the house the ladies decided on their bonfire outfits and something special from their day shopping underneath, just in case. Soon they were back outside and standing around a roaring bonfire. Doug worked on what they both had to admit was a pretty cool looking dinner. True to form it wasn't long before Doug launched into one of his speeches.

"The Mayan calendar was right," Doug yelled into the night sky standing a safe distance from the heat of the fire. "The world has entered a new age, the age of the hunters and gatherers ended eight thousand years ago, and now the age of great discovery has come to an end. The world has turned upside down and the people have lost their way. If a new direction is not found, and found soon, the people will start falling off the edge."

"What!" Ashley exclaimed with the amazement of a bottled up writer who wished that just once she could come up with an opening line like that.

"The age of discovery isn't over," Kim yelled back in challenge, seeing potential in this bonfire debate. "And last time I checked Newton's Laws are still in effect."

"Of course there is more out there to be found, but it's limited to finite research and expensive deep sea and space type exploration, not available to the average man. So where does mankind turn for meaning, money, power, religion, nothing new there, and worse, nothing good coming from it. So what is the new age going to bring?" He asked the ladies.

Ashley looked at Kim but neither came up with an answer, "What?" The ladies ask in unison.

"Nobody knows," Doug yelled back, "the Mayans left that part out. They did say that the world would turn upside down, and one look at the daily news will prove to anyone that that's already happening."

"So the Mayan's meant that day to day life would be turned upside down, not the actual world like everybody was saying," Kim yelled back. "But how could they have known that?"

"Who knows, a thousand years ago they saw that the end of the age of hunting and gathering and the beginning of the age of civilization had taken place some seven thousand years earlier. They also saw that the change had marked the beginning of a new age for mankind, the age of civilization and discovery. Amazingly, if you look at the archeological evidence of when mankind's move to civilization became inevitable, the Mayan's got it just about right. A new age that marked mankind pursuit from a fight for survival to a quest for knowledge. From that observation they calculated and devised the Mayan long calendar and predicted that this new age of discovery would last 7880 years."

"Is it the age of civilization or the age of discovery?" Ashley shouted across the fire.

"Both, the age of civilization, the age of discovery, a move made possible by the discovery and implementation of farming, both agrarian and livestock. The ability for a single individual to produce enough food to feed more and more people made the move towards larger communities and occupational specialization possible. Occupations like architecture, engineering, religion, medicine, and science. Small groups began to spring up, and then tribes. The tribes became communities, then societies, then states and nations. Specialization led to great and small discoveries in all areas of life, with both positive and negative in consequence. Money, power, religion, engineering, and exploration, are just a few of the fields of thought that became the driving force for mankind's existence in this new age. The need for the societies to grow led to wars, and war led to the drive to invent the tools to fight them."

"Civilization didn't lead to war," Kim countered.

"Of course hunters and gatherers fought to protect the space they needed to live, that's evident in the animal kingdom today.

But the reasons for war became more political and less survival oriented. The Mayans saw all of this and calculated that it had happened more or less six or seven thousand years earlier. The Mayans also saw the end of the age of discovery and predicted that would end in a thousand or so years. Thus the Mayan long calendar and the ending date of the age of discovery, December 21, 2012. Now for mankind to survive we need to find a new purpose, a new challenge, a new meaning, or the age of man will surely come to an end. And looking at the news of the world today, I would say it will end at our own hands," Doug proclaimed with a tone of doom.

"Unfortunately I'm not so sure you're not right," Kim said laughingly, "but what do we do about it?"

"The Mayans never figured that out, or maybe the answer just didn't survive the test of time," Doug yelled back. "But clearly for mankind to survive it will need a new direction, a new purpose. I'm not smart enough to see what that will be, but I am smart enough to see that something is wrong."

"I thought you knew everything," Ashley joked.

"Of course I know everything," Doug yelled back, "I'm a writer after all."

"And just exactly how does that work?" Ashley asked. "Simple, if I'm ever wrong I just hit delete," Doug answered.   "Is anybody smart enough to figure it out mankind's next great challenge?" asked Kim, not ready for the debate to end.

"I'm not sure," Doug yelled in answer, "but I'm quite certain that it's nobody currently trying to claim that they know. Obama will tell you he's got us on the right road. Personally, I don't think he even knows what direction the road we are on is heading in. He doesn't see the fork in the road that we are currently facing. He, like all the others, is just forging ahead into the darkness. It's not just Obama, I don't think there is a single person in politics, democrat or republican, American or foreign, or in religion, be they Christian, Muslim, Buddhist, Hindu, or in science or in the media that has any idea where the road mankind is on is actually going."

"That's true," Ashley yelled across the bonfire starting to get the feel of the debate, "I've heard a lot of politicians talk about being on the right or wrong road, but I can't remember any of them saying where the road is going."

"I agree that exploration has seen its finest hour, at least for the foreseeable future, but as for the end of the age of discovery, I think you're way off on that. You should see the advances in medicine that I see almost daily," Kim argued. Then looking across the fire at Doug she added, "But I still don't understand what the options are if we really do need to find a new direction."

"If you believe Hollywood, we are still in the era of exploration and conquest," Doug yelled back, knowing that he was beginning to lose Ashley to reality, "The question is that without Hollywood's special effects, will mankind survive till space travel is possible. Of course we can all hold our breath and hope for the aliens to come to Earth. That could take care of both exploration and technology." "I thought they were going to conquer us," Ashley yelled back, "Or blow us up."

"Well, if they really are intelligent they should probably blow us up," Doug joked. "But till that happens, mankind needs to look towards its next great challenge." Looking at Kim he added, "Possibly in art, hopefully with compassion towards the wellbeing of the Earth, maybe ending poverty and war, resolving geopolitical and religious differences, or at least working towards acceptance of the views of others. Even with all that I'm not sure it would be enough to for mankind to survive and move into a new era. As far as everything being invented, of course there is more to be discovered. Just remember that using the Mayan calendar the age of hunters and gatherers ended almost eight thousand years ago and there are still hunters and gatherers living on at least three continents today."

"Three?" Ashley challenged.

"South America, Africa, and some of the Aborigine tribes in Australia. Hunters and gatherers to a certain degree anyway," Doug offered.

"I'm not sure were in a new era of mankind," Kim yelled, "I find it hard to believe that everything has already been discovered or invented, we just need to look harder. Besides the world will end with the apocalypse, at least that's the way I learned it."

"I've been thinking a lot about the apocalypse," Doug said, his voice changing from argumentative to reflective. "Remember Harold Camping and his end of the world prediction a few years back?" The ladies nodded grudgingly not really wanting to get into a serious discussion tonight, especially not one about Harold Camping. It was worse than the ladies feared. "How can anyone look at his followers that sold everything they owned and started warning everyone that the end is near, and still say that religious addiction doesn't exist?" The ladies turned away, "No, no, no wait, that's why I've been thinking about the Apocalypse. I don't know enough about higher mathematics to figure it out, but I'm pretty sure that the Apocalypse is actually a mathematical equation with no answer. The more data you feed into the equation the bigger it gets, and the more consumed you will be by it, but you will never find an answer because there in none. Harold Camping's followers were addicted to religion, but Harold Camping isn't addicted to religion, he's addicted to a mathematical equation that he can't solve, remember that he is an engineer."

"The apocalypse is a math equation?" Kim yelled in a voice that was half way between mocking and shock.

"Think about it, it's brilliant," Doug urged. "All a preacher has to do is start adding data to the apocalyptic equation during a sermon and the entire congregation starts to feel the effects of the vacuum effect that the unsolvable equation produces. Then the preacher passes around the collection plate and the people fill it with money. If the preacher wants more money, all he has to do is add more data to the equation, thus sucking the congregation deeper into the vacuum of the equation. When the preacher gets as much money as he thinks he can get, he stops adding data to the equation and the vacuum disappears. Fear of the apocalypse doesn't work like other fears. Most fears don't just vanish when you stop adding to them. And if you check it out, most of the major doomsday proficiencies based on the apocalypse were started by people who had mathematical backgrounds."

"Didn't the Mayans practice human sacrifice?" Ashley yelled to Kim as she started separating the stack of moving blankets that the three of them had been using as ground blankets around the nightly fires. "I didn't spend the day trying on outfits a Victoria Secrets to wind up leaving one on," She added with a glance at Kim and a quick wicked smile directed at Doug.

Grabbing the ends of one of the blankets to help Ashley spread it on the ground, Doug looked at Kim and said, "Even better, the High Priest at Machu Picchu was the only male said to be permitted in the City in the Sky. Beautiful virgins were recruited from far and wide to labor and serve his every need. I wonder what a three hundred and threesome would be like?"

"Hit delete writer," Ashley told him, "Machu Picchu was Incan."

Chapter 16

One of Doug's passions was golfing and with the arms of a man who had spent his life building heavy furniture, the thighs of a cyclist, and the hands of a craftsman, he was good at it. Since becoming a bestselling author and having no particular schedule to keep, it was not uncommon for him to be invited to play as a fourth with some powerful people. Doug knew how to keep the executives entertained with his wild theories and crazy plans. Even more important, he knew how to make himself scares when the conversation turned to business. These golf outings were also how Doug often found himself with the kind of tickets for events that you can't by at any price, even if he did get them on a second string sort of basis. This time he was invited to play on one of the Jack Nicolas designed courses near Traverse City on Thursday morning. The truth was he didn't really know any of the other three men he would be playing with, but he loved playing The Bear golf course, so after checking with the ladies he accepted. After checking the weather report Doug suggested that the three of them take the boat up on Wednesday and stay in a hotel for a short vacation. They had tried sleeping in the aft cabin of the Searay but it had proven to be a little small for three. The ladies loved the idea and readily agreed to the plans. They had been hearing about some shops in Traverse City that they wanted to explore. They also wanted to see the famous Sleeping Bear Dune that was located along the shoreline that they would be passing. Doug thought about telling them that Sleeping Bear Dune had "blown out" twenty years ago, but decided to let them find out for themselves. So with only a slight chance for a shower that afternoon they left the marina in Grand Haven on Wednesday morning and headed north.

The Great Lakes are known for their violent pop-up storms, a thousand or more ships resting on the lakes bottom are testament to that. Though the storms are more common in the winter and spring months the summer storms are no less dangerous. Three hours out of Grand Haven the winds began to pick up and the sky grew dark. From what Doug was seeing in the sky and on his Doppler radar he knew they were going to be hit with a bad one. He changed his dash monitor to show the navigational maps then keyed his GPS to give him an exact fix on their position. From the Doppler radar he knew the storm would be on them in about 25 minutes and he would have to turn the boat into the wind at that point. The Searay was capable of 32 Knots maximum speed, so Doug had the Navigational Map draw a circle fifteen miles around their current location. It would be possible for them to make it to shore, but the map wasn't showing any area of refuse that they could make it to in time and they were too far North for Doug to have any personal knowledge of the area.

"Get below and secure anything that's loose, then get in the aft cabin and get ready for wild ride," Doug told the ladies with an attempt at bravado, but they could see he was worried. "And get your life jackets on," he added reaching for his own.

Kim and Ashley quickly went about securing all the gear they had been using, but when it came to riding out the storm in a windowless cabin, they decided that the cabin would be scarier than staying topside with Doug. "We're riding it out with you," Kim told him as she and Ashley sat back down on the bench seat next to the captain's chair. Doug thought about arguing but he wasn't so sure he wouldn't do the same thing in their place. It was academic at this point anyway, the storm was upon them.

The Searay Sundancer is a very popular boat on the Lakes,

not only for its sleek sporty appearance and stylish well planned layouts, but also for its sea worthy hull and powerful engines. Doug was not an experienced pilot having only purchased the boat three years ago, but he was a good pilot, he had the feel, the right stuff. At only 29 feet, Doug's Sundancer was still considered a "small craft", but she and Doug had seen storms before, none worse than this but as they moved deeper into the mayhem Doug knew they would be alright.

"YEHA," Ashley yelled as the bow broke deep and sent a wall of water over their heads. The sudden yell caught Kim and Doug off guard and they both looked at her and started laughing. Kim gave her a hug. Doug yelled that he was glad she was enjoying herself. With the tension broken Kim reached out and adjusted the Doppler radar.

"About twenty more minutes," Doug yelled reading her thoughts.

"They pass about as fast as they start," Kim yelled back.

Doug was about to agree when Kim yelled in a panicked voice and pointing over Doug's shoulder, "What's that," she yelled. Ashley and Doug looked to where she was pointing.

"It's a water spout," Doug yelled. "It's sort of a tornado over the water. I've heard of them, and seen them on the news, but I've never seen one in person before."

"Is it dangerous," Kim asked.

"Yeah, if you're in its way, this one is already past us. See if you can find it on the radar," Doug yelled to Kim. Suddenly an unusually loud call came over the radio. The radio had been busy threw-out the storm, but this one came through loud and clear, obviously from very near.

"Mayday, Mayday," a man's voice repeated. Doug reached for the mike but before he could respond a Coast Guard vessel in the area came on requesting information on the emergency. "I've got a wife and two kids on a sail boat and there's a waterspout heading right towards me," a panicked man's voice responded.

"What are your coordinates, over," the Coast Guard radio

operator requested. There was no response. "Repeat, what are your coordinates, over," Again there was no response to the Coast Guards radio call. "I've got your coordinates as approximately 44 17 degrees North by 86 42 degrees West, can you confirm, over." Doug nodded to Kim who was already plugging the coordinates into the boats GPS. As the Coast Guard continued trying to raise the endangered sailboat the Searay's GPS showed the position given by the Coast Guard relative to their own, they were close, real close. Doug instinctively began throttling up the Searay's twin 260's but stopped and turned towards the ladies.

"Go," The ladies yelled in unison.

"Hold on," Doug yelled to them. Then almost to himself he said, "This is going to get dicey."

The Searay had performed well facing the 12 foot swells and 4 foot waves head on, now he turned the small boat 140 degrees to Port, a maneuver that could roll the boat or swamp it from the rear. He was putting them all in danger and he knew it. According to the radar the storm would last for less than fifteen more minutes, but Doug knew that only meant the sky would start clearing, the swells and waves they would face could last much longer. He finally got through to the Coast Guard and informed them of his position and intentions to attempt to lend aid. Three other boats in the vicinity had called in before him, and more were trying to call in, but from what he could tell they were the closest to the endangered sailboats last suspected position. It didn't take long for their proximity to the endangered sailboat to be confirmed and their worst fears to be realized. After traveling less than half a mile in the choppy water Ashley pointed to something in the water off the starboard bow.

"What is it?" Kim yelled. Doug's heart sank, he knew what it was.

"I don't know," yelled Ashley then looking at Doug she asked, "Is that part of a sail boat?"

"Yes," Doug yelled back, "It's a spinnaker boom, and it didn't come off easy." Kim and Ashley looked back at the rod of aluminum bobbing in water as Doug's words registering in their heads. Soon the rod disappeared and they were surrounded by walls of water as the Searay road to the bottom of another swell. When the small boat reached the top of the next swell all three knew they had found the sailboat, or at least what was left of it. The crest of the next swell was only 100 feet or so in front of them, yet it was barely visible through the rain and the spray from the water. The 4 foot waves inside the swell seemed to play a hide and seek game with what they all knew was the wreckage of the sailboat. "If they had her sealed up," Doug yelled, "she would have imploded just like a house in a tornado."

"Who cares," Kim yelled back, the emergency training of the CICU where she worked taking over. "There are four people out there, two adults and two kids." With her words Doug and Ashley snapped out of the shock of seeing the debris field.

"You look to the right," he told Kim, "Ashley, keep looking to the left, I got the front. If they got their life jackets on they should be florescent yellow or orange," Doug yelled then realized that his life jacket and the ones the ladies were wearing were of less visible and more fashionable colors. He grabbed the radio mike from Kim and reported the coordinates of the debris field to the Coast Guard. The Coast Guard was about 45 minutes out but several other boats were closer and heading their way, the closest still being more than 15 minutes out. Doug looked at the amount of debris around them. There was a large amount of miscellaneous plastic and buoyant items that had probably been inside the sailboats cabin, but it was all light items that would have traveled the farthest in the winds of the waterspout. What was missing were any large pieces of the hall and mast. There were small pieces of fiberglass from the hull in the flotsam, and they had seen the aluminum spinnaker boom, but there was not enough for this to be the waterspouts point of contact with the sailboat.

"We're still on the outskirts of the wreckage. This is all light stuff," He yelled to the ladies. "We need to find the center. I'm going to try to get up on that next swell and run the top as long as I can." Pointing to a piece of fiberglass from the sailboats hull that was floating nearby he added, "Look for larger pieces of that." The ladies signaled that they understood. He gunned the engines and got the boat to the top of the swell in front of them. As he turned to attempt to run the top of the massive swell the Searay started sliding down the opposite side causing the small boat to lean about forty degree to the port side. Doug shoved the throttles forward and steered into the slide, the twin 260's of the Searay managed to get the boat back to the top of the swell. Doug took a deep breath and quickly glanced over at Kim and Ashley wondering if they realized how close they had all come to taking a swim. Back on top of the swell they could see debris in every direction. Even with the ferocity of the storm and the intensity of the search it was heartbreaking to see the amount of debris surrounding them. They all knew their efforts might be in vain.

"There!" Ashley yelled, pointing to something about 40 yards in front and a little to the right of them, "What is that?" Doug made a sharp right turn till the Searay was at the bottom of the swell them he turned back to the left to take a closer look at Ashley's find. As they approached they could clearly see two small windows on the 3 foot by 7 foot piece of floating fiberglass. A sizable chunk of the cabin, yet still small enough to be susceptible to traveling a long distance in the wind, not the proof Doug was looking for.

"Keep looking around," Doug yelled, "Don't get fixated on one point." Then off in the distance Doug thought he saw what he was looking for. Going forward at the bottom of the swell about 150 yards then turning left to re-cross the swell they had just ridden, Doug hoped would put them close to what he thought was a large section of the stern of the sailboat. If the engine is still attached, he thought, it would be as close to ground zero as they could get.

"You're going backwards," Kim yelled.

"I think I saw something," he yelled in response. As they crested the swell he regained sight of what he had seen but realized that he had overshot it and was preparing to adjust their direction a few degrees left when suddenly.

"There they are," Yelled Ashley excitedly, pointing to the right about 20 degrees. Doug and Kim looked to where Ashley was pointing but didn't see any sign of people, just the same debris that was scattered all around them. "There they are again," Ashley yelled.

"I see them," Kim added pointing to a spot about 70 yards ahead. Doug cold see them as well, sometimes visible, sometimes disappearing as they bobbed in the choppy waves.

"Can you get to them?" Ashley yelled to Doug.

"I'm going to," Doug yelled, "They're almost to the crest of that swell. I'll try to get beside them in the trough on the other side," Doug yelled back. They were relieved to see that the people in the water were not only alive, but where thrashing around trying to get their attention. The ladies waved and yelled and Doug sounded on the boats horn to signal them that they had been spotted. "Get the ropes out from under the back seat and run one of them through the cleat, then tie the ends to each of your life jackets. Use one of the other ropes to throw to them," Ashley hesitated trying to figure out the order but Kim, who was more experienced in emergencies, grabbed her and started to the back of the boat to make preparations for the rescue.

"Which side?" Kim yelled, not sure Doug could hear her over the noise of the storm and the engines.

"I'm going for starboard, but be ready for either," Doug yelled back. The people in the water were just about to crest the oncoming swell and Doug knew that going lateral to the storm would be dangerous and hard to control. His plan is to turn directly into the oncoming swell and go over it and past the people in the water. By doing this he hoped to be able to use the next swell like a surfer uses a wave to make a tight U turn and bring his boat beside the survivors. The waves were high and choppy, the swells massive, visibility was terrible, the target he was aiming for was only visible for a few seconds at a time as they disappeared amongst the waves, and he had never tried anything like this before, he said a prayer. Luck was on his side, as he finished the U turn the people in the water emerged in front of him, not dead on but close enough that he could safely maneuver the boat next to them.

"You have to get them on board quickly, I can't keep the engines shut down for long," he shouted back to Kim who had also seen the survivors. She was leaning over the side ready to throw the rope when the people got close enough. Ashley was behind her still tying a dock bumper to the end of her rope to make it easier to throw. The sides of the Searay are too high for people to climb over, and it was doubtful that even together Kim and Ashley would be strong enough to pull the people on board. Fortunately the stern of the Searay has a swim platform only a foot above the water. If Kim could get the rope to the people in the water, and the people had the strength left to hold on after their ordeal, then Kim and Ashley could reel them in to the back of the boat and help them on board. The problem is that the propellers are located just below the swim platform, so as soon as the survivors are close the engines they would have to be stopped for safety, not a safe thing to do in the rough waters.

"There they are," yelled Ashley spotting the three swimmers clinging to each other now just twenty five feet from the Searay. As Ashley prepared to throw her rope Kim let hers fly first, it landed short.

"It's farther than it looks," Kim yelled pulling her line back in for another try, she wouldn't get the chance. The thin, studious looking English teacher from Overland Park Kansas somehow threw the fifteen pound dock bumper five feet past the swimmers with the rope landing on top of them. "Great throw," yelled Kim dropping her rope and taking hold of Ashley's. They could see the people in the water clearly now, a man, a woman, and young boy about ten years old. The man was busy securing the rope around the others, and both adults were yelling something but with the storm and engine noise Kim and Ashley couldn't tell what they were saying. "We realize there's one still missing," Doug's voice announced over the Searay's PA system. "We need to get you on board first. Secure yourselves to the rope and let us do the work. I will pull forward while we reel you in." He said this last line as much to Kim and Ashley as the people in the water, "We will bring you to the back of the boat and bring you on board with the swim platform." The man in the water waved that he understood and Doug began inching the boat forward as the ladies pulled the three survivors in with all their strength.

"Ask if they are injured," Kim yelled to Doug.

Doug hesitated; he realized that he had a nurse on board but knew that there was nothing they could do till they got the people on board as well. "Do you have any injuries that will require help getting on board?" he finally asked over the PA. By this point they were able to answer by shouting to Kim and Ashley. Looking back Doug saw that the ladies had things pretty well in hand so he made one last call on the PA in the hope of calming the survivors a little. "Several other search boats are in the vicinity can you give us a description to aid them?"

"Barbra is thirteen and wearing blue shorts with a yellow top," Doug heard the woman yell to Ashley who turned towards Doug to relay the message. Doug waved Ashley off letting her know that he had heard the woman. "Is she wearing a life jacket, if so what color?" He yelled to Ashley and the people in the water.

"Yes, it's green," The man in the water yelled. Ashley and Kim both turned to make sure Doug had heard, realizing he had they went back to maneuvering the people in the water closer to the swim platform. Still looking behind ready to shut down the engines when the three people in the water were close enough to reach the swim platform, Doug switched from PA to radio mode and began relaying the information to any boats in the area through the Coast Guard that three of four swimmers had been recovered, and to concentrate the search on a lone teenage female in a green life jacket.

Doug cut the engines long enough for Kim and Ashley to help the three people into the boat. Kim immediately went into nursing mode and started asking medical questions as she and Ashley led the rescued boaters below deck. Ashley returned to the deck to help with the search for the missing girl and not unexpectedly it wasn't a minute before Bill, the father, also joined them on deck worried about his daughter Sarah. Bill's wife Karen also joined them briefly on deck but was in such a state of panic that they all realized she would be better off below deck. Kim did what she could to calm and reassure Karen and to get her below with her son, but she was only having limit success. With Doug driving, Ashley sitting next to him and Bill standing to their left they resumed the search. The pop up storm was almost past now but Doug knew it would still take twenty minutes or so for the waves to calm. Though they exchanged few words it was clear to Doug that Bill was an experienced boater.

"The three of us were thrown off the port side, but I think Sarah was thrown aft," Bill told them.

"We saw a large section of the canopy, and I have an idea where ground zero is, do you know what direction you were heading when you went overboard," Doug asked.

"I don't know," Bill yelled, "We got thrown overboard when she started spinning."

The Searay's bow lifted as Doug maneuvered her towards his best guess as to where the sailboats stern would have been pointing based on what he had seen in the debris field. As her bow made a hard entry into the water they all heard a loud crash that seemed to come from the boats cabin. Doug and Bill gave each other a quick look; they both knew that the crashing sound they had heard was more than just the bow breaking the water. Without a word Bill hurriedly headed down to the cabin to find out what had happened.

"What was that sound?" Kim asked as Bill entered.

Relieved to see that they were alright Bill asked, "Could you tell where the sound came from?"

"From up in the bow," Karen said pointing nervously. She was hugging her son Tyler with all her might, "Have you found Sarah yet?"

"No not yet, but there are a lot of boats searching, don't worry we'll find her," Bill said with as much reassurance as he could muster. He quickly made his way to the bow and began opening the storage compartment doors.

When Bill returned to the bridge Doug could tell news wasn't good, "How bad?" he asked.

"There's a hole in the port storage locker about six feet from the bow. She's taking on water but if you keep her moving you should be alright," Bill yelled in response. "From what I could feel the hole is rectangular about 6 inches by 10 inches. You might have come down on the base of my mast."

"Did you have a sail up?" Doug asked.

"No I had gotten them down," Then looking at Doug, Bill realized what it meant, "If the mast broke clean and entered the water it would have made a sea anchor."

"And that would make this ground zero," Doug agreed. Both men realized they were heading in the wrong direction. Using his dashboard compass for guidance Doug turned 120 degrees to starboard and pushed the throttle forward hopping to gain enough speed to form a vacuum and suck some of the water out of the now slowly sinking boat. "Well keep searching till more boats show up then transfer you to one of them and I'll make a run for the closest port," Doug yelled.

"You should be OK as long as you're moving," Bill said absently, his attention now back on finding Sarah. He didn't have to wait long, with the boat now on the correct heading and moving fast it was only a minute or so till they caught sight of Sara's green life vest almost directly in front of them. By this time the waters had calmed considerably and Doug was able to pull his boat within feet of Sarah without any additional maneuvers, but all was not well. Even from a distance they could tell that Sarah was unconscious, only the life vest was keeping her head above water. As soon as they got even with her lifeless body Bill dove out of the boat and swam to her.

"Get Kim," Doug yelled to Ashley, who was already moving towards the cabin door. Soon Kim and Karen joined Ashley on deck and Doug had made his way to the swim platform to help Bill.

"She's alive but she has a big cut on the back of her head," Bill yelled as he grabbed the line that Doug had thrown him.

"As gently as possible let's get her on the platform." Kim instructed the men when she joined Doug on the swim platform. After carefully lifting Sarah onto the platform, and getting Bill back onboard, Kim started her examination. She gently felt the back of Sara's head for swelling around the site of the laceration, not happy with what she found she checked Sara's eyes, "She has serious head trauma," Karen told them. Then looking at Doug she added, "We have to get her to a hospital as soon and as gently as possible." As Doug headed for the radio he knew that a small, damaged boat in rough water was not what was needed. While informing the Coast Guard of their situation and requesting a helicopter he spotted a 65 foot Horizon motor yacht about a quarter mile away that had joined the search. Raising the yachts captain on the radio he found he was in luck, not only was the owner a physician, but they were cruising with two other couples that were also doctors. After explaining the situation to the boats captain the Horizon started making its way towards the Searay. Doug headed back to tell Kim what he was thinking. Kim agreed that they had to get Sarah off the swim platform and that transferring her to the Horizon to wait for the rescue chopper wouldn't be any more dangerous than moving her to the deck of the Searay, deep down she knew that both were dangerous.

When the 65 foot yacht pulled its starboard side next to the Searay's stern and the swim platform where Sara lay, it was clear that the doctors had been busy. They handed down a table leaf from the Horizon's dining room to use as a backboard. Then two of the doctors climbed down carrying several tie-down straps and a roll of duct tape. With Kim's help they carefully maneuvered the table leaf beneath Sarah and secured her to it with the straps and tape. The Horizons side rail was several yards above the Searay's swim platform and getting Sarah aboard was going to be a problem. Fortunately the Horizons upper deck was equipped with a small crane that was used to lower her 14 foot runabout and two jet skis down to the water. The captain lowered the 14 foot runabout down to the level of the swim platform and they carefully lifted the table leaf, with Sarah strapped to it, from the swim platform and into the small boat. Using the runabout as a gurney they were able to safely lift her to the upper deck of the Horizon where she would need to be for the rescue chopper to pick her up. Soon Bill, Karen and their son Tyler were aboard the yacht. Kim looked back at Doug.

"Meet you at the hospital," Doug said then turning to Ashley he added, "You go with them too."

"No I'm staying with you," Ashley answered heading for the pilot seat.

"If anything happens that's just another person who will need to be rescued," Doug shot back.

"I don't care, I'm staying," Ashley said stubbornly.

"Well if you're going to stay get below and see how much water we've taken on," Doug said angrily as he brushed by her on his way to the controls. He got the boat moving and checked his GPS to find the closest marina. Pentwater and its manmade entrance to an inland lake were about 27 miles away. The only other option was to head directly to shore and beach the boat till it could be recovered. The shore could be reached in about twenty minutes and Pentwater's Marina in about an hour.

"The water in the cabin is about 3 or 4 inches deep," Ashley told him when she returned from the cabin. Sitting down next to him she added, "The storage compartment up front was completely full, but it emptied pretty quick when we started moving."

"Could you tell if there was water coming in from anyplace else?" Doug asked, giving her a one armed hug and a kiss. He knew it would be safer if he was alone but deep down he was still glad that she had stayed.

"It has to be," She replied after thinking for a second. Realizing he didn't fully understand what was happening below she added, "The front storage compartment was full of water but it wasn't spilling over. The water has to be coming in from somewhere else. I can't tell where."

Doug took a moment to let this new information sink in, "OK, We'll head to the shore and then stay as close to it as possible while we try to make it to Pentwater." As he talked he showed her what he meant on the GPS screen. "Pentwater should take about an hour to reach. What I need you to do is to monitor the water level about every five minutes or so, but first take the controls, I want to take a look for myself." Ashley and Kim had both driven the boat several times in the last two months so once Doug gave her a heading and showed her what they were doing on the GPS she confidently took the wheel as Doug headed to the cabin to see the damage for himself. When he returned topside he sat down next to her and put his arm around her shoulders leaving her to steer, "It looks to me like it's stabilized down there, but I'll check again in a few minutes." He radioed the Coast Guard with his plans, position, and the condition of the boat. The Coast Guard then gave him a progress report on the rescue chopper.

"I hope they're alright," Ashley said showing the first signs of emotion. Doug gave her a supportive hug, suddenly aware of the emotions returning in him and the pride he had in all three of them.

"They'll be fine," he whispered into her ear, "they've got Kim looking after them."

A half an hour later with Ashley and Doug hugging the coast line but confident that they would make Pentwater Marina they got a message from the Coast Guard. Sarah had been airlifted and was on her way to a hospital in Muskegon. Kim, Karen, Bill, and 11 year old Tyler, had been transferred to a Coast Guard Cutter that would take them to Muskegon as well. The Coast Guard also reported that arrangements had been made with a repair shop and marina at Pentwater and Doug was given directions and contact information for getting the Searay out of the water. It was the best news they had had. Soon Doug had made arrangements by cell phone with a friend of his from Ludington. He would meet them up in Pentwater and take them to the hospital in Muskegon.

When they arrived in Pentwater's harbor the boat yard had

a trailer already backed into the water waiting for them. Doug maneuvered the boat onto the trailer and after being secured they were pulled onto shore. Once on dry land Ashley and Doug disembarked and along with the boat yards owner and chief mechanic inspected the damage. Bill had been right, there was a 6 foot by 8 foot hole in the inner hull of the double hulled boat, it was hard to say what happened to the outer hull, most of it was missing. The outer and inner hulls both had extensive cracking. It was clear to everyone that the boat would not have stayed afloat long had it not been moving. With very little chance it could be repaired Doug made arrangements to store the boat at the marina till he could decide what to do with her, or more likely, how much he could make stripping her for parts. With the money from the movie based on his first book that was about to be released and a second book well on its way, Doug had been thinking about buying a new boat anyway, he would just be buying it a year or two before he had planned.

The Coast Guard had gotten Kim and the Young's to the hospital in Muskegon by the time Doug and Ashley arrived. Sarah had arrived by chopper a few hours earlier. As they had arranged by cell phone Kim met them in the lobby, "The news is bad, but it could be worse," Kim told them as they made their way to the intensive care waiting room. "Sarah has a 3 inch laceration on the back of her head, and x-rays show a hairline fracture in her skull about an inch long. The hospital has a Neurologist who is working with her and came and talked to us. Sarah has been awake but still hasn't spoken which the doctor said really didn't surprise him at this point. He also told them they had given her a full range of physical response test and that Sarah had passed every one of them."

"That's sounds good," said Ashley. "Did the doctor say when she would be able to talk?"

"He doesn't know. The problem right now is the possibility of swelling inside the brain, they gave her a CAT scan but we haven't gotten the results yet," Kim went on.

"So if it is swollen will they have to operate?" Doug asked.

"Possibly," Kim answered, "I called a friend back in Kansas who's a surgical nurse in neurology. She said the extent of the surgery, if any, depends on the results of the CAT scan and some of the physical tests that Sarah has already passed. Her best guess was that if surgery was needed it could be just a matter of drilling a small hole through the skull to relieve the pressure."

"Just a matter of drilling a small hole," Ashley said softly echoing Doug's thoughts.

"Have you told any of this to Bill and Karen?" Doug asked. "As little as possible," Kim told him. "I'll let the doctor tell them what he wants them to know. Bill's an engineer by the way, works for a bridge repair firm in Grand Rapids." Doug cringed at the thought that Kim was a member of the medical community and its passion for keeping people in the dark.

"I figured he was smart. He did a good job out there, you all did," Doug said putting an arm around Kim, a gesture that quickly became a much needed hug that Ashley joined in on.

"So how are Bill and Karen holding up," Ashley asked.

"As well as can be expected I guess, I gotta admit that I'm a nervous wreck too. It's easier being the nurse than the patient," Kim told her as they navigated the maze of the hospitals hallways.

Doug and the ladies soon joined the Young's in the waiting area. After some small talk and thank you's, and with no new news from the medical team to share, they did what all people in an intensive care waiting room do, they waited. Before long Doug talked Bill into going with him to the hospital cafe for coffee and some food. Along the way they decided that Doug would get a rental car for all of them to use and two hotel rooms. They knew that Karen wouldn't leave Sarah and that Kim wasn't going to leave Karen. With Ashley being a school teacher the plan was to return and pick up Ashley and 11 year old Tyler, and take him out for dinner, then if possible back to the hotel and let him watch TV and get some sleep. When the men returned to the waiting room with the coffee, still no news, the ladies agreed with the plan and Doug took off to set the plan into motion. After about an hour he returned and he, Ashley, and Tyler, headed off to a Denny's restaurant that Doug had seen. Doug didn't have much experience with kids and was amazed at the resiliency Tyler showed. After watching Tyler eat a huge hamburger platter and what seemed like an even bigger fudge and ice cream dessert, they headed for the hotel. Along the way they passed a miniature golf course and with a disapproving look from Ashley, Doug and Tyler decided to play a round. After the golf Tyler said he was tired so after a quick stop at a local Meijer's to buy Tyler some cloths, they went to the hotel. Kim and Ashley were in constant communication both by phone calls and text messages, and they learned that Sarah did have some swelling on her brain but that the doctor was going to hold off on operating for now and put her under constant observation. It was going to be a long night. The next morning Ashley called Kim for a progress report on Sarah while Doug woke Tyler who had fallen asleep on the extra bed in their room watching TV. After being in contact all night it didn't surprise Doug when Ashley told Tyler that Sarah was still asleep but that the operation was getting less likely with every passing hour.

"Has she said anything yet?" Tyler asked.

"Not yet," Ashley told him trying to sound positive, "But your mom and Dad have been in to see her a couple of times during the night." Tyler thought about the news for a minute then he went into the connecting room to change for the day. After Tyler left, Ashley told Doug that Kim wanted them to bring Tyler to the hospital for breakfast. Hospital rules prevented an 11 year old from entering the intensive care unit, and everybody agreed that it would be best if they keep him out of the hospital as much as possible. Kim was hoping that by bringing Tyler in the dining room for breakfast she could get Karen to eat something. She had been able to get some food into Bill during the night, but at this point Karen was running on caffeine and stress. The Young's had made arrangements with a friend in Grand Rapids, who also had an 11 year old boy, to pick

Tyler up in Muskegon and stay with them in Grand Rapids for a few days.

Around one o'clock Karen's parents arrived from Indianapolis, and Karen's best friend had made her way to the hospital from Grand Rapids. Bill's parents lived in Atlanta and hadn't decided whether or not to come yet. Kim was still reluctant to leave but when the Coast Guard showed up to finish their reports it made for a good opportunity for Doug and Ashley to get Kim out of there. Leaving the hotel room keys and taking the rental car since the Young's wouldn't need it now that their friends and family had arrived, they said their goodbyes. It was quiet on the forty five minute drive from the hospital to Doug's house till Doug finally broke the silence, "Well I was thinking about buying a new boat anyway."

"O' I'm sorry," Kim added lightly, happy for any relief from the stress, "I forgot to thank you for a lovely the day on the lake."

"Well you two were looking for adventure," Doug said. "I think I've had enough of adventures," Kim said. "Me too," Ashley added.

"Me three," Doug added. In their current state of exhaustion it gave them all a much needed laugh.

As soon as they got inside the house Kim headed upstairs and crawled into bed and Ashley crawled in next to her to keep her warm. Doug went to his office and checked on a few things including calling Pentwater Marina about the boat, but it wasn't long before he crawled into the bed as well. They all thought the terrible adventure was over, they were all wrong.

Chapter 17

Water spouts on the great lakes are a normally harmless phenomenon that captures the locales imagination. If anyone can capture one on camera, the pictures are certain to make the weather segment of the evening news. Boat wrecks and rescues are more likely to be the make the evening news top story, when you combine the two it can become a national news story. When you're a bestselling author with a Hollywood movie based on your first book about to be released, a second book on the way, and a publicist and movie studio advertising department who would love nothing more than to get some free publicity, then you've got a problem. To have the author of a solo adventure story, Thought On A Long Lonely Road, make a daring rescue a few months before their film was to be released was more than the studio promo department could hope for, to have him do it with his two girlfriends was more than they could dream of. As soon as Doug checked his messages the next morning he began realizing how big a problem he had.

"We need to talk," He yelled from his office to the ladies when he heard them talking in the kitchen.

"What's wrong?" Kim asked rushing in and expecting the worst. Ashley was at her shoulder and from the look in their faces Doug realized what they were thinking.

"No, it's not about Sarah," Doug said to the relief of the ladies. "I just got a call, and several emails, inquiring about the possibility of the three of us going on a media tour about the rescue. The thing is that the real reason for the media tour would be to promote my book and the upcoming movie."

"Sounds kind of cheap," Ashley commented. "What are we talking about, the Today Show, CNN, that kind of stuff?"

"Exactly, most of those shows are so desperate to fill air time they will put just about anything on, and this really is a pretty good story. It would also involve photo shoots and interviews for magazines and internet home pages. The movie ad people seem to be pushing it, but my publisher is in on it as well, with all of them involved it's hard to say what they would come up with. How long it would last would depend on how long the story is of any interest to anybody," Doug explained. "There is money involved."

"How much money," Kim asked.

"Depends on how long people are listening, how long we can make it entertaining. Probably in the ten to fifty thousand range. If you're interested you would need to work that out with the advertising firms involved," Doug told her, "But let me introduce you to my lawyer before you sign anything."

"For a couple weeks work," Kim exclaimed. "I'm in the wrong business."

Ashley as usual finally brought up what they were all thinking, "What about us?" She said putting an arm around Kim and looking at Doug. What followed was an awkward silence.

"How long before you head back to Kansas?" Doug asked. "About a month," Kim told him.

"Well, I would be very surprised if this lasted more than a week or two," Doug said, the pain of thinking about the summer ending, or of wasting the time left was obvious in his voice. "Kansas isn't that far away, and it's not like I have a real job."

"You don't have a real job, and we don't have a real home," Ashley said.

"Come on Ashley," Kim said, "we need to talk." As the ladies walked away Doug realized that he didn't care about the movie or the book that carried his name, he only cared about them.

"Personally I don't care about the money, but it is important to remember that this is Doug's livelihood," Kim told Ashley when they were alone.

"Taking a whorl wind tour of the talk show circuit would have sounded like a dream come true a few months ago. Now, I don't know, I guess I just love being here so much," Ashley said with tears forming in her eyes.

"My vote is to support Doug however we can, but I want to suggest one other possibility," Kim said putting an arm around Ashley. "He was right about the people asking what's wrong with the mental health system after the Sandy Hook shooting. I'm not sure, but I think he might have the answer. If he does, or even if he doesn't but he has enough to get the debate started, it could change a lot of lives for the better."

Ashley pulled away realizing the magnitude of what Kim was saying, "You're talking about taking on the AMA. It could cost you your job."

"Maybe, but I doubt it. Doug was right about one thing, psychiatrists don't get much respect in the hospital. Anyway, you're the one who wanted an adventure. Trying to get a movement started, or a bill through Congress, now that's an adventure," Kim said with enthusiasm.

Ashley smiled as she met Kim's eyes, "We need to talk to Doug," she said.

Doug listened as the ladies explained that they were willing to do the talk show circuit to help him promote his books and the movie, but that they wanted more. They agreed with him that the mental health care system in America is in need of change. They also acknowledged that after some of the recent violence people have started asking about problems in the world of psychology and not just looking at the gunman like they did after the Virginia Tech shooting. They had heard the case that Doug had put before them and even though they didn't know if he was right, they did believe that he had enough to get the debate started. They also told him that they believed it was important.

"I've been thinking about trying to making my case," Doug told them as he reached into his desk and pulled out a flash drive, "But I was planning on doing it with a book."

"A good time for both," Kim said.

"If an organized movement were to catch on there would be a lot of money in it, money and fame," Ashley offered.

"I can live without the fame," Doug said, "But I wouldn't turn down the money. I do need a new boat."

"That's nice," Kim said sarcastically. "It's up to you how you do it, but I really think you should share what you've found."

"In order to do this we would have to play a game with the movie company ad people," Doug said, then thinking about it he added with a smile, "I guess that doesn't bother me too much. What does bother me is the idea of drawing swords against the AMA, the psychologists, the universities, the pharmaceutical companies, and organized religion, especially the Catholics who own a lot of the hospitals. Any one of them could and would crush us like bugs."

"No guts no glory," said Ashley.

Kim and Doug looked at each other, "How far along are you with your book?" Kim asked.

"These talk show tours are really boring. All you do is sit around waiting your turn to go on," Doug answered with a positive air. "If we get any momentum going... I can finish the book in time to take advantage of the publicity. It's all written, it just needs to be cleaned up for publication." Kim jumped into his arms with Ashley close behind. "We need one hell of a game plan," Doug told them, not entirely sharing their enthusiasm.

"No," said Ashley, "we need one hell of a lesson plan. We are teaching the public after all."

Doug called his publisher and told him that they all agreed to do the media tour. They would start with a couple of local interviews around 2:00 that afternoon, followed by a private flight to New York around 5:00 that evening, and hopefully the morning talk shows the following day. Someone from the ad agency would be on the flight to discuss compensation with the ladies. "So much for the mile high club," Doug joked. Ignoring him Kim plugged the flash drive into her laptop and started reading through what Doug had already written.

"I do my lesson plans in outline form," Ashley suggested.

"I don't do outlines," Doug told her. "I write like I do woodworking, I start out with a mental picture of what I want, then start breaking it down into individual pieces. I guess it is sort of an outline."

"Keep going," Ashley encouraged.

"Well, after I have all the individual drawings done, or with writing a paragraph or a line, I just start doing it. I get on the computer and look everything over and usually one thing or another catches my eye and that's where I start," Doug explained.

"Then that's where we start," Ashley said as she got a yellow legal pad out of Doug's desk.

"Get me one too," Kim told her, "This could get complicated." The three sat down and began listing all the points that Doug could think of, and that the ladies could remember, for the reason that change was needed. They made a list for the reasons that changes were needed and a second for the changes they would recommend to address them. Even with the almost constant phone interruptions by the movie studio's promotional team that would be handling their interview schedule and travels for the next week or so, the lists soon started taking shape. Refine, combine, and eliminate, as Ashley called it, would come later. Then it would be Doug's turn to write short articles about each of the changes they would propose, and the reasons that they felt the changes were necessary. They had come together as a team on the rough waters of Lake Michigan and they now felt empowered and invincible. Yesterday the lake, tomorrow the airwaves, and soon the mental health system. They keep at their work till they needed to get dressed for the afternoon interviews, and pack for their next adventure in New York. They would inform the world that the forgotten need their help.

On the plane to New York the ladies signed contracts that could be worth up to $100,000 with the promotional company. Doug informed them it would be closer to the low end. "Never believe anything an ad man tells you," he told them. The ladies assured him they had already figured that out. It turned out to be an interesting flight, Doug, Ashley, and Kim, trying to work on the outline for a plan of action without letting the ad people know what they were up to, and the ad people trying to work on their story of the rescue for the upcoming morning talk shows, all being done on a cramped 13 seat corporate jet.

"You were right, no mile high club today," Ashley whispered to Kim and Doug.

"You probably should have read the small print on those contracts you signed a little closer," Doug whispered back, "We'll be lucky to find any time alone for the next week."

Kim just rolled her eyes, "You two are incorrigible," She whispered.

When they finally arrived at their hotel room they had all had more than enough of the enthusiasm of the advertising company's buffoons. The three conspirators, or so they felt, ordered a snack tray from room service and got back to work on their plan. It had been a long day and they had an early wakeup call, but before turning in on the first night they managed to put together a short list of changes they would propose.

First- Give the psychiatrist's limited use of the prescription pad so they can prescribe psychotropic drugs.

Second- Require psychological testing to be added to the Diagnostics and Statistics Manual's existing requirements for diagnosing mental disorders, when such testing is applicable and available.

Third- Shift the percentage of tax payer funded research away from research in theoretical psychology, and invest in research aimed at supporting clinical psychology. Support research designed to develop structured step by step procedures for treating specific disorders to aid counselors in working with clients. Support research designed to provide follow up testing to measure the effectiveness of medications and different forms of treatment for individual disorders.

Fourth- License psychologists and mental health counselors by the type of approach they use and the areas that they specialize in.

Fifth- Require mental health treatment facilities to be licensed by both the type of treatment they provide and a scale of what level of care they cater to.

Sixth: Challenge the members of the psychologies Ivory Tower to be more clients oriented in their approach to research. Recommend that the colleges and universities be more career task oriented in the education of future mental health workers. Take the names out of the text books.

"Would it be possible make the psychiatrist use psychological test to support their diagnosis?" Ashley asked as they discussed the list.

"It would be easier to get the word out to the clients to request testing rather than to make a doctor do anything," Kim replied, "Unless you get the malpractice lawyers involved."

"I would think that making psychological testing required through the DSM prior to the psychiatrist making a diagnosis would bring the lawyers into play. If the psychiatrist makes a wrong diagnosis and prescribes an unnecessary medication and they didn't follow the recommended testing requirements then somebody should be held accountable," Doug said.

"It would depend on how much authority the DSM has over mental health providers. From what I've heard there are some psychiatric hospitals that are already abandoning the new DSM-5 because of all the changes they made to it. If that's true it means that following DSM guidelines is voluntary. I still agree that it should be part of the DSM guidelines, and that might give the lawyers something to work with," Kim told him, "At the very least it's more than they have now, and they do need to stop the psychiatrists from guessing, if that's really what they are doing."

"Getting the psychologist limited use of the prescription pad is the most important part of this. A lot would change if that was the only thing we are able to do. The clients do deserve the right to choose, and having the choice would bring competition that would put pressure on the psychiatrists to get it right the first time. We really need to get the media to start investigating the quality of psychiatry, and show just how wide spread the incompetence is. I'm afraid that if I say how bad they are based just on my experiences it will look like just one disgruntled mental patient and nobody will listen, or worse one crazy person who shouldn't be listened to. If we can make a case for the psychologists getting the prescription pad and put the field of psychiatry on the chopping block then I doubt that there is much the AMA won't do to save it, possibly even forcing the psychiatrists to use available testing," Doug added. "Taking the names out of the text books isn't going to happen either," Kim said. "We need to find a way to get the media to stop using the wasted psychology research for comedy fill, and start asking the researchers how their findings are relevant to psychology clients, or mankind as a hole for that matter."

"All of these stations that do those fleecing of America type stories and then turn around and make money by mocking the wasted psychology research are guilty as well," Doug added sadly. "Unfortunately that might work against us if they decide to protect the material they use in there programs."

"You need to be careful of saying things like that," Ashley cautioned. "If any of the stations have done stories on questionable use of research grant money in psychology it could come back and bite you."

"Do you remember when I told you about the professor I had who ask the class why do research psychologists do what they do?" Doug asked.

"Yeah, they did it for peer recognition," Kim said.

"Well, when I was thinking about what he had said, and started forming the idea of taking the names out of the textbooks, I did a little research. I went to the college bookstore and started counting the names in text books for different subjects," Doug said beginning to put together a plan.

"Do tell," encouraged Kim.

"What I found from just randomly picking books in various subjects, and then counting the names on about twenty or so pages in each book, was that the eight psychology text books I looked at had an average of 3.4 names per page. I also picked books in Sociology, Philosophy, Civil Engineering, Physics, and Art. Art came in second with just under one name per page, the others had roughly one name every three or four pages, it wasn't even close," Doug told them.

"If we could get that out to the general public then people with any interest in what you're proposing might try counting names in textbooks themselves," Ashley said looking at Kim.

"If the people prove to themselves that the egos of psychology's ivory tower are out of control then it might take care of the research problem for us. And ironically it would do it with the same driving force that's causing the problem, peer pressure," Kim added getting excited about the idea. "So it might be as simple as telling that story and seeing what happens."

"How about requiring that the people who are working with clients be given mental health evaluation before being licensed?" Doug asked.

"I've heard your stories about how crazy some of them are, but is there any research to back your stories up?" Kim asked.

"And can you do it without eliminating people who have successfully dealt with issues from entering the field? Or removing some of the people who have gone to the trouble of getting the licenses but are still dealing with their own mental issues? You did say that when they changed the rules for certification in counseling that it took personal experience out, and as a result the quality of counseling dropped. If some of the best counselors have successfully dealt with their mental issues the disorders still might show up on the tests, if so then they would be removed from the field," Ashley reminded them.

"That's true, it's also something the media and the day time television shows might jump on since it would be an easy story to prove and doesn't violate the client privacy laws. We better leave that alone for now," Doug concluded.

"If we get any momentum going, it would also be a quick fix the politicians could use to make it all go away. Go after the little fish and leave the big fish alone," Kim added.

"What's really needed is an independent investigation that's not done by the mental health providers or by the patient. A group that has the legal authority to penetrate the entrenched, secretive world of the mental health care system," Ashley pointed out. "How do we make that happen?" Kim and Doug looked at each one another but couldn't come up with an answer, at least not tonight.

They decided that since none of them had any professional credentials in psychology that taking on the changes in DSM5 would be dangerous. It didn't mean they couldn't question the changes if they came up during an interview, or discuss their concerns on the web site Ashley was preparing. As a high school English teacher Ashley had taught and encouraged the kids to design their own web sites. Now her expertise would be put to the test for the first time, and it made her feel alive.

The biggest question still remained unanswered, how to shift the interviews from water spouts to mental health. They decided that in the morning they would try to introduce it by making changes to mental health treatment and research the topic of Doug's next book. They would deal with the ad people and Doug's publisher after the first interviews. With all that accomplished the three conspirators went to bed, the morning wakeup call would come all too soon.

The following morning Doug, Ashley and Kim, were driven to an independent television studio. They were scheduled to appear on three different morning shows, all at about the same time. The three interviews were to be aired live so in order to make an appearance on all three without rushing from studio to studio they would all be done from this remote location. Via teleconferencing they were able to talk briefly with each of the three hosts who would be conducting the interviews prior to the actual on air interview. All three stations would use file footage of a waterspout, and a brief description of the phenomena by their respective weather persons as part of the interview. The first interview would lead into the story with the waterspout footage.

Doug and the ladies were relieved when all three stations decided that since none of them could explain their relationship they would simply not mention it during the interviews. Doug did tell the interviewers that his next book was based on his personal experiences in the dysfunctional world of psychology, and that he would like to plug his upcoming book. The three interviewers all said they would try to find time. The movie ad people didn't know what Doug's next book was about and they didn't care, they wanted any plugs to be for the upcoming movie, not Doug's next book. In their minds books were at best a secondary form of entertainment. Doug's publisher Jim Spears did know what Doug's next book was about and he realized that something was up. With the busy schedule of three interviews in an hour and a half, and not wanting to cause any problems with the movie people, Jim only had a minute alone with Doug.

"I've read you're manuscript on psychology and it's good, but I thought we were going to publish the Alaska response team book first," Jim asked Doug when they were alone.

"I keep thinking about the questions people were asking after the Sandy Hook shooting. What's wrong with the mental health system instead of what's wrong with the individual? I decided that I wanted to test the waters for the psych book first," Doug explained, not entirely lying. "The Alaska book won't be on the shelf for six months or more anyway, and let's face it nobody's going to remember a plug for it on this interview by then."

"Well, I'll have to think about that," Jim said not entirely happy. "I guess we own the rights to both books, but I wish you had told me your plans first, it's a shock hearing them in a pre-interview interview."

"Sorry," Doug said with sincerity, then looking over at Kim and Ashley added, "It kinda came as a shock to me too."

Jim looked at Doug, then at Kim and Ashley. He had known Doug for three years, and he knew all about his strange life. What made Doug a good writer was that the twenty years he had spent outside of societies social circles he hadn't exactly spent inside himself either, he had spent the decades observing the interactions of others. The longing Doug had felt to be a part of society, and the anger and frustration he had experienced from not quite fitting in had at times made him suicidal, it had certainly added to his insanity. It also made his writing rich with emotion, and gave his characters a deeper understanding. Jim decided to go with Doug's instincts for now. After all he was right that nobody would remember a plug for a book that wasn't going to be released for six months.

During the first two interviews the conversation was all about the waterspout and rescue. The ladies did great with Ashley's calm delivery and the confidence she had gained from years of teaching stealing the show. She was quick to tell how Kim and Doug had saved the day with their heroic actions and skill. She laid it on so thick that Kim and Doug had to resist the temptation to laugh at times, but the camera was eating it up. The interviewers made time to plug the upcoming movie since it was the movie studios that had made the interview possible. At the end of each interview they did give Doug a few seconds to plug his next book, but it came off quick and cheap. It wasn't till the third and last interview of the morning that they got the break they were looking for. This time the interviewer wasn't just an on air personality who was more interested in keeping the viewers entertained and the advertisers happy. He was a former political insider who actually listened and understood the deeper purpose of his job. He had watched the first two interviews during breaks in his own broadcast, and he had seen something that he felt had some merit. After giving the waterspout story minimal attention, and barely acknowledging the movie, he dug in and pursued the mental health angle.

"I'm curious, is you're next book about your experiences with mental health system, or an effort to recommend changes to the mental health system," Stewart asked.

"It's recommending changes based both on my experience in the system and my attempt to go back to college in psychology to help some of the people I met along the way," Doug explained.

"We've made a list of six changes that Doug has identified," Kim added seizing the opportunity. As she said this she pulled a 3 X 5 index card out of her pocked and showing it to the camera in front of her.

"I'm almost out of time," Stewart told her, "Give them to me quick." Kim read the six recommended changes they had written the day before almost too fast in her excitement. "It sounds to me like you might be on to something," Stewart said with a nod designed more to encourage them to continue their work than playing for the cameras. "It's certainly a system in need of change," he added before praising them for the rescue and closing the segment.

Not much for the morning's effort the three of them agreed, but it was something. Even more important, or at least more fun, was how upset it made the movie people that they had wasted valuable air time talking about something as insignificant as the proposed changes to the mental health system.

Jim Spears bumped into Doug's arm and making sure Kim and Ashley heard, told him in a no nonsense voice that they needed to talk. When they finally did get some time alone, Doug and the ladies told Jim of their plans, and explained in detail each of the six changes they were proposing. When Jim was satisfied that they were serious about their quest he shocked all three of them with his response. The world of literature that Jim had spent most of his life involved with was full of people who were either in, or in desperate need of psychological treatment. Jim had been aware of the shortcomings of the mental health system for some time, so two years earlier when he had first read the draft of Doug's book proposing changes, it had peaked his interest. Jim also knew the value of being in the lead of such a program. Doug's first book had made the best sellers lists and made them all millions. If Doug could write the book that launched popular or even political support for a detailed agenda of change in the treatment of mental health, it would be worth tens or even hundreds of millions. "We did some preliminary research when you first gave us the manuscript for this book," Jim told them. "Have you made any changes to it since then?"

"Yes," Doug said handing Jim a flash drive with the revised manuscript. "It's sort of a work in progress, I pull it up and add a page or two when I find out new things, or get any new ideas. I've been adding a lot since they announced the changes to the DSM. So what kind of research did you do?"

"We looked into what you are proposing to see if it was anything we wanted to get involved with for starters. What we found might surprise you, you're not alone. There are several other individuals, and several small organizations that support more or less the same things that you do, but they can't seem to get together and form anything big enough to get anyone's attention. That and the fact that the subject is just so unnerving for some people that most media outlets won't touch it seem to be keeping any progress towards recommending changes from reaching the general public. What they need is a leader, a voice that they can rally around, or a book."

"A voice would be better," Kim said looking at Doug.

"Both would be best," Ashley added.

"How fast can you publish it?" Doug asked, pointing to the flash drive in Jim's hand.

"Let me worry about that," Jim said with a nod of confidence, "If your plan is to try setting this in motion using the media, you're going to need some help. I have a friend in the Boston area who works for a group called Citizens for Change. CFC is a small but high powered group of lobbyists, lawyers, and media types, who work with grass roots groups to help them get their causes public attention, and help them navigate the political landscape. It was about a year ago when I talked to my friend at a party and mentioned that I had an author who was writing a book that dealt with changes in mental health care. To my surprise he jumped on the prospect of getting CFC involved with the mental health issue. He told me that CFC had meet with several groups who are working on changes, but that as a group they hadn't gotten behind any of them to date. I didn't tell him your name, and only hinted at your ideas, but he told me that it would be something CDC would be interested in hearing more about. I can give him a call if you want. I've got to warn you though CFC plays hardball, and what you're doing involves taking on some very powerful people."

Doug, Kim and Ashley, looked at each other for a minute. They had run out the door with high hopes and big dreams, and now they were seeing a clearer view of the daunting road before them. Feelings of excitement, hope, and the urge to run like hell, all shone in their gaze. "I would very much like to talk with him," Doug said breaking the spell. Both ladies immediately moved closer to his side, their path uncertain, their resolve strong.

"Let the adventure begin," Ashley said proudly, as she put her chin on Doug's shoulder and grabbed the front of his shirt. All four had to laugh when the movie advertising clowns came rushing over to repair any wrinkles she had put in his cloths.

The afternoon schedule was hectic but well planned. Many of the big name talk shows book their guests days or weeks in advance so most of the interviews they did were for lesser known programs. Doug and the ladies were able to mention mental health reform in some of the interviews but with the interviews mostly being prerecording's and subject to editing, they could not be sure if their ideas would make the final cut. The ladies, especially Ashley, were stealing the show, a fact that Doug didn't mind at all and a relief to Jim Spears who had seen Doug's so-so performances during interviews following the release of his first book. Late in the afternoon they did get to appear live on two of the cable news networks. With all the practice they had had telling the story both interviews went exceptionally well, but only WSTD news allowed Doug any time to present his mental health proposal. Still it seemed to be enough, not only were they getting calls from news and talk shows interested in having them tell their rescue story and exploit the current media sweetheart, Ashley. They were also getting calls from interested parties looking for more information on Doug's next book, and exactly what changes he was proposing. Granted it wasn't many calls, but it was a start.

By this time the people from the movie company advertising agency had figured out that something was happening that they weren't entirely sure if they should be happy about or not. Even though it was too late for them to do anything about it they still they demanded a meeting and a full explanation ASAP. For fifteen years Ashley Johnston had been teaching high school kids. For fifteen years she had been trying to build the teen's confidence in their writing skills. For fifteen years she had been reading the crap the kids laid on her desk. For fifteen years she had been dealing with the immaturity and antics of America's youth, the movie company advertising people never had a chance and were seldom heard from again.

By 7:00 pm the interviews were either done or had been taped to air later in the night. Jim had arranged for a teleconference to introduce Doug and the ladies to a small assessment group from Citizens for Change at 8:00 pm. The four of them ordered room service and eat dinner as they prepared to present their ideas. It had already been a long day, but all the interviews had served as practice and had actually helped to make their presentation look more polished and rehearsed.

At 8:00 pm Doug, Ashley, Kim, and Jim Spears, joined four members of Citizens for Change by teleconference. Doug presented his six proposed changes and gave his reasons for believing that they were necessary. The four members of the CFC assessment committee asked Doug several questions about how he had derived his ideas, what research he had done, how much he had done to present the ideas to the public, and what his future plans were. The CFC members seemed especially interested in the book that he was writing to present his ideas to the public, and when the book would be ready for publication. The members of CFC explained that they had been approached several times to aid in presenting programs designed to bring about changes in the treatment of mental health. To date they had refused their services due to the single mindedness of the recommendations the various groups were proposing. Religious groups wanted to base treatment on a more Pray away the pain type approach for all types of disorders. Other groups wanted to eliminate religion from treatment altogether. Some groups wanted to rely more on pharmaceuticals, others wanted to eliminate pharmaceuticals. Some felt that talk therapy was the answer, others Cognitive-Behavioral. Some groups felt that social psychology including censorship of movies, books and television was needed. Proposals CFC had declined included mandatory separation from society for psychiatric patients, mandatory sterilization for patients, and mandatory testing for all school children.

The CFC members felt that Doug's six proposed changes were neutral enough to appeal too many of the groups, yet inclusive enough to bring about the changes that are needed to the mental health system. They realized that Doug's theory about psychology researcher's vanity being a major reason for the lack of effort spent on building supportive evidence and providing clinical applications for the researchers theories would be hard to prove. They also felt that he was probably correct in believing it. The theory that researchers were being pushed for quantity of research by universities they had heard before and knew had some merit. The CFC members did see that a shift from theory to clinical application in psychology research was needed. "Take the names out of the text books" was a good sound bite, or a basis for debate that could catch on with the public, actually doing it however would at the very least a challenge to the US Constitution. Doug Hines was a known and gifted writer capable of composing a book that could get the public's attention, however the CFC assessment team realized that his ideas lacked supportive evidence. Without the supporting research Doug's the book would just be the opinion of one man. Without the book there would be no money for the research. It was just one man's guess, granted it was based on twenty years of personal experience, but it was still just one man's guess.

In the end the CFC assessment committee saw enough to make the recommendation to pursue Doug's application for their aid further, but not to recommend acceptance at this time. To that end they would send one of their members to meet with and possibly aid Doug till a final decision on the application was made. Doug and the ladies didn't know it at the time but the CFC's help would be crucial in the coming weeks.

The next morning as Doug and the ladies were preparing for a late morning interview they were introduced to Don Peterson. Don was an image maker and consultant with Citizens for Change who had experience with the media talk show circuit. Don was also a lawyer and had worked as a political lobbyist for CFC on other issues. It would be Dons job to assess whether Doug Hines truly had a realistic proposal for changes to the mental health system, or if he was just a disgruntled psych patient with an ax to grind. Don also had to determine if Doug had the ability to present his plans for change, and if so, to what extent Doug's contribution would be most effective. Don had studied Doug Hines on the plane and during the morning by researching him on the internet and by reading as much of Doug's book as he had time to. Don had worked with several mainstream individuals who seemingly out of thin air had come up with brilliant ideas that needed to be presented to the public; in fact he specialized in it. Doug Hines, he thought might be different. The proposals were too deep, to well thought out, and they had been done over a long period of time. The book Doug had written was based on the deep thoughts Doug had during a bicycle ride that he took in this early twenties. Don's research indicated that Mr. Hines was of above average intelligence, and accomplished in several fields. Could it be that the alcoholism and psychological problems had worked as a temporary road block for Doug, and now that he had them under control he was starting to show the true person the diseases had been masking? Could it be that Doug Hines had spent twenty years in the mental health system dealing with serious issues, while in truth he was often the most intelligent person in the room and the one who was paying the most attention to what was going on? Doug was an endurance athlete with a high IQ and a passion for pursuing his thoughts and ideas to unusual depths. If this was all true, he could be looking at a diamond in the rough and if properly handled Doug Hines could become a valuable asset in the future. With all of this in mind he prepared for his initial meeting with Mr. Hines and the ladies.

Preparing for the initial interview Don Peterson decided to do his assessment of the ladies first, since in his mind they were not going to be major players down the road. He had researched Ashley Johnston and Kim James and found them both to be well respected in their respective fields of employment. Both of the ladies had strong credit ratings, no history of legal problems, and from the tapes he had seen of their recent interviews, he knew they could both handle themselves on camera. Having only met Doug a month or so before and being uncertain about their future plans, combined with their lack of knowledge in the subject matter, made it risky for CFC to involve the ladies any more than they had to. During the initial interview he found them both to be much as he had expected, friendly, outgoing, intelligent, strong, and most important for the role he saw them playing, attractive. In short order he concluded that his initial assessment of them was correct and moved on to Mr. Hines.

Through body language and vocal tone Don immediately found Doug to be uncomfortable even with social chit chat. Doug's demeanor grew stronger and more confident when he was talking about his personal experiences with psychological treatment, his house, or woodworking. Doug also had an attribute that in Don's mind was missing in most people, the ability to say that he did not know, if in fact he didn't. Don found that most people answered questions, or worse rambled on, when ask about something they had no knowledge of. It was a fault that left most people open for attack. Don realized that although Doug's evidence was limited to personal experience, conversations with others, and a small amount of schooling and research, that his conclusions were hard to dismiss. Don also found that Doug's passion when discussing topics that he was comfortable with was contagious. He also noted that when challenged Doug's body language became withdrawn, and his answers tended to be scattered and poorly presented, but still not lacking in substance.

Don concluded from his initial interview that Doug's ideas deserved further research. Don also realized that like many people whom he had worked with, Doug Hines was an introvert, but in Doug's case he was not shy about it. Unlike most people who believed that introvert and extrovert were descriptive words for how people communicate, Don knew that introvert and extrovert were actually descriptive words for how people thought, how their minds worked. Introverts doing their best thinking alone and in a quiet setting, while extroverts needed a sounding board or some form of give and take to do their best thinking. Don knew that the media talk shows were dominated by extroverted thinkers and that if an introverted thinker got on one of these programs the extroverted panelists would talk faster to prevent the introvert from having any say at all, or worse they would make the introverted thinker appear slow and stupid. It was one of the many flaws with the current trend in television, the last person talking, or the loudest person, usually was seen as the winner when very often the truth was just the opposite. Don concluded that if CFC accepted Doug's proposal, that Doug himself could present his ideas, but that CFC would have to send professional debaters to defend it.

Chapter 18

The next few days went by in a blur of airplane flights and interviews for Doug and the ladies. The waterspout rescue had captured the public's attention and they were in constant demand for appearances coast to coast. Their proposal for change to the mental health system was gathering momentum and interest from the people who were already concerned with, or working on bringing about similar changes, but it had not caught on with the general public as of yet. Doug did manage to get some credit points with the general public on one late night talk show when he talked about a futuristic vision of treatment based on Doctor McCoy's tricorder from the original Star Trek series. Doug explained to the audience that when Doctor McCoy passed the tricorder's cylindrical medical doohickey over the patient that it was in fact picking up the resonant energy of the human body, what some call the aura, and sending it to a computer to be decoded. The result would be that the body itself would tell Doctor McCoy what was wrong with the patient. Doug explained to the audience that it was no longer science fiction, and that there already exists several research companies trying to decode the language of the human body and that they were doing it with some success. He explained that there are cell phones already available to the general public that omit low level energy to aid in sleeping and controlling some moods. Then Doug suggested that for the several psychological disorders that are currently proving to be drug and treatment resistant, the key might be that the disorders are in fact caused by electrical malfunctions in the body and not by chemical malfunctions or thought processes.

"Someday," he told the audience, "it might be possible to get an app for your cell phone to control some mental health issues." Doug and the host then had some fun pointing out all the missuses of such research. Devices to promote gambling, sexual arousal, and cell phone apps that worked like love potions were the audience favorites. Doug suggested adding electrical impulses of greed to the oxygen and booze that are already being used to increase gambling in casinos. The host argued that greed would keep the money in the people's pockets, lust would be more effective. Doug agreed he might be right but pointed out that nobody was going to gamble when there was a Roman style orgy going on, the crowd went nuts. Kim added to the conversation by saying that they were already using some prototypes of tricorder type devices in the cardiac ICE unit where she worked. Doug and the host then discussed where the next multibillionaires would be coming from till their time ran out. The segment did nothing to get the general public to look at the proposed changes in mental health, but it did arouse interest in Doug and in his next book, and the book would discuss the proposed changes.

By the fifth day of their quest to propose changes in the mental health system, it was about a fifty-fifty mix of interviews based on the waterspout rescue and interviews asking for more information on Doug's plan for change. Not that the proposed changes were taking off however, more because the waterspout story was dying. With the help of Doug's editors at the publishing house the book was almost ready for the printers. It wouldn't be the most polished book ever published but it didn't need to be, shelf life wasn't a concern. To speed up the printing it had been agreed to make the book available in paperback first and then print hardback copies if they were needed. E books would be available almost immediately. With the help of CFC input and Doug's writings, Ashley's web site was beginning to take shape and have the look of a professionally built site. More important it was starting to get hits with comments and inquiries for more information.

That afternoon just before a scheduled radio interview strictly about the state of the mental health system, Don Peterson's worst fears and biggest question about Doug's ability to handle a live debate came into play. Five minutes prior to going on air the radio talk show host informed them that they would be joined on air by a minister, Reverend Solomon, who would be representing the current methods used in treatment centers. Don knew of the Reverend Solomon, he was a professional bible thumper and antagonist who had made a name for himself by arguing against gay rights, abortion, or issues like the teaching of evolution in public schools on debate programs. Reverend Solomon had his own following of fanatics and was popular on the talk show circuit since his appearances almost always led to at least one verbal altercation, which in turn led to higher ratings.

"You can't beat this guy at his game," Don told Doug. "The Reverend is quick on his feet and cares little about facts. When cornered he will just start quoting bible verses till he thinks of some way to make them sound like they apply to his point. The truth is that he probably doesn't know anything about the mental health system. His thing is to sell the power and glory of religious fanaticism to religious fanatics."

"So how do I approach him?" Doug asked, having gained considerable respect for Don's advice during the past few days.

"Let him have his points, they're setups and he'll be ready to trap you if you bite on one of them. I've made you a list of key words to listen for. If you hear one of the key words that I've listed then when it's your turn to talk try to use a word from the corresponding list to move the conversation in another direction. Whatever you do don't get bogged down on any one topic. If you do he will turn the interview into a sermon," Don cautioned him, showing Doug the list of words he had made, and a second list of suggested topics he could try if needed. Doug thanked him and after giving Kim and Ashley each a kiss and a hug for luck he entered the sound proof booth.

Starting the discussion off on a friendly note the reverend condemned both Doug and the DSM for blasphemy for condoning same sex relationships, and praised the treatment centers that were doing God's work to cure the dysfunctional gays and lesbians. Doug just thanked him for pointing that out and sat quietly listening for any issues that he was there to discuss to come up. After Doug similarly blew off the Reverends rant about the terrorists being a sign of the impending apocalypse the reverend finally got to the issue of drug abuse. The reverend pointed out that drugs were undermining society. Doug quickly agreed and then pointed out that the overuse of psychotropic drugs and misdiagnosis of psychiatric patients was undermining the treatment of mental health. The reverend countered by saying that it was the under use of Christian teachings in treatment that was the real problem facing recovery. Doug looked at the list of key words that Don had given him. One of the words on the list was Christianity, next to it were several suggested words for Doug to base his reply on, holistic medicine caught his eye.

"I am a strong believer in holistic medicine, or faith based medicine if you prefer. I however don't limit it to Christian faith or Biblical teachings. Caregivers in all areas of medicine should not discount the power of the human mind and the human spirit in recovery. The problem is that it's not 100% effective, so if we have modern medical procedures, including pharmaceuticals, that can increase the effectiveness of treatment. We need to use both holistic and modern medicine to give the client the best chance for recovery. Medical doctors are just beginning to use holistic methods in their treatment of medical patients. We need all the hospitals and treatment centers to start using both holistic and medical methods as well. Meditation and relaxation training are very important in dealing with mental disorders in day to day living. We also need the treatment centers to improve their accuracy of diagnosing the client by using psychological testing," As Doug was saying this, the reverend started talking over him with a loud voice in an attempt to obscure his point. Much to Don's surprise Doug simply slowed his speech and raised his voice a few decibels above the reverends, thus making his comment the one that was heard.

"Woodworking," Ashley said seeing Don's surprise.

"You should try his hands," Kim added with a smile when she saw Don's thoughtful look. Don thought about the need to talk over woodworking equipment in a busy shop and agreed that the skill was probably transferable. Kim's comment he decided to take on her word.

"Let's look at one of the world's lonely people, Eleanor Rigby," Reverend Solomon scoffed at the inclusion of this mythical figure, but Doug just raised his voice again and continued. "You all know her, if not she can be found picking up rice at the church after most weddings. The minister at the church probably thinks he is doing her a service by making her feel wanted and needed, and he is. He would be doing her an even greater service if he found a way for her to get the mental health evaluation, and the treatment she needs, in order to help her in dealing with her depression, or social phobias, or the physical or sexual abuse she faced as a child, or whatever the underlying cause of her social isolation is."

"God is the great healer..." The reverend broke in. "Absolutely,"

Doug immediately agreed, "That is why he gave us a mental health system. Then while receiving professional help she could use the church to enhance the recovery process, and find friends so that the next wedding might be hers," Doug hurriedly added over the reverends angry sermon. "The church is a great place to go to enhance recovery and to find support during the recovery process. It's a terrible place to go to find help for psychological problems that many church leaders are not adequately trained to deal with, or worse, church leaders who use the sufferers to do their dirty work."

That was too much for the Reverend and he went off on a long and loud rant about the glory of the church and its infinite power to heal it held for all who seek its help. Doug just calmly sat back and watched. When the Reverend finished Doug turned to the host and explained, "The big three in the mental health system are psychologists, with their talk and Cognitive-Behavioral therapy, and their use of psychological testing. Psychiatrists, with their medical approach and pharmaceuticals, and holistic, which in this country is predominantly religion. For the client to have the best chance at recovery, all three approaches should be used in harmony, and in the percentage that they are needed for each individual client. The problem is that the big three are often fighting for absolute control of the system, and the client is the one who suffers by receiving lopsided treatment from providers that are reluctant to use, or flat out refuse to use, treatment techniques developed by what they seem to feel is the competition. In today's provider controlled system, the client very often doesn't even know what kind of treatment is being offered till after the treatment is under way, and they only know it then if they realize that there are other treatment choices available. Unfortunately, I don't think that any of the big three currently have the competence or the maturity to take over the entire system and utilize all three pieces properly to insure the highest chance of recovery for the clients. I do think that the infighting has to stop, and that the mental health system needs to be brought under one governing body for both clinical and research purposes. That could be done by committee, or if we do need to pick a winner out of the big three, then Psychologists would be my choice to take over the entire system, but that's only if the psychologists agree to certain conditions. The most important of which is that the client always comes first, in both the clinical setting and the research world."

The rest of the debate went back and forth with nether side scoring any significant points. In Don's mind it was a victory for Doug given the surprise addition of the reverend and the fact that the reverend was a professional antagonist and debater. Doug had been able to take his best shots in stride, and he even scored some points along the way. As the hour long program came to its final segment the host gave each of them twenty seconds to make a final statement. When the reverend finished his three and a half minute biblical rant it was Doug's turn, "As comforting as it would to be to know the truth, as you do, I thank God for the wisdom to seek it," was all he said.

Don was ecstatic; any sound bites that would come from the show were Doug's. As far as the audience was concerned it really didn't matter what Doug said since most of the people who listened to this particular program were just listening for the fights, the topic often being irrelevant. The reverends followers who had listened would support him regardless of meaningless things like common sense and facts. Doug was exhausted and dissolutioned, in his mind he hadn't won anything. He felt he had just run into another of the walls that psych patients know all too well. The ladies did what they could do to comfort him, and Don assured him that he would take charge of all upcoming appearances to make sure that this kind of stunt would not be repeated.

Don also told him that the researchers at CFC headquarters were coming to the conclusion that Doug's plan for change had validity, not perfect, but strong enough to form a solid platform to open realistic debates on the need for changes in both the treatment and research currently used in the field of mental health. Through Ashley's web site CFC had been able to contact several small groups already working to change the system, and plans were under way to consolidate as many of them as possible under the name The Silent Voice Coalition. Steps were being taken to establish a central headquarters for SVC, and to write a constitution and elect leaders for a run at Washington. Consolidating scattered groups under one banner was a technique CFC had used before to gain political and public exposure. Slowly but surely thing were starting to come together.

Chapter 19

A few days later in a conference room in Washington DC a meeting was being held. It was a meeting of political lobbyists for some of America's most powerful organizations, the AMA, the American Psychiatric Association, the pharmaceutical companies, and lobbyists for religious organizations that own many of the treatment facilities. This would be the first time the pharmaceutical companies had sent their lobbyists to one of these strategy meetings on how to deal with Doug Hines and the Silent Voice Coalition movement. Their proposals intended to reform the research and treatment of mental health was becoming troublesome. Financially the pharmaceutical companies had the most to lose, but they were also the most realistic of the groups. They had seen that changes to the treatment of mental health issues were inevitable and they were not altogether opposed to them. They were attending the meeting to insure that those changes would be in their best interest.

They had all heard rumors of the book outlining the changes that Doug Hines had written and was being prepared for release. They had seen that Mr. Hines's efforts, along and that of the Citizens for Change group, had managed to form a loose alliance between several groups supporting changes in the treatment of mental health. They also knew that even with an organized coalition for change that they had enough combined power in Washington to stop any Bills that might be introduced. What they feared was that

Mr. Hines's book would coincide with another mass shooting, or a terrorist attack that was perpetrated by an individual who had received prior treatment for a mental health issue and that the book would gain wide spread public interest and spark demands for changes that they could not stop.

The three factions agreed that due to the unpopularity and uneasiness that any discussion of mental issues causes in the general population, and the political dead end it offered the politicians, that the best approach was to silence the current voice of change and hope the people would forget all about it. Contingency plans would have to be made in case the population still demanded change so that they could guide the changes to their mutual advantage. As lobbyist for some of America's most powerful players they all knew that the politicians would be easily handled. This Silent Voice Coalition group that was now making trouble for them had been in place in one form or another for a long time, but it worried them that it might continue to grow and gain public support if it found a strong and popular leader. All in attendance at the meeting knew that the Silent Voice Coalition was currently gaining momentum due to its leadership and the fact that Mr. Hines had an actual plan for change that they could rally around.

Having done their homework they knew Mr. Hines had only taken nine psychology classes and was in fact a college dropout with a track record of losing in his personal life. The lobbyists had also seen that Mr. Hines was holding his own on the talk show circuit, but only holding his own. In truth it was the more experienced and polished voices of the Silent Voice Coalition that were scoring most of the points. They decided their best move was to cut the head off and hope the body would die, but how. If they tried to discredit Mr. Hines they feared coming off as bullies and making a martyr out of him, thus giving the SVC group the sympathy vote. The group concluded that they had to make Mr. Hines discredit himself in some way, but how?

"You've been invited to speak to the House of Representatives," Ashley yelled, running into the room where Doug, Kim and Don Peterson were working.

"The United States House of Representatives in Washington DC," Doug responded in shock as he took the letter Ashley was waving and read it for himself.

Reading the letter over Doug's shoulder, Kim could barely contain her excitement, "We've done it, we've done it," She kept yelling.

"We haven't done it yet," Ashley warned her, "Doug still needs to give the speech."

"And a speech doesn't change anything, we still need a vote," Doug reminded them.

"But we got it into the capital, that's all we started out to do," Kim reminded them, "Somebody's listening," she added clutching Doug's shoulder.

"Can I see that?" Don asked, not sharing the exuberance of the others who were gathering. Don Peterson had been doing this type of work for a long time, and thought he smelled a rat, "When Congress has questions they call for a subcommittee hearing on the issue and ask the questions themselves. Being invited to speak before the house is usually reserved for dignitaries, astronauts, or generals, someone who is invited more to be recognized than to presenting new ideas," Don told them. Don had gained a great deal of respect for Doug during the ten days that he had spent with him. The research he had done on Doug prior to their meeting had not given him high expectations, but Doug was getting the job done, there was a certain air about him. Intelligence, common sense, style, flair, they all combined in Doug and gave him that 'X' factor that couldn't be found in any research. All of that aside, Don also had a great deal of respect for Doug's limitations, and he knew that others might see Doug's limitations as well.

Doug and the ladies watched as Don read the letter, the

enthusiasm in the room seemingly on hold. They looked at Don as their hired gun, and it was clear he wasn't sharing in the celebration over this unexpected invitation. As Don dialed a number on his phone he said to them, "They just don't give out invitations to speak in front of the house very often, I've never seen this before."

"So is this phony, some type of joke?" Doug asked with Ashley and Kim on his shoulders and all of them now looking at Don. Don shrugged but didn't answer them instead he turned his attention to the person on the phone. Kim, Ashley and Doug, listened in trying to gather what was being said from one side of the conversation. It was an agonizingly long time till Don hung up and turned back to them.

"It's a real invitation," Don finally announced when he hung up the phone, "But there's more to it. The best we can figure is that you were not invited to speak by the members of the House, you were invited by the lobbyists who work for organizations that oppose the changes you are suggesting."

"Is that even possible?" Kim asked.

"The lobbyist would have to do it through members of the House," Don told her, "but if they have enough power then it could be done."

The ladies murmured, doubting what they had just heard. "Promotion to the point of incompetence," Doug said in a faraway voice.

"That is exactly what the opposition is hoping for," Don agreed. "If you get up there and fail in any way, you lose credibility and the entire movement loses momentum and possibly falls apart. If you give a good speech then we get a minor move forward that will be forgotten long before anything comes up for a vote."

"Then he just has to give an incredible speech," Ashley said stubbornly with a challenging look at Don.

"Remember that were dealing with mental health issues. He could give a Mr. Rodgers Goes to Washington quality speech and it still might not get any air time, Don said discouragingly.

Realizing that Doug was leaning towards declining the

invitation, Kim pointed out that the Congressional Representatives and the media would still be there.

"By making the invitation before the public gets firmly behind the movement the media presence will be small," Don explained. "Without the media to pose for, the Rep's probably won't bother to show up. You will most likely be talking a handful of pages with everything to lose and not much to gain."

"Well played," Doug nodded with grudging respectable for the opposition.

"Do you have any experience in giving speeches?" Don asked, already knowing the answer.

"Not very much," Doug said.

"That's not true," Kim challenged, still very much in favor of accepting the invitation, "You give speeches all the time back home around the fire, your good at it."

"That's true, you're always going on about something," Ashley's comment being greeted with smiles and restrained laughter. "I mean you're good at it," She added.

Don realized that they might have a point, giving a speech was giving a speech whether it was in front of a fire or in the House Chamber. "Are there other people at these fires?" he asked.

"Yeah, a lot of the time," Doug replied, "In my heart I think I can give the speech."

"I'll set it up if that's what you want, but I'm not sure this is a good idea," Don told him.

"Give us 24 hours," Ashley suggested, then looking at Kim and Doug she added, "Let's get a first draft of the speech before we move." They all instantly agreed that 24 hours was a good idea. Kim, Doug and Ashley, started setting up for a think tank and speech writing session, Don got back on the phone. Don knew that conventional wisdom said to turn down the invitation, and that his colleges at CFC would push for Doug to decline it. But Don believed in the X factor, he believed that Doug had it, and he knew that if Doug could pull the speech off, that even though it wouldn't give the movement much momentum, it would give it strength, it would make it very hard to stop.

As he had expected, Don Peterson had a difficult time convincing his colleagues at CFC that Doug should go ahead with the capitol speech. What he didn't expect was that another point he thought would bring objections, not bringing in a professional speech consultant to work with Doug, but letting Ashley Johnston coach him instead, turned out to be what convinced the other members of CFC that Doug could pull the speech off. Don told his colleagues that when he had first seen Doug's home office he had noticed three stuffed bears that seemed out of place in Doug's bookcase. He had assumed that they had something to do with the relationship between Doug, Ashley and Kim, and he hadn't pursued it any farther till Ashley had told him that they were one of keys to his success on the talk show circuit. It turns out that Doug had won the bears playing games at the Michigan State Fair midway ten years earlier, and that he kept them as a trophy and as a reminder of the work and courage it took him to overcome his panic attacks. Ashley explained how Doug had practiced visualization and relaxation exercises to train his thoughts to be able to find a safe place in his mind before attempting to challenge the panic attacks using systematic desensitization. She told him about the metaphoric water droplet in the waterfall, and of the cliff that overlooked the waterfall where Doug had been delivered and had found peace. Ashley explained to Don how Doug practiced calming his thoughts by visualizing the waterfall and the cliff for six months and then he had gone into places that were sure to cause panic attacks. Doug would then allow the attacks to happen and at the same time use the visualization of the cliff to calm himself by using what he called the floating technique to remain in the situation till the attacks passed. Doug continued this process going to more and more frightening settings till he was able to eventually overcome the panic attacks through repetition. She told him that the midway at the Michigan State Fair was one of Doug's last challenges to himself, and that he had done the work so well that he didn't have any symptoms of the panic attacks at the fair. She said what Doug did find that was by applying the same relaxation techniques before playing the games at the midway significantly improved his chances, and that was how he had won the three bears.

As Don told this story to his colleagues during the morning meeting they began to realize that Doug Hines was perhaps a bit deeper than they had previously thought. The plans for change were a result of Doug's observations, and ultimately they knew that the speech was his decision to make. The Silent Voice Coalition was being built based on his work and would need a strong leader in its early stages to prevent a power struggle before a charter could be put in place and elections could be held. Doug was the obvious choice for the leadership position, and he was CFC's choice. CFC knew the speech could solidify that position and give them time build a strong infrastructure in SVC. It still wasn't a unanimous vote, but it was decided that CFC would support Doug's decision to give the speech.

Chapter 20

Doug was already a nervous wreck and the speech wasn't till tomorrow afternoon. They had decided to stay at the house in Michigan that night and fly to Washington in the morning. The plan was to give Doug one last chance to practice the speech in front of an audience, and to try to keep him as calm as possible till they left for Washington.

"It looks like everybody is coming," Ashley said, looking out the window to where their friends were gathering. Doug had worked hard practicing the visualization exercises he had used to overcome panic attacks, now he would use the same techniques to overcome his nerves in the Capitol Rotunda. Tonight he would deliver his speech in front of a fire with a group of friends around, tomorrow they hoped the fire would be inside him. "Where is he?"

"He was walking along the river bank a few minutes ago," Kim answered, putting her arms around Ashley from behind. "I saw some people going over to talk to him. He's not the only one who's nervous," Kim said as Ashley leaned back into her. The two of them stood silently looking out the window until they saw Doug and a small group of friends heading towards the fire.

As the ladies approached the fire there was a feeling of electricity in the air. Doug's, and now their friends had heard him talk about changing the world before, but this time he was really doing it. They had followed the progress of his proposed changes in the papers, on television, and on the internet, and they were excited to be a part of the movement, even if it was only as a practice audience. When the ladies reached Doug they all agreed the excitement of the evening would be missing tomorrow.

"Don't expect many of the Representatives to be in the rotunda tomorrow," Don Peterson told him.

"They will hear the speech on tape won't they?" Ashley asked. "One of their aids will monitor the speech, if the aid feels it's worth passing on then they will either show the reps the speech, or more likely give them a synopsis of the key points. Doug's real job is to impress the staffers," Don explained. "We'll deliver a copy of the speech, along with a synopsis of Doug's plan to every reps office in the morning. The trick is to get the reps themselves to actually read it, and not just a staffer. There's been enough public attention over the last couple of weeks that the representatives will have heard of the movement and the proposed changes, but they're busy and they probably haven't paid much attention to it yet. Doug's job is to put it on their desks."

The crowd of about a hundred people settled down as Doug approached the replica of the house podium that he had built for practicing his speech. He raised his hand to quiet the few remaining howls of encouragement and began to speak. From the start Don Peterson could tell that Doug was only reciting the words. Doug's body language was tight and nervous, the emotional rise and falls in his voice sounded forced and practiced. Twice Doug had to refer to his index cards for help remembering his lines. It could have been a worse practice speech, but if Doug repeated this night's performance on the floor of the Capital in the morning it would not have the legs to reach into the Congressional Offices. This performance could stall the movement and bring Doug's leadership qualities into question. Don Peterson returned to his hotel that night wondering if he had made a big mistake. The speech was good, the audience listening had responded to the points that were being made, some even debated the points as they were being presented, but it needed wings to make it fly in Washington, and Doug had to give it those wings.

In the morning Doug and the ladies boarded the private jet to Washington. Don Peterson and a few other members of CFC and SVC discussed the responses they had heard from the crowd the night before. The suggestions for changes or additions to the speech were mostly ignored due to the copy of the speech that was already being delivered to the Reps offices, and the fear of introducing last minute changes to an untested speaker. The emphasis of the talk on the plane was the delivery, Doug would get one chance and he had to get it right.

Sitting with Kim by his side and Ashley across the aisle Doug leaned over to Kim, "I can't help thinking that for this to work what I really need is a Virginia Tech type shooting, or a Boston Marathon style terrorist attack to really get the media to take notice," Doug whispered to Kim, "Does that make me a terrible person?"

"No," Kim assured him in a soft voice, and then putting her head on his shoulder she added, "It just makes you a realist."

Upon arriving at the airport in Washington they were met by several other members of the Citizens for Change group who led them to three cars that would take them to the Capital building. The mood was somber but there was a sense of power throughout the procession. Entering the Capital Building through a rear door the small group was escorted to a waiting area before entering the Capitol Rotunda. Doug would be allowed two guests to accompany him onto the main floor of the chamber. The rest of the group could watch Doug's speech from the balcony of the great hall. To no one's surprise Doug asked Kim and Ashley to walk with him. Soon the Sargent at Arms entered the waiting room and informed the group that it was Doug's turn to speak.

Entering the great hall the three were overwhelmed both with the halls magnificence and the significance of what it represented. Afraid to do anything wrong the ladies gave Doug a final good luck gesture not with a hug but rather with a firm squeeze of his hand

and a quick word of encouragement. As Doug stepped onto the rostrum of the great rotunda and next to the podium he looked around at the thirty or so pages that were mulling about. Then his eyes gazed up at the circular balcony and a tourist group that was being seated and instructed to remain silent. He found where Don Peterson, Jim Spears, and the small group of CFC and SVC members were being seated. Finally he looked to his right on the floor of the great hall to where Kim and Ashley had been instructed to sit. Doug smiled when he saw that Kim was fingering his favorite Zippo lighter that he had used to start so many fires over the years. It was a good visual aid, but it wasn't needed. To Doug's surprise he did not feel nervous at all, he felt empowered, a great force had built in his chest, a feeling of tremendous strength and power, and he liked the feeling. After being introduced he stepped up to the podium and began.

"I have come to talk to you today about a silent killer. A killer not of the body, but of the mind. A killer of hopes and of dreams, a killer of careers and marriages, like time and weather it slowly erodes the fabric of one's life and leaves people desperate and alone. A desperation that all too often reaches our eyes and our ears. A desperation that all too often tears at our hearts. A desperation that we often hear referred to with words like suicide, addiction, divorce, or murder. How often have we heard that these desperate people had attempted to find help, attempted to be heard, attempted to find peace before they reach our eyes and our ears on the crime page, or in the obituaries. Who are they reaching out for help to? Why are their cries being heard on our radios, our televisions, and in our newspapers? Hasn't somebody created a system for these people to reach out to?

"My name is Doug Hines and I reached out to that system for help. I am here today to give you my report on the mental health system that I found over the last twenty years."

Even from the balcony of the Capitol Rotunda, Don Peterson could tell that the "X" factor was in full force within Doug. Doug's body language was one of power and confidence, his voice flowing with emotion. Doug had the look and the demeanor to pull it off. Still Don sat on the edge of his chair hardly able to contain himself. "Come on Doug, come on, come on," He whispered to himself.

"I have met a lot of good people in the mental health system during the last twenty years." Doug's voice going sullen "Friends I met in the treatment centers, friends I made in the homeless shelters, and in the hospitals. Friends that I have sat with for the endless hours of waiting, waiting and hoping, waiting and praying, maybe this time, maybe this drug, maybe this diagnosis, maybe this counselor will be the one, the one that gives me my life back. And there is reason for such hope," his voice rising with enthusiasm, "The researches committed to unlocking the secrets of the human mind are making impressive strides forward in identifying and understanding the workings of the human mind. The use of PET scans, the work of neurobiologist's, psychologists, psychiatrists, and others. The pharmaceutical companies are developing and introducing new medications for a wide variety of psychological disorders with impressive regularity and impressive results, when they are properly administered," The last words he said in an ominous tone. "So I ask you why the rate of recovery in America has remained the same for so many mental health issues over the past century. Almost 70 percent of clients going into a mental health facility will return within a year. Teenage suicide rates are rising, military suicide rates are skyrocketing, anorexia and bulimia are killing young Americans, homelessness is on the rise, school and workplace shootings that are committed by individuals with prior contact to the mental health system are seemingly becoming everyday news. The success rate in treating heart disease, liver disease, cancer, even the simple pimple, has increased dramatically over the same period, so why not psychology and psychiatry. Why?" he paused briefly, "Some say that a more complex society is to blame for the increases in teenage suicide, Madison Avenue is to blame for the increase in anorexia and bulimia, glamorization by the music industry is to blame for the drug and alcohol use, school shootings are blamed on insufficient gun control laws or violence on television. Many people put the blame on the clients themselves. Through all of the theories I see one common denominator in all of these problems, and that one common denominator is the quality of care available in America's mental health system."

"As a client receiving treatment from a psychiatrist I was diagnosed as psychotic and prescribed the antipsychotic drug Zyprexa. For four years the drug took control of my life and made me, for the first time in my life, psychotic. During this four year period I also dealt with severe paranoia first time in my life, paranoia that was caused by the drug I was being prescribed. Paranoia that was so overwhelming at times, that it made me a threat to society. The sad truth is, and psychological tests verify, that I am not psychotic. The power that psychotropic drugs have on the mind is unimaginable, and when they are improperly prescribed can cause irreparable harm both to the client, and to society as a whole. In my case the antipsychotic drug that the psychiatrist prescribed made me experience psychotic symptoms, so when I went back to my psychiatrist for my fifteen minute monthly medication review I was told that they had given me the right diagnosis, and were prescribing the correct drug, but that they needed to increase the dosage. And the psychiatrist did increase the dosage several times, each time making the problem even worse," Doug said shaking his head. "They were the worst four years of my life and it was all totally unnecessary. A simple psychological test could have told the psychiatrist that I was not psychotic. It is amazing and unbelievable just how often clients are diagnosed and treated for the wrong disorder. Often the disorder the client is being improperly treated for is also the disorder that the latest wonder drug has been introduced to treat. We need to take the guessing out of diagnosing mental health issues for the good of the client and the safety of the American people. Psychotropic drugs are Godsends when properly administered, but they are far too powerful to be handed out on a trial and error basis."

"Today's mental health system seems to work best, and it

seems to be dependent on intuitive super professionals like the ones portrayed on television by celebrities like Oprah Winfrey and Dr. Phil McGraw. These super intuitive and perceptive professionals do exist within the mental health system, and from personal experience I can tell you that it was a blessing when I found one of them. Unfortunately these super professionals make up a very low percentage of the doctors and counselors available to the client. Certainly there are not enough of them to improve the unacceptably poor accuracy rate in diagnosing mental health disorders," Doug voice rising and falling for effect. "Still psychiatric diagnosis's for deeply rooted mental issues are being doled out, and psychotropic medication prescribed, during a consultation with a psychiatrist that on average lasts only one half hour, and is then followed up with fifteen minute monthly medication reviews. The use of currently available psychological testing such as the MMPI to confirm the psychiatrist's initial diagnosis is almost unheard of in this country. Psychological testing prior to diagnosis and the administering psychotropic drugs would certainly improve the low accuracy rate currently being achieved by psychiatrists. So why aren't they using them? Most people would not take blood pressure medication without first having their blood pressure tested. Yet in the treatment of mental health disorders people are being prescribed reality altering medications on what amounts to a first impression."

"Psychologists generally do use the psychological tests that are currently available when making a diagnosis. Psychologists generally spend an hour with the client and often see the client for hour long individual or group counseling sessions often on a weekly basis. Unfortunately for the client, the psychologist cannot prescribe psychotropic medication when they are needed, so the clients are often being forced to see a psychiatrist. Due to the high cost of treatment most clients cannot afford to see a psychiatrist and a psychologist, and most insurance plans only cover a limited number of mental health visits per year, this effectively prohibits the use of both of these specialists. This means that the client who is in need of medication for their illness is for all practical purpose being forced to receive their mental health treatment from a psychiatrist. I personally, and many other clients currently receiving treatment for mental health issues would prefer to receive that treatment from a psychologist," Doug said emphatically.

"One of the problems with relying on psychological testing to improve the accuracy of diagnosing clients with psychological disorders is that there are not enough accurate tests available," Doug explained. "The most accurate tests that do exist are predominantly broad spectrum tests that provide a probable diagnosis by a statistical comparison. In many of the available tests the client is asked to answers to a series of questions, tell a story based on provided images, or identify standardized images. The client's answers are then compared with a large cross section of society, in some of the tests a structured follow up interview is also conducted. These tests are designed to provide the test giver with a probable diagnosis such as bi-polar, ADHD, or depression. The existing tests do little to identify specific problem areas that the client will need to work on in therapy if they are to be successful. Available tests in psychology also fail to give any indicators as to which of the many medications available for many specific disorders would best serve the client. Bi-polar disorder for example is currently being treated with one of six different medications. It is not uncommon for a properly diagnosed bi-polar client to spend over a year taking several of the six medications on a trial and error basis before finding the medication which best treats their symptoms."

"We need for more accurate tests, and more specific tests to be developed, unfortunately these tests take time to develop and perfect," Doug said returning to his normal voice. "Many of the psychologists currently being assigned the responsibility to further the treatment of psychological disorders in this country are instead attempting to further the scope of our understanding of the human mind in ever expanding arenas. /many of the research psychologists have lost sight of the individual client and the need to focus their research on accurately diagnosing and treating already identified and named disorders. The requirement for a high volume of publications that researchers face at some colleges and universities in order to receive tenure also restricts the long term research that is needed to develop tests and procedures aimed at supporting clinical psychology. One area that needs to stop is the use of tax payer funded research to get the schools name on the Tonight Show monolog, or morning talk radio, to make the university appear as a fun school," Doug said with as much contempt in his voice as he could muster. "Having gone through years of counseling with their graduates, I can assure you that the results are anything but fun."

"I feel that the client would be better served if the schools stopped teaching their students about the researchers and the many psychological theories, and moved to a more clinically responsible curriculum. Practical application of the theories that the prospective counselor can use with the client, along with in-class role playing and an apprenticeship program similar to that found in education could help standardize treatment, and provide much needed inroads to what is really working in the treatment of mental health issues. Research designed to give prospective counselors structured plans, road maps if you will, based on effective and proven treatment procedures. These plans need to be developed to treat different disorders, and the different disorders common co-morbid maladies. Practical experience, proven procedures, a client based education for the counselors, now all we need is to empower the client," Doug suggested with a whimsical hint.

"Many times clients are advised that the most important factor in choosing a counselor is to find one they like. For some clients filling the need for human contact and friendship will give them some temporary relief from their pain," Doug in a semi mocking voice. Then getting serious he continued, "I have observed that long term relief from ones problems often requires change. What I found was that the counselors whom I trusted but that did not always agree with me, the ones who challenged me to addressed topics of my life that I did not choose to look at on my own, did me the most good. When I first entered the mental health system I was not looking for a Woody Allen type lifetime introspective journey, I simply had a few issues and wanted help in dealing with them so I could move on with my life," Doug said with his hands raised. Switching to a sullen voice added, "But that is not the treatment that I have received over the last twenty years. Endless talk therapy with no particular direction or outcome in mind seemed to be the norm. Counselors skilled at breaking the client down, but stopping far short of building the client back up, were all too common. The emotional release of exposure is after all what is needed, that's what we as clients were told anyway. For me all it did was to open up old wounds, it did not make them go away, or help me deal with them. Twenty years in the system, hundreds of thousands of dollars spent on treatment, all for advice I could have gotten from my mother or any average person off the street," Doug shook his head as he said this.

"I hope to improve the care that individuals in the mental health system receive by giving client's access to the full range of mental health care professionals that the client can pick and choose from," Doug announced to the hall in a loud voice filled with power. "By introducing competition into the stagnant mental health system, supplemented with changes in the direction of psychological research, and adjusting training required to enter the field, I hope to improve the quality of care available to the client. By providing the client with the information they will need to make informed decisions on what type of treatment they will receive, and how that treatment is to be administered, I hope to force the providers to be competitive in developing more reliable procedures, and be more accountable for their results," Doug said in his loudest voice. "I want to remove the unknowns from the mental health system in the hope of opening the door to treatment for those experiencing minor psychological issues less intimidating. I want to end the petty feud that has existed between the psychologists, the psychiatrists, and religion, for centuries. A feud that seem to be based on the egos of the caregivers, and is designed to insure their market share. A feud that is often detrimental to the client. I hope to empower the client by forcing corporations and individuals that provide mental health treatment to disclose the type of treatment they offer. I hope to remove the confusion and expense that is created by the unnecessarily layered mental health system that is in place today. To that end I am proposing six changes to the mental health care system that I feel will break the stagnant establishment, improve the quality of care, and empower the client."

"First- Give the psychiatrist's limited use of the prescription pad so they can prescribe psychotropic drugs."

"This will allow the clients to choose between seeing a psychologist or a psychiatrist. Giving the client the right to choose will bring much needed competition into the field of mental health, and will make the success rate in recovery a priority in order to secure market share in that competitive environment. Some say that the Medical Doctors understanding of the anatomy, physiology, and the chemistry of the human mind, is essential in properly administering psychotropic drugs. It is true that medical school students are instructed in brain function and chemistry as part of their overall curriculum. The psychology PhD candidate's curriculum is entirely dedicated to the understanding of the human mind including its chemistry, physiology, and anatomy. In my opinion the addition of psychotropic drug interactions with the brain and the body is not past the psychology PhD candidate's ability to grasp. The fact that the rest of the medical students curriculum is of little use in diagnosing psychological disorders, compared to the psychology PhD candidate's curriculum which is entirely dedicated to understanding and diagnosing psychological disorders, makes the psychologist the clear choice to be given the responsibility to prescribe and track psychotropic medication," Doug offered.

"This is the most important of my recommended changes due to the declining state of the psychiatric profession. Personally

I support giving the psychologists the ability to prescribe psychotropic medication. However," Doug continued in an ever more pleading tone, "if it is decided to not give the psychologists the authority to prescribe psychotropic medication, then I beg of you to please take action to insure the future of psychiatry by passing a law that will make it impossible for the psychologist to get use of the prescription pad for at least thirty years," Doug paused to let this odd request sink in before continuing.

"It has been almost twenty years since a bill to give limited use of the prescription pad to psychologists was introduced before Congress. The bill was never brought before this chamber for a vote. Subsequent efforts to reintroduce the bill have also failed. The effort however, did not go unnoticed by the students in America's medical schools. The result has been to reduce the number of quality medical students that are entering the field of psychiatry. Students who once might have thought about a career in psychiatry are exploring other areas of medicine that have more certain futures. This uncertainty of the future of psychiatry has resulted in residency programs in training hospitals seeing fewer applications to fill their psychiatry positions, and hospitals are often forced to lower their standards, or turn to graduates of foreign medical schools, to fill the slots once coveted by quality American medical students. The reduction of the quality of individuals entering the field of psychiatry has resulted in a decline in the level of psychiatric care given to the client, due to the decline in the quality of the individuals that are providing that care. The quality of care is also getting worse every year with the retirement of the older generation of competent psychiatrists, for whom the study of psychiatry was their first choice," Doug was now pleading in an effort to make this point understood.

"Imagine going to a psychiatrist only to find that they can barely speak English. Diagnosis's by psychiatrists, whether they use psychological testing or not, are dependent on verbal interaction between the psychiatrist and the client to determine variations from what is commonly seen as the "norm" and what the client is experiencing in their thought processes and in the their ability to interact with society. I find it hard to believe that psychiatrists for whom English is a second language, and who have very little experience in American society, are able to accurately diagnose deeply rooted mental health issues, in many cases without the aid of any form of testing, and do so in the first half hour of contact with the client."

In the balcony Don Peterson pumped his fist. This was one of the tongue twisting lines that Doug had struggled with the night before.

"Personal experience and the rate of re-admittance into the mental hospitals support my skepticism. This misdiagnosis by psychiatrists who can barely speak English might sound like a bad joke from some movie," Doug said in an angry voice, "but it is already common place in America, and has happened to me on three separate occasions."

"The client deserves the right to choose who they will receive their treatment from." Doug stated sternly slapping his hand on the podium.

"Second- Require psychological testing to be added to the Diagnostics and Statistics Manual's existing requirements for diagnosing mental disorders, when such testing is applicable and available."

"We need to stop the revolving door that exists in the treatment of mental disorders," Doug stated in a powerful voice, and with a note of frustration. "Regardless of your feelings regarding the need to have medically trained doctors prescribing psychotropic medication, the simple fact is that the percentage of misdiagnosis proves that psychiatrists are not doing a very good job of accurately identifying and treating mental disorders. Requiring the use of available psychological tests before a client is labeled and treated for a specific disorder is a simple and inexpensive way to improve the accuracy of the doctor's diagnosis. If the reason psychiatrists are not using psychological testing has anything to do with the childish feud that exists between psychologists and psychiatrists, then in my opinion, any misdiagnosis resulting from the lack of testing is nothing less than acts of criminal negligence by the psychiatrists."

"Third- Shift the percentage of tax payer funded research away from research in theoretical psychology, and invest the money on research aimed at supporting clinical psychology. Support research designed to develop structured step by step procedures for treating specific disorders to aid counselors in working with clients. Support research designed to provide follow up testing to measure the effectiveness of medications and different forms of treatment for individual disorders."

"The ivory tower world of psychology has seen unbounded growth during the last century. Research in social psychology, Humanistic psychology, Behavioristic, Environmental," Doug began listing with increasing speed, "Biological, Developmental, Comparative, Cognitive, and Clinical psychology," Doug stopped and took a deep breath before continuing "Developmental, Educational, Existential, Paranormal, Sports, and Structural psychology, form a only a partial list of the range of specializations now studied under the heading of psychology. While the research world of psychology has extended its reach for understanding of just about everything, its grasp on the treatment of mental health disorders has remained pretty much the same. Treatment in mental health facilities has remained for the most part unchanged for the last hundred years. Some real world gains in treating psychiatric disorders have reached the clients from the Cognitive-behavioral psychologists during the last fifty years. We have seen the development of a few psychological tests that are helpful in diagnosing clients when they used. Still the overall advances in the treatment of mental disorders have not been in keeping with other areas of medicine. The last major stride in the treatment of mental health disorders didn't even come from the psychologists in the ivory tower. It came from an unemployed stock broker by the name of Bill Wilson and a shaky handed proctologist known lovingly too many of us as Dr. Bob. Together Bill W. and Dr. Bob, along with some friends, introduced the Alcoholics Anonymous program in 1935, and millions of us who suffer addiction problems owe our lives to them."

"To be fair major strides in any field do not come every day, and these breakthroughs cannot be contracted for, we can only hope and pray for them. Major strides are often the result of expanding ones vision of sight and looking at known facts in previously unknown ways. I congratulate the members of ivory tower of psychology for its willingness to look to the skies for miracles," Doug said in jest, then he added, "but if it's not too much trouble, could some of you come down and see if you can help the clients that need you."

"It seems to me that the quest for professional recognition, personal grandeur, the possibility to have ones bust displayed next to Skinner, Pavlov, or Freud, and the pursuit of knowledge for the sake of knowledge, has distracted the researchers in psychology's ivory tower from focusing on their most important job, helping the client."

"Several significant strides in our understanding of the functioning of the human mind have been made by psychologists over the last century. Some of these advances such as behavior modification have even made it into the treatment centers, but we need more. The problem is not that psychologists are not working to introduce new and better techniques for treating mental health issues, or that they are not working on developing new tests to improve their ability to diagnose psychological disorders, they are. The problem is that the main focus of psychology, the priority of psychological research, and the bulk of the work being presented, seems to be directed at chasing butterflies of some greater understanding, rather than clearing the cobwebs of discord from the client's minds. In fact both are important pursuits, and both deserve our support. In my opinion we do not have to change psychological research from the ground up. However in my opinion we do need to shift the priorities of psychological research away from pure knowledge and towards the client. We need to focus the majority of the research psychologist's efforts on client first research, at least until we see some positive results in lowering the percentage of clients who continue experiencing psychological problems after they have received mental health treatment," Doug suggested.

"In the academic world practical applications of psychological theories such as systematic desensitization are often theorized, discussed, and when possible their effectiveness in treating mental illnesses is being tested. The problem is that most of these theories are not producing treatment procedures that are making it into the mainstream clinical settings. The tools of the trade that the psychologists in the ivory tower are theorizing, debating, and testing, in their experimental clinical settings are not reaching the counselors in a form that can be helpful to the average client. We need to shift the bulk of research money currently being spent in psychology away from the theoretical psychologists, who already have a stockpile of theories in place. We then need to then invest that money in the work of researchers in the field of applied psychology who are working to get practical procedures derived from the theories into the hand of mental health clinicians. By doing this it is hoped that researchers will be able to give clinical psychologists and counselors more tools to help in the treatment of the clients," Doug urged.

"Even the systematic desensitization training that I received has been around for decades, it's hard to find, but it's nothing new" Doug told the few pages who were actually listening "Systematic desensitization training, and the Twelve Steps of AA, were the only forms of structured treatment that I received over the last twenty years. The rest of the treatment was talk therapy with very little structure and with and no practical end in sight."

"While some disorders, such as phobias, are being effectively treated with structured procedures such as systematic desensitization, others are more resistant to structured forms of treatment," Doug began in a slow, instructive tone, "I have been diagnosed, and I am taking medication for bi-polar disorder. In counseling bi-polar disorder is often treated in a general way through talk therapy. I feel it would be more helpful if the psychology researchers took the issues commonly associated with bi-polar disorder, such as sleep problems, social phobias, addictive behavior, and problems concentrating, just to name a few, and developed a semi-structured interview that the counselor would give to the client during their initial assessment. The semi-structured interview would be designed to produce a list of the common issues often experienced by bi-polar individuals that the individual client that they are working with is experiencing. The counselor now has a list of areas that the client needs to work on developing management skills to deal with. With the input of the client, the list of issues is then prioritized and each issue is then dealt with in the order that the counselor and the client agree on. By structuring the treatment the counselors can then give specific feedback to researchers on exactly what was tried, and what was successful. Using this data the researchers can then develop guided procedures that have proven to be successful in working with other clients. Researchers then provide the counselors with these guided procedures listed by their know effectiveness. The counselor can then share this information with the client and allow the client the chance to pick which procedure they feel will best suit their needs. The counselor will then give the client specific guidelines, and case studies, on the procedure they have selected. These guidelines, procedures, and case studies, are designed to aid the client in working on their own recovery inside and outside of the treatment setting. This will put the combined knowledge of psychology at the client's disposal, and lesson the dependence on the skills of the individual counselor. By providing several proven options to help the client deal with each individual issue that the client is experiencing allows the treatment to be tailored to the specific needs of each individual client. This system would also provide the client with a specific treatment plan that they helped develop, specific goals for the client to strive for, and an overall understanding of the recovery objectives with a clear end in sight. Structuring counseling in this way would take the unknowns out of mental health treatment, which is a major cause of stress, and give the client clear obtainable goals to help the client with the feeling that no progress is being made."

"If this type of standardized counseling were available, I would choose to utilize it for my own recovery. Others might choose to take part in more the more traditional form of talk therapy which often deals with life's problems as they come up. I feel that both forms of treatment, as well as the style offered by religious practitioners, should be available, and that the client should have the choice of which to use," Doug concluded.

"All that being said, exactly where are the statistics on recovery coming from?" Doug asked the tourists sitting in the balcony. "During the last twenty years I have been to six alcohol and drug treatment centers, five mental hospitals, fourteen counselors, nine psychiatrists, two psychologists, and I have yet to be asked to fill out a follow up assessment by any of them. Unless you count the ones they give you before you leave the hospitals that is," Doug said bluntly. "I have often seen recovery percentages advertised on television, some for institutions that I have been to, and I wonder to myself how in the world they calculate these recovery rates if they aren't doing any follow up research. More important, if nobody is checking to see what works and what doesn't, how do they make changes to improve their services? I understand that part of the problem in doing follow up research involves the patient confidentiality laws, and the issues some clients have with the social stigma attached to mental health treatment. It seems to me that a simple waiver offered to the client at the end of treatment would allow researchers to contact willing individuals. Personally I have filled out a stack of wavers giving my permission for researchers to contact me after leaving treatment, I just haven't been contacted. Simply doing some follow up research could improve overall performance simply by finding out what worked and what didn't. Some say that they are already doing follow up research, but you can't confirm that by me. The lack of follow up research is also indicative of a stagnant system that is set in its ways, and is resistant to change," Doug suggested knowing it wasn't his strongest argument.

"Fourth- License psychologists and mental health counselors by the type of approach they use, and the areas that they specialize in."

"For over a decade I have been seeing an orthopedic surgeon for my knee. Last year I sprained my ankle and called to make an appointment with him, I was told that he only did knees and I was referred to another orthopedic surgeon who specialized in ankles. This type of specialization is common practice in almost all fields of medicine. Specialization is also common practice in the study and research of psychology. So why are the psychologists, psychiatrists, and counselors, not making their selected field of study, and their approach to therapy available to individuals seeking help for a mental disorder? Unavailable that is for all practical purposes or at a reasonable price" Doug added,

"Psychologists in the academic world specialize in their approach to understanding, researching, and treating mental disorders by the discipline they most closely believe in, and that they have been instructed in. These disciplines include Cognitive-Behaviorist, Psychoanalysis, and Humanistic, just to name a few. Theoretically these disciplines also determine the type of treatment a client will receive from the psychologist, and to some extent they do. In order to give the client the best chance at recovery it is essential that the psychologist is trained in, or at least has a working knowledge of, all of the disciplines available. That does not mean that the individual psychologist is not biased to a particular style of treatment. To the informed client knowing what discipline the psychologist is trained in, and is licensed to provide, would give them the ability to choose the type of care that they prefer to receive. Licensing psychologists by discipline would also help in creating a specialization in the mental health system that currently is all too often giving a generic form of treatment to all its clients,"

Doug argued. "It would also help to create competition that in turn will drive result oriented research."

"Theories of how mental disorders develop and manifest themselves, how disorders should be researched, and how disorders should be treated, are often debated based on the beliefs that form the basis for the various disciplines. Unfortunately by the time the client meets with the counselor these disciplines seem to become blurred with the result being a generic form of counseling commonly known as talk therapy," Doug's voice now echoing the hollow feeling known all too well by clients in the system. "Some clients do respond well to talk therapy. The problem is what happens if the client does not respond to talk therapy, where does the client turn?" Doug asked, his hands lifting in a gesture of bewilderment. "Today any licensed counselor can claim that they have been trained in various forms of counseling, in truth this mean that they went to school and listened to the instructors explain the theories, and the personalities instrumental in developing the theories, for the various psychological disciplines. Perhaps the students read a few case studies as part of their education. Specific step by step instruction through role playing with other students, and hands on experience with real clients through apprenticeship are not required curriculum, or even offered as part of the curriculum in most programs that train mental health counselors. Psychology, social work, and counseling are popular online degrees. Prospective clients are often told to "come on down we offer all types of services" by the treatment providers, but what is the client really getting?" Doug asked.

"One of the personal issues I had to deal with was panic attacks that I experienced in social situations, agoraphobia to be specific. After years trying to identify and resolve some kind of deeply rooted experience that was the cause of the attacks through talk therapy. And having done this with four different counselors at three of different counseling centers, all with no positive results, I wanted to try something different. Since I was suffering from a phobia the next logical step was to try systematic desensitization. Every counseling center I tried clamed to offer systematic desensitization counseling, but when I started with the counselor they assigned me to it turned out to be more talk therapy," Doug said in an exasperated voice. "I did finally find a counselor in private practice that did understand how to prepare and guide a client in systematic desensitization, and he did successfully guide me through the process. With his help I was able to overcome the panic attacks in a matter of months, as opposed to the two years that I had wasted unsuccessfully discussing my childhood and current events in talk therapy."

In the balcony Don Peterson cringed. Doug had wanted to take a shot or two at the overuse of talk therapy in counseling, but he had convinced him to edit the shots out of the speech, Doug was adlibbing. "Stick to the speech you wrote," Don whispered to himself.

"To some extent there already exists specialization in counseling. Specialized fields such as alcohol and drug abuse, end of life counseling, family crisis counseling, anger management, and marriage counseling, are examples of specific issues that the client is able to look for specific counselors for help in dealing with. Today licensing and advertising specialized counseling for the treatment of psychological disorders such as bi-polar disorder, or obsessive-compulsive disorder, where no specialized treatment is currently available may seem a little like putting the cart before the horse. My hope is that the competition for the clients business that the advertising of treatment specialization will bring, will also drive the research needed to eventually make the need for training and licensing of specialized counselors for specific disorders seem obvious," Doug concluded.

"Fifth- Require mental health treatment facilities to be licensed by the type of treatment they provide and by a scale of what level of care they cater to."

"There are several different ideologies that mental health treatment centers employ to treat clients. Some facilities that offer specialized treatment such as aversion therapy, or hypnotic therapy, generally do advertise the style of treatment they offer. The more traditional treatment facilities generally base their treatment on one of three ideologies, a psychological approach, a psychiatric or medical approach, or a religious approach," Doug began, "In the business of providing mental health treatment it is best to be seen as offering all three of these approaches in any given facility. In truth this is rarely the way it happens in real life. Reliance on one of the three approaches, with limited use of one or both of the other approaches is more common. I do not feel it is realistic to expect the mental health treatment facilities to responsibly advertise the type of treatment they provide if it would potentially reduce their admissions. I do feel it is the right of the client to choose the style of treatment they desire to receive. To achieve this I recommend that licensing by type of treatment, or types of treatment that the institution offers be and mandatory. Mental health care providers would then be required to list the type, or types of treatment that they are licensed to provide in all advertising. Responsibility for insuring that the mental health care provider is in fact providing the type of treatment, or types of treatment they are advertising would be the responsibility of the licensing board," Doug recommended. In the balcony Don breathed a sigh of relief. They all knew it was a stiff dry section, but Doug had hurried through it in a clear voice and had made it relatively painless, which would make it easy for him to regain his momentum.

"I told you earlier that I have been to five mental health hospitals. Three of the hospitals I should never have seen the inside of. The first one provided a religion based style of treatment designed to help people who have lost their way in life find direction and guidance. While this type of treatment is of great help to some, I was suffering from a chemical imbalance in my brain that needed to be addressed with medication before any type of counseling would be of much help. This religious based treatment facility did claim to offer psychological and medical assessments, but they were poorly done and I walked out after graduation in exactly the same condition that I had walked in."

"The third and fourth mental hospitals I was in were for individuals with severe psychiatric conditions. Most of the clients were on disability and would probably remain on public assistance for the rest of their lives. Few clients who are in need of this level of treatment are likely to ever achieve a fully functional lifestyle. The reason that I was in these two hospitals was the result of misdiagnosis and psychiatric problems caused by incompetently prescribed antipsychotic medication," Doug explained.

"What I needed, and in two hospitals I found, was something in the middle. A treatment facility that offered medical diagnosis, and medication if needed, along with counseling designed to treat clients for a moderate psychological disorder stemming from a medical condition or the result of faulty thought patterns. The reason I went to two of them was due to the inaccuracy of the diagnostic ability of the psychiatrists, the psychiatrist's refusal to use psychological testing, and the unwarranted medications that I was prescribed," Doug added with distain.

"In treatment terms, I am a high functioning psychiatric client. Prior to seeking treatment I had taken three college classes in psychology. I knew what I type of treatment that I wanted to receive but I was unable to find it in the real world. That's not to say it didn't exist, it just wasn't advertised so that the choice would be mine to make. The hospitals were just one part of a whole world of unknowns that once you walk in the door of the mental health system, you will be assigned a place in, all dependent on the intake counselor you draw. That's just not right!" Doug said slapping his palm on the podium, "The client has the right to choose more than just whether or not to enter the dark halls of the secret society of psychology. The client has the right to choose the type of treatment that he or she wants to receive. In order to make this possible I am recommending that treatment facilities be required to list not only the style of treatment they offer, but the level of care they specialize in treating. Functional clients who are in need of direction and counseling would be a level one, functioning clients who are experiencing symptoms of a mental disorder or facing life altering issues that they cannot control, would be a level two, low functioning clients experiencing disabling mental conditions would be a level three. By forcing treatment facilities to adopt these guidelines it will give the informed, functional client the ability to make informed decisions about their own treatment," Doug paused and took a drink of water. Even here the thought of the whorl wind tour of the mental health care system that he had been led through angered him.

"Sixth- Challenge the members of psychologies Ivory Tower be more clients oriented in their approach to research. Recommend that the colleges and universities be more career task oriented in the education of future mental health workers. Take the names out of the text books."

"To a great extent client first research can be achieved by requiring researchers in the field of psychology to explain how their research is applicable or beneficial to clinical psychology when applying for tax payer funding. Together with a more responsible assessment of the research goals by those charged with evaluating research grant applications, will help in redirecting the priorities of psychology researchers."

"I am asking all collegiate psychology departments to focus their instruction on the practical application of psychological theory in a clinical setting, and away from instruction on the theories themselves. A degree in psychology should mean that the recipient is prepared to step into a clinical setting and work with clients. A degree in psychology should not mean that the recipient has only a theoretical knowledge of what might be discussed in a clinical setting, but no practical tools or experience to go along with this knowledge."

"I am asking all research psychologists to voluntarily remove their names from the publication of their research, and to place their emphasis on the application of the results of their research and how their research will benefit the client, society, or the overall knowledge of mankind. Until we see more encouraging results in the diagnosis and treatment of mental disorders there is really nothing for them to be proud of anyway.

I challenge college and university psychology departments to go ten years without being featured in every B rated college T&A movie coming out of Hollywood. I also challenge them to go one month without having any psychology research results used in late night television monologs or morning radio banter. One thing many of the schools could do to achieve this is to eliminate the quantity of publication that some schools are currently requiring for tenure, and replace it with quality of publication requirements. "I believe that I am a victim of the mental health system as it exists in America today. If I had been given reliable psychiatric testing that pinpointed my bi-polar disorder at any point during the sixteen years I that I dealt with misdiagnosis and improperly prescribed medications, I could have avoided years of pain and frustration. If I could then have found counseling that was geared to individuals with bi-polar disorder and bi-polar disorder's specific issues, and provided by counselors who were trained and experienced in treating individuals with bi-polar disorder, then my experience with the mental health care system in America could have been brief and productive. Instead I first went to a Christian based treatment hospital that used outdated testing, some from as far back as the Korean conflict, pray away the pain type counseling, and games designed to build life skills, and I left that hospital with no diagnosis and what amounted to a ten thousand dollar pep talk. I then went to a mental hospital that did provide medical diagnosis and treatment, but did not employ any form of psychological testing. There I was given the wrong diagnosis and began a four year nightmare from taking the prescription psychotropic drugs I was prescribed but were developed to treat a disorder that I do not suffer from. During all of this I saw multiple counselors and spent endless hours discussing personal experiences that had nothing to do with the problems I was dealing with, and that could not be directly attributed to my mental disorder. The last thing in the world I wanted to be was 'in the system'," Doug said with his hands as well as his voice, "All I wanted was to receive a proper diagnosis, and the proper treatment for the problems that I was having, and then to move on with my life. Now twenty years later I am still 'in the system' and have seen the system from every conceivable angle due to incompetent diagnostic techniques and endless open ended counseling."

"As a taxpayer, I want to invest in psychological research to help further mankind's understanding of the human mind. Even more importantly I want to invest in psychological research that provides reliable help for those who find themselves in need."

"As a taxpayer, I do not want to invest in psychology research that provides morning DJ's and late night talk show hosts with comic material, or research that aids Madison Avenue type advertisers in targeting their prospective customers."

"As a taxpayer, I want mental health care services available for those who cannot provide for themselves to be reliable and effective. I do not want government mental health care hospitals to be used as dumping grounds for mental health care workers who cannot make it in any other setting."

"As a taxpayer, I do not want a mental health care system that is so inept at diagnosing psychological disorders that individuals in need of public assistance are being denied that assistance, and individuals seeking to exploit public assistance are able to access disability services with ease."

"As a client in the mental health care system I want to have the same ability to choose my mental health care provider that I have in choosing health care providers in other areas of medicine."

"As a client I want anyone authorized to prescribe psychotropic drugs to be held accountable when these drugs are unnecessarily prescribed due to misdiagnosis, especially when all available diagnostic tools were not utilized."

In a loud voice filled with the pain acquired from years of being shuffled in and out of the system, the pain of a thousand hopes and dreams seen withered and blown away, the pain of burying so many of his friends, Doug raised his arms towards the domed ceiling of the great house and cried, "Can't anybody hear me, can't anybody help me, I am tired and it hurts inside." now yelling with the voice of a wounded animal. "I want to be a man, I want to take my part, I want to be like you, I want to be whole, I want my life back," As Doug cried out this last line he brought his hands down onto the podium with such force that it sent pieces of the wooden podium flying across the great hall. Doug looked at what he had done to the podium. He then looked at his right hand. He couldn't tell if it was broken, but it was clearly dislocated. A small bone about the size and shape of a bouillon cube was protruding out the back of his hand. Without thinking he used his left thumb to push the bone back into place. Even without the amplification of the sensitive microphone the corresponding crack would have been heard by every person in the hall, with the amplification it sent shivers down the spine of all that heard it. Doug barley winced, he looking up at the shocked faces and a strange smile formed on his face. Picking up the microphone with his left hand he continued, "Physical pain," he said slowly, "it's so much easier." Then with a throaty laugh he added, "And they don't double your co-payments." A moment later, after gaining control of his emotions and the pain he continued, "I do not know if the changes I am proposing to you are the best options available, or for that matter if they would even work at all. I do know that the mental health system that we have in this country today does not work. I came here today to ask for your help, not just for me, but for my friends who are still looking for help in a broken system. As I leave I will ask you to send a message to my friends. I will ask you to sit in your seats, put your feet on the floor, your hands on your desk, and your eyes on your work. I will ask you to show my friends that you have heard them. I will ask you to show my friends that you are ready to work this problem. Thank you for your time," Doug said stepping away from the podium, then turning back he added, "And sorry about your podium." When Doug had finished he looked up from his broken hand at the empty seats of the great hall, and the thirty or so pages till in the hall. About half the pages had sat down as he had asked. The rest stood looking from the chairs, to him, then to each other, unsure what to do. The small group of tourists in the balcony, and the small group who had accompanied him to Washington were applauding. It made only a faint, empty sound in the great hall. With a quick smile, a chuckle, and sideways nod of the head, Doug made his way down from the speaker's platform to the isle way where the ladies were waiting. Led by the House's Sargent at Arms Doug and the ladies made their way out of the great hall.

Once outside the house chamber Doug was informed that he didn't qualify for treatment in the Capital hospital located in the basement, but they had arranged to have him driven to a nearby hospital. Doug climbing into the electric cart they had provided to drive him to the exit. Ashley got in by his side and Kim climbed on his lap and facing him, straddled his legs with hers. Putting a hand on either side of Doug's face Kim could see that his eyes were far away and that he was crying, "You did it baby, you did it, I'm so proud of you," with tears in her eyes she kissed him.

Looking up for a brief moment Doug looked into Kim's eyes and softly said, "Yeah, I did it," then looking down at his wounded hand he added, "but was anybody listening?"

The end

www.ingramcontent.com/pod-product-compliance
Lightning Source LLC
Chambersburg PA
CBHW070106290526
45789CB00005B/1941

9 781499 633665